THE POETRY OF PAUL MULDOON

THE POETRY OF
PAUL MULDOON

Jefferson Holdridge

The Liffey Press

Published by
The Liffey Press
Ashbrook House, 10 Main Street
Raheny, Dublin 5, Ireland
www.theliffeypress.com

© 2008 Jefferson Holdridge

A catalogue record of this book is
available from the British Library.

ISBN 978-1-905785-30-8

This book has been published with the assistance of grant aid
from the Arts Council/An Chomhairle Ealaíon

Printed in the United Kingdom by Athenaeum Press.

Contents

Acknowledgements

I would like to thank all those who helped me to complete this book, especially Dillon Johnston, Guinn Batten, Omaar Hena, Phil Kuberski, John McNally, Candide Jones, and Sarah Winkler.

I would like to extend gratitude to all my colleagues at Wake Forest, but especially the three serving Chairs of English, Gale Sigal, Eric Wilson and Claudia Kairoff, for providing a creative intellectual environment in which to work.

Warm recognition goes to my students for posing and often answering difficult questions. And, if I now thank my students, I must thank my own professors, particularly Declan Kiberd.

I thank the Irish Arts Council of Ireland, as well as the Graduate School and Archie Fund of Wake Forest University for their generous support of this project.

David Givens of The Liffey Press has also been of significant service, as has the proofreader, Penny Harris. I thank them both.

Gratitude also goes to Paul Muldoon for his encouragement and to Faber and Faber for rights and permission to quote from Muldoon's poetry.

All errors herein are attributable to me and no one else, but the cast above has certainly endeavoured to make sure there are fewer mistakes than there might have been.

Per Wanda, per tutto, come sempre.

Introduction

It's hard to make a poem these days that is absolutely clear
and direct — if the poem is really to be equal to its era. This is
not an era in which clarity and directness, however much we
hope for them, are entirely justifiable, because so much is unclear and indirect. I'm not just talking about willed obfuscation and crookedness, though, God knows, there's plenty of
that. I'm just talking about a realization that very little is as it
seems, that everything has within it massive complexities —
maybe even the inappropriateness of being certain about
things. A proper awareness that things are just not at all as
they seem — one would wish for more of that, particularly on
the political front. Wouldn't you love to hear the president or
someone say, "Well, you know, I'm not absolutely clear on
that?"[1] – Paul Muldoon

THOUGH THIS STUDY OF PAUL MULDOON'S poetry alludes to his
life, especially where it is germane to the discussion of the poetry, it is not a biographically inspired reading of the work. Instead, it is meant to provide an introductory critical perspective,
upon which, it is hoped, readers may wish to elaborate. That said,
a brief biographical outline as a way of introduction is sure to
help anyone entirely unfamiliar with Muldoon's poems.[2]

The oldest of three children, Paul Muldoon was born on June
20, 1951 in Portadown, County Armagh, Northern Ireland. He has
a younger brother Joseph (born 1954) and sister Maureen (born
1953). The latter's recent death is the subject of the powerful poem

"Turkey Buzzards". Muldoon grew up in Collegelands, on land once owned by Trinity College Dublin, near Moy, a village located eight kilometres (five miles) from Dungannon, County Tyrone, Northern Ireland. Both places frequently appear in his poetry. His mother, Brigid (Regan), was a teacher, while his father, Patrick Muldoon, worked as a labourer and as a commercial grower of mushrooms. Both were Roman Catholics. Paul Muldoon was raised in their faith, and attended St Patrick's College in Armagh. He proceeded to study at Queen's University in Belfast, where he met the group of Ulster poets with whom, as a younger writer, he is often associated: particularly Michael Longley and Seamus Heaney, the latter of whom was his tutor. Yeats was an early influence, but Muldoon's interests soon concentrated upon those whose verse he felt was more closely aligned to his. One of the major influences upon Muldoon's work has always been Louis MacNeice; however, Muldoon also read Auden, Frost, and Edward Thomas, and they (especially Auden and Frost) have remained important precedents throughout his career. After receiving his university degree, Muldoon went to work for the BBC in Northern Ireland. He was a radio and television producer there for thirteen years. Muldoon published his first full collection, *New Weather* (1973), when he was just twenty-two.

From the pastoral meditations and linguistic openness of *New Weather*, reflecting his upbringing and his poetic education, he moved to the rejection of polarities, especially human and animal, in *Mules* (1977), his second collection of poetry. Then came speculations on the nature of perception in *Why Brownlee Left* (1980), which subsequently took on violent uncanny, familial forms in *Quoof* (1983). Muldoon received the Eric Gregory Award in 1972 and the Faber Memorial Prize in 1982 for *Why Brownlee Left*. Both *Why Brownlee Left* and *Quoof* carry the burden of the Northern Troubles, and wear the mark of the beast in light of the mixed human-animal formulations of the earlier volume *Mules*. Muldoon was Judith E. Wilson Fellow at Cambridge University (1986–1987), Writing Fellow at the University of East Anglia (1987), and Visiting Professor at both Columbia and Princeton (1987–1988). In

1990 he began teaching at Princeton, where, since 1993, he has also been Director of the Creative Writing Program. Additionally, Muldoon was President of the Poetry Society of Great Britain from 1996–2000, and was made Professor of Poetry at Oxford University in 1999. He married poet and novelist Jean Hanff Korelitz in 1987. The transformations of *Meeting the British* (1987) illustrated the increasing complexity of Muldoon's mature craft, always complex, but now particularly challenging. The volume also reflected the influence of the American political and poetic scene on his work. This became apparent in the daring cultural and philosophical combinations of *Madoc: A Mystery* (1990), which considers the relationships between philosophy and colonisation in the New World, while reflecting on the complicit role of the Old World in the colonial project. Life, in the birth of his children, and death, in the deaths of parents and friends, intervened, and led to the beautiful elegies ("Incantata" and "Yarrow") of *The Annals of Chile* (1994), a volume for which he was awarded the 1995 T. S. Eliot Prize of the Poetry Book Society.

In *Hay* (1998), Muldoon entered what might be said to be his mature style. Engaging in self-parody of his own overweight, middle-aged, suburban, Americanised life, he wonders how he is to find suitable material for poetry in this well established existence. In this volume, there is also middle-aged consciousness of memory and loss, which avoids epic formulations. In Muldoon's *oeuvre*, there is no sense that art is unfolding its truths, but there is instead a disorienting feeling that the progression of form is associational and dreamlike, with no determinate end in sight beyond the record of sensation, and the cataloguing of culture. *Moy Sand and Gravel* (2002), Muldoon's ninth book, extends the example of *Hay* and is concerned with deracination and disorientation. Even though Muldoon had explored these themes in earlier volumes, they are particularly visible in both *Hay* and *Moy Sand and Gravel*. His most recent volume, *Horse Latitudes* (2006), like *The Annals of Chile* (1994), is moved by personal loss to elegiac heights; only now the savagery with which Muldoon has viewed political realities enters into his elegy and infects his perspective on poetry itself. Muldoon has also edited *The Faber Book of Contemporary Irish Poetry* (1986), *The Essential Byron* (1989) and *The Faber Book of Beasts* (1997). Among other publications he has written a television play called *Monkeys* (produced in 1989), and provided a libretto for Daron Hagen's 1989 opera *Shining Brow*, based on a love affair between Frank Lloyd Wright and the wife of one of his clients, as well as the recently published essays on poetry entitled *The End of the Poem: Oxford Lectures on Poetry* (2006). Though these literary efforts will not be central to my concern, which is the poetry that has made him famous, they will be examined when they are relevant to the discussion. [3]

The two important full-length critical studies of Muldoon are Clair Wills's *Reading Paul Muldoon* (Bloodaxe, 1998) and Tim Kendall's *Paul Muldoon* (Dufour, 1996). At risk of simplification, the chief difference between Kendall and Wills is that that former is more historical and the latter more aesthetical. Both books, however, very ably cover the forms and themes of Muldoon's major volumes of poetry to the date of their publication, with some coincidental examination of his other works. They are thorough assessments of a significant poet; yet both critics admit the attendant complexities that confront the reader of Muldoon's work. Kendall writes that undertaking "a study of Muldoon's poetry brings peculiar difficulties". He then goes on to say that Muldoon has "described his poetic technique as a means of reassuring readers that all's well, then leaving them 'high and dry, in some corner of a terrible party, where [he has] nipped out through the bathroom window".[4] Wills states that her critical work is as much a "record" of being "read by Muldoon" as it is of "learning to read him".[5] The emphasis is on double-edged "reading" because Muldoon is a poet whose content often seems intentionally obscure and whose highly accomplished style is often bewildering. Any reader, invited or not to the "party", must, in the end, answer the question of whether he or she is glad to have come to a place where one is read and must read.

Reading Muldoon, then, requires a variety of methods – formal, historical, etymological – as well as perspectives – local and international. Wills and Kendall engage in a critical investigation of Muldoon that is meant to answer, if not necessarily negate, various criticisms of his poetry. For example, Muldoon has been accused by John Carey of "cliquish nonchalance" and by Helen Vendler of having "a hole in the middle where the feeling should be". The poet, of course, aims for this effect and so describes his own polished clever lyrics as "whimful".[6] The purpose of this present study is to introduce the general reader to some of the main critical questions surrounding Muldoon's work as well as to introduce his general themes, major poems and concerns. This book also aims to show readers how vital a role the American context and aesthetic plays in understanding Muldoon's poetry.

For her part, Wills admits that at some level the above negative criticism of Muldoon's poetry is just, but she also insists that these aspects are necessarily part of his poetic. In a subtle introductory reading of the poem "Twice" (from *The Annals of Chile*, 1994), she ably shows how the poem "… remains absolutely balanced between two separate visions, teasing us with our inability to choose between the real and the copy. More than just a playful image, this doubleness is integral to Muldoon's work. It ensures that we can never be quite sure how to take him; above all, this is a poetry which preserves doubt."[7] For the rest of the book, Wills remains true to this judgement, showing where the critics may have a point and where they do not. From her interpretation of the early poem "Dancers at the Moy" (*New Weather*, 1973), to those of later poems such as "Yarrow" and "Incantata" (*The Annals of Chile*, 1994), Muldoon's poetic device of concealment and discovery, of the creative hole in the middle of the poem, is seen as evidence of what Wills, in a beautiful phrase, calls the "displaced knowledge of 'forgotten' suffering".[8]

In his early work, Muldoon seemed to suggest that the aestheticising role of poetry may potentially cure painful emotions by transforming or burying them. By the third volume *Quoof* (1983), Wills sees that poetry as purgation is as much "a symptom as a cure".[9] In Muldoon's most recent volumes, she concludes that poetry is often implicated in the violence it tries to understand. The

very transformation of experience into the aesthetic object requires an act of violence. Wills therefore maintains that there are
two sides to Muldoon's poetic. For while being "imbued with a
postmodern suspicion of poetic efficacy", he is nevertheless "attuned to the traditional reflexes of romanticism", and so believes
that poetry may still offer some solace.[10] One perspective presents
a traditionally romantic vision of the redemptive possibilities of
art, while the other displays a more sceptical postmodern view.
Two examples from his poetry make this dichotomy clear.

The latter side of the dichotomy, "[Vico]", is from *Madoc – A
Mystery* (1990) and portrays the philosopher of history, Giambattista Vico (1668–1744), trapped in a system of copies that, for all its
complexity, has no origin or purpose and reduces the Italian's
conception of historical cycles to the ridiculous:

> A hand-wringing, small grey squirrel
> plods
> along a wicker
>
> treadmill that's attached
> by an elaborate
> system of levers
>
> and cogs and cranks
> and pulleys
> and gears ...
>
> ... to a wicker
> treadmill in which there plods
> a hand-wringing, small grey squirrel.[11]

This is a picture of the closed postmodern aesthetic – elaborate, but repetitive – where a baroque frame surrounds an absurdity. The only sign of life here is Muldoon's exuberant language.

The second example is from "Incantata", in *The Annals of Chile*
(1994), and contains all the elegiac wistful lyricism and redemptive possibilities of the old Modernists:

> I thought again of how art may be made, as it was by André
>   Derain,
> of nothing more than a turn
> in the road where a swallow dips into the mire
> or plucks a strand of bloody wool from a strand of barbed
>   wire
> in the aftermath of Chickamauga or Culloden
> and builds from pain, from misery, from a deep-seated hurt,
> a monument to the human heart
> that shines like a golden dome among roofs rain-glazed and
>   leaden.

The "golden dome" as image of art and religion offers some redemptive hope for the slaughter of the Scottish at Culloden or of the Union and Confederate Soldiers at Chickamauga. If we take these quotations as statements of his central dual poetic, Muldoon has not moved beyond Yeats's "The Circus Animals' Desertion" – no more than had Frost, Auden, or MacNeice, poets more typically seen as Muldoon's predecessors. Art aims to assuage the pain and transform the ugliness that conceived it in "the foul rag and bone shop of the heart".[12] Yet, if we cannot look to Muldoon for an extension of what Yeats is implying, we may yet allow his tone and technique, his witty vulnerability and elusiveness to embody our contemporary style of confusion. As Wills states, Muldoon's style is "superbly equipped to capture that insistent modern experience – the sense that it is precisely when we think we know our place that we are furthest from home".[13]

This praise is not meant to dismiss Muldoon's tendency to hide behind cliché or the parody of cliché, or to engage in too many puns, too many poses, in glibness or unnecessary obscurity, but it is meant to accept these as the terms of his poetry, and perhaps, as Wills and Kendall both show, those of his being. In this respect at least, Muldoon is heir to Wallace Stevens, and his poetic powers may be best appreciated in that light, although with a contemporary twist, which may be best represented by Muldoon's part in a rock 'n' roll band called "Rackett" since 2004. In a sense the cursed poet, wayward troubadour, badboy rockstar combine

in Muldoon. Admitting the strange basis of this mix, he declares
in his own website about the band: "When Cole Porter meets prog
and punk or Ira Gershwin glam and grunge, you're looking at
what can be described only as three-car garage rock."[14] The poet
also tellingly writes in a recent poem, "Bob Dylan: Oh Mercy"
(from the sequence on pop music cleverly called "Sleeve Notes",
in *Hay*, 1998):

> All great artists are their own greatest threat,
> as when they aim an industrial laser
> at themselves and cut themselves back to the root
>
> so that, with spring, we can never be sure
> if they shake from head to foot
> from an orgasm, you see, sir, or a seizure.

With this self-indicting thought the reader may put Muldoon into
perspective, to be easy with not being sure, to understand and
appreciate the power of contingency and hallucination in his
verse. As Mick Imlah put it in his review for the *Observer*: "Muldoon seems to require such exacting schemes to get himself going;
but his virtuosity would count for nothing were it not at the service of the deepest poetic which is to say, unparaphraseable thinking. He may be said to have reinvented the possibilities of rhyme
for our time; and the way his words slip in and out of each other,
marrying, transforming or dissolving, carries a constant metaphysical charge."[15] What more can be said of a poet than to say he
has invested questions of form with metaphysical significance
that is suitable to our times.

Endnotes

[1] Interview with Paul Muldoon in Charles McGrath, "Word Freak", *The New York Times*, November 19, 2006.

[2] For biographical detail, the following is indebted to Clair Wills, *Reading Paul Muldoon* (Newcastle upon Tyne: Bloodaxe, 1998); Tim Kendall, *Paul Muldoon* (Chester Springs: Dufour, 1996); and to the Chadwyck-Healey author entry: *Twentieth-Century English Poetry*, Muldoon, Paul, from *Literature Online Biography*; adapted

from data developed by the H. W. Wilson Company, Inc. Copyright © Bell & Howell Information and Learning Company 1996–2000), H. W. Wilson Company, Inc.   http://gateway.proquest.com/openurl?ctx_ver=Z39.88-2003&xri:pqil:res_ver= 0.2&res_id=xri:ilcs-us&rft_id=xri:ilcs:ft:ref:2815:0

[3] A list of Muldoon's publications can be found in the bibliography at the end of this book. I have also decided not to discuss *The Prince of the Quotidian* because Muldoon chose not to include it in the Faber edition of his *Poems 1968–1998*. I have taken his editorial decision as definitive.

[4] Kendall, *Muldoon*, 7.

[5] Clair Wills, *Reading Paul Muldoon*, 23.

[6] Quoted in Wills, *Reading*, 11–12.

[7] Wills, *Reading*, 17.

[8] Wills, *Reading*, 181.

[9] Wills, *Reading*, 87.

[10] Wills, *Reading*, 22.

[11] Paul Muldoon, *Poems 1968–1998* (London: Faber, 2001) 4; all subsequent quotations of Muldoon's poetry are from this edition unless otherwise stated.

[12] W. B. Yeats, *Collected Poems*, ed. Daniel Albright (London: Dent, 1992).

[13] Wills, *Reading*, 217.

[14] See http://www.rackett.org/index.html

[15] Mick Imlah, "*Hay*, by Paul Muldoon," *The Observer* 15 November 1998.

1

New Weather (1973)

PAUL MULDOON'S FIRST VOLUME, *New Weather* (1973), was criti-cised for not having an organising principle;[1] yet it does seem to be organised around the themes of landscape, nature and the question of the social unit, whether family, community or nation. Here is a list of some of the dialectical tensions that underlie these themes: culture *versus* nature; universal *versus* local; modern *versus* primitive; imitation *versus* authenticity; father *versus* mother; fallen worlds *versus* innocent ones. The difficulty arises in trying to figure out exactly what Muldoon is trying to say about their relationship, or which category he prefers. Then again, the ambi-guities and ambivalence one might feel about these oppositions (who would really want nature without culture? or who would completely prefer primitive to modern?) probably tells us more about how they interact than any forthright declaration of prefer-ence. This is what makes this first volume so rich, even if it is somewhat inchoate when compared to later more mature ones.

From the first poem of the volume, "The Electric Orchard", we witness one divining concept at work. Here, the old paradigm of nature *versus* culture takes on a modern industrialised twist. The first line, "The early electric people had domesticated the wild ass", lets us know that nature, in the guise of the sexual image and pun of the wild ass, must be domesticated.[2] After that come im-ages of original sin and the fall. The connection between nature and original sin has a long lineage in Irish literature, and indeed in all literature, but in Ireland it takes on specific historical forms. Muldoon writes:

The electric people lived in villages
Out of their need of security and their constant hunger.
Together they would divert their energies

To neutral places. Anger to the banging door,
Passion to the kiss.
And electricity to earth. Having stolen his thunder
From an angry god, through the trees
They had learned to string his lightning.

Muldoon's allegorical skills are wide-ranging. The electricity of the people is like the mythical fire stolen by Prometheus for the benefit of humankind. The energy it represents is also part of human nervousness, a human sense of wrongdoing, the guilty curse of self-consciousness, which drives us into communities for security. In the poem, the people then translate or sublimate suffering and desire into "neutral places". That phrase is vague in psychological terms; it could just mean safe, or it could mean those places that won't be contested. In Irish terms, the phrase is more specific: it is a political stance that challenges both sides of the national question. In this scenario, the sense of transgression is connected to the historical wrongs of colonisation, while the electricity and security are the energies and fears that history has wrought in Ireland. The rest of the poem, not included here, takes the image of falling from the electric poles, with all that signifies (both negative and positive), as its centre. Falling means historical awareness in the Irish context and also means falling into consciousness in general. And the electric people learn to circumscribe all attempts at awareness and consciousness. They surround the electric poles with barbed wires and no-trespassing signs, but significantly none of the signs can "describe / Electrocution, falling, the age of innocence". This is both a local (e.g. the source of the "Troubles") and universal dilemma; much of Muldoon's work is an attempt to describe that fall and to imply what innocence was lost.

In "Blowing Eggs", the third poem in the volume ("Wind and Tree" is second), Muldoon tries to capture the natural boyhood transgression or fall from grace. Here destruction and beauty, like sexuality and pain, are inextricable. "This is the start of the underhand," writes Muldoon. The boys' stealing of the egg, pilfering and ruining the nest, is both studied and brutal. Soon it is revealed to have sexual analogies, a sadomasochistic rehearsal of masturbation: "This is the breathless and the intent / Puncturing of the waste ... / ... his wrist, surprised and stained." The conception that any one thing is inevitably like another, in this case blowing eggs like masturbation, does not make them exactly the same; nevertheless, the similarities are difficult to deny. And, more importantly, in Muldoon's way of registering behaviour, the implied consciousness is analogous. The poem "Thrush", about a love letter, has similarly violent sexual undertones, and uses the fist as symbol of passion, anger and desire.

In poems such as "Wind and Tree", "The Glad Eye", "Hedges in Winter", and "Macha", philosophy, myth and landscape come together. "The Glad Eye" centres round another childhood memory, placed ironically in a philosophical frame of subjectivity (the "glad I"). Here, the speaker remembers being bored by "Ascham and Zeno" and going "onto the lawn" where he fired an arrow that struck his brother's eye. The eye of the title is the "glad" one, in a piece of mordant irony that has come to characterise Muldoon's poetry. The eye becomes an evil eye, a talisman that "inveigled [him] to standing stone". It is "deeper than the Lake of the Young" and "Could look without commitment into another eye". That ability to be disinterested is at the base of the aesthetic gaze, as if the gaze were the result of being injured and needing protection. In the driving beat and powerful spondees of "Hedges in Winter", the presiding myth is a natural one in which landscape and culture are profoundly intertwined:

> Every year they have driven stake after stake after stake
> Deeper into the cold heart of the hill.
> Their arrowheads are more deadly than snowflakes,
> Their spearheads sharper than icicles[.]

Readers must be impressed by the command of form in such a young poet, one whose formalism is complex but seems effortless, whose rhymes are so well placed. This has become another trademark of Muldoon; his poetic is postmodern, his sense of form is traditional. Yet, the postmodern often works off an eclectic model, borrowing from the past in a pastiche that has a contemporary edge. The people of the poem have taken their weapons from the landscape and weather, have moulded a new weather, with which they threaten nature itself. Nevertheless, they are reliant on the landscape for images that they desire, "whittling the dead branches to the girls they like". In the end all are shaped from nature itself, which, because it holds their secrets, cannot be overcome:

> Whittling the dead branches to the girls they like.
> That they have hearts is visible.
> The nests of birds, these obvious concentrations of black.
> Yet where the soldiers will later put on mail,
>
> The archers their soft green, nothing will tell
> Of the heart of the mailed soldier seeing the spear he flung,
> Of the green archer seeing his shaft kill.
> Only his deliberate hand, a bird pretending a broken wing.

Even if the soldiers become more civilised, or more artificial in chain-mail, their protective skills are more indicative of their natures. The "soft green" is the trick and riddle of nature, "pretending a broken wing", seeking protection in camouflage, feigning injury, but remaining deadly withal.

Why Irish nature writing should so often emphasise allegorical and mythological renderings of nature is difficult to say. It may be because the pressures of colonial history have forced Irish writers in general toward a mythological conception of nature, or it may be that they claim an original world before the "fall" of colonisation. What Paul Muldoon writes in his collection of lectures *To Ireland, I,* of the Irish love of liminal worlds, may well apply to Irish nature writing as somehow connected to various versions of home (one thinks of Yeats's paean to Sligo, "Under Saturn", or of so much of MacNeice, or Heaney): "This idea of a parallel universe, a grounded groundlessness, also offers an escape clause, a kind of psychological trapdoor, to a people from under whose feet the rug is constantly being pulled, often quite literally so."[3] Muldoon's poem "Wind and Tree" is a fine example:

> In the way that the most of the wind
> Happens where there are trees,
>
> Most of the world is centred
> About ourselves.
>
> Often where the wind has gathered
> The trees together and together,
>
> One tree will take
> Another in her arms and hold.
>
> Their branches that are grinding
> Madly together and together,
>
> It is no real fire.
> They are breaking each other.
>
> Often I think I should be like
> The single tree, going nowhere,
>
> Since my own arm could not and would not
> Break the other. Yet by my broken bones
>
> I tell new weather.

When seen as an expression of the age-old Irish view of the family as a political unit, this early poem about individual identity and the danger of families of trees becomes a natural allegory in which the poet seeks "a grounded groundlessness", to be "a single tree going nowhere" in a country where the felling of trees was symbolic of colonisation. Perhaps this move into nature provides a fed-up Muldoon with a way of escaping Irishness. It will not, however, help him escape history. There is a type of surrender to the empirical fact that where there are few trees to be

16

found, standing trees reflect the circumstances in which they grow. History is a wind and the individual a tree that is shaped by the direction in which it blows. Nevertheless, there is a poignant simplicity about the escape into solitude and nature, which shows that being and nature are not interchangeable with history, but have some mythological quality that transcends circumstance.

Nature provides the fundamental *mythos* of *New Weather*, as the beautifully sculpted poem "Macha" makes clear:

> Macha, the Ice Age
> Held you down,
> Heavy as a man.
> As he dragged
>
> Himself away,
> You sprang up
> Big as half a county,
> Curvaceous,
>
> [...]
>
> The day you fell,
>
> At the hands of men,
> You fell
> Back over half a county.
> Clutching a town
>
> To your breasts.

This poem is based on the story from the Bronze Age epic *The Táin Bó Cúailnge* in which the pregnant Macha is made to run a race against the men of Ulster. Upon falling into childbirth during the race, she curses the men of Ulster saying that they will suffer the pangs of childbirth in the hour of their greatest need. *The Táin* had recently been made current by Thomas Kinsella's modern translation of the ancient text and by Louis le Brocquy's modern ink drawings which adorned the Dolmen edition; both the translation and the illustration use the primitive aesthetic of Modernism to highlight the lines of the original text.[4] For Muldoon, the pregnant Macha is the figure for the landscape of the drumlins, the rolling hills made soft and steeply undulant by the Ice Age, which define the border counties between Northern Ireland and the Irish Republic. Her suffering becomes emblematic of the position of people caught between warring tribes, but she also represents the earth and nature, violated by the struggles of men. Taking "half a county" to her "breasts", she represents nature suckling culture, but is not an image which offers much relief in the end. Many of these early poems endeavour to represent a return to nature and innocence, to represent a space before the fall, but what Muldoon shows us is the constitutive violence and modernity of these imaginative spaces and returns, where the modern (Northern Ireland) is the primitive (the Ulster Sagas) and vice versa.

In "Dancers at the Moy", nature is again shown to underlie culture. And, again, history and myth converge. Kendall explains: "Having heard that Greeks were arriving at the Moy's fair to buy horses for a war of independence, the people in the area ... brought all their horses to be sold. Unbeknown to the Irish, peace had been declared a week previously, leaving the Moy overrun with starving horses."[5] Rather than foregrounding the pathos of the actual incident, Muldoon roots it in the historical and mythological connections between Ireland and the Mediterranean:

> No band of Athenians
> Arrived at the Moy fair
> To buy for their campaign,
>
> Peace having been declared
> And a treaty signed.
> The black and gold river
> Ended as a trickle of brown
> Where those horses tore
> At briars and whins,
>
> At the flesh of each other
> Like people in famine.

The war that has ended in Greece could have been the Trojan War, or a war against the Turks, it matters little ("One or other Greek war"). And the hunger of the horses mirrors the Irish famine in its composition if not in its facts. Like myth, history is as important in its underlying structures and movements as it is in its surface details. Muldoon is allowing the essential truths of the misfortune to shine through until we see how history and myth define culture:

> The local people gathered
> Up the white skeletons.
> Horses buried for years
> Under the foundations
> Give their earthen floors
> The ease of trampolines.

Muldoon's macabre sense of humour is most evident here, but also evident is his belief that history defines us in profoundly subconscious ways, so that the movements of the dancers at the Moy are shaped by the bones of the horses. Beauty and destruction, love and pain are intertwined.

We already see at this early stage of Muldoon's career that he has a gift for parable, "allegorical or emblematic elements, dream logic, Everyman protagonists, a concern with questions of identity, interest in narrative, and the creation of a special world".[6] Many of these characteristics have already been discussed. The poem "Identities", as the title suggests, is concerned with questions of identity. The narrative, told in the form of parable, is one of love under political duress of some kind, a theme that fits into the Northern Irish frame:

> When I reached the sea
> I fell in with another who had just come
> From the interior. Her family
> Had figured in a past regime
> But her father was now imprisoned.

Identity, it seems, flows like a tributary toward one all-encompassing stream (where the two characters were to be married), but the speaker seems to wander off, for those from the interior know a different reality, that streams flow singly, even if they "had once flowed simply one into the other / One taking the other's name". The marriage is a conditional dream-image of streams flowing into each other and to the sea; the reality is the missing declaration of inalterable difference.

In "Clonfeacle", nature mirrors language in the tradition of *dinnseanchas* ("poems and tales which relate the original meanings of place names and constitute a form of mythological etymology",[7] as Heaney writes). This poem is influenced by Seamus Heaney's own place-name poems, "Anahorish", "Toome" and "Broagh", from the volume *Wintering Out* (1972). The name Clonfeacle means the "meadow of the tooth", the derivation of which is explained in the first stanza:

> It happened not far away
> In this meadowland
> That Patrick lost a tooth.
> I translate the placename …

The rest of the poem follows this meditation along familiar lines: water coursing along land and through stones is like language coursing through the mouth. The poem ends vaguely, but seems to point out how Patrick, and his sermons, end "in the air", that is, leave the pagan roots in the Christian desire for transcendence. In "February", we return to the same theme of trees as emblems of suffering that we found in "Wind and Tree". The human references are even more explicit and perhaps less suggestive, but there is a self-criticism of Muldoon's own impersonal mode within the stanza:

> He had never yet taken time to grieve
> For this one without breasts
> Or that one wearing her heart on her sleeve
> Or another with her belly slashed.

It is a welcome critique. The tensions between the impersonal and the personal, as well as the sentimental and cynical, are some of the most fruitful in Muldoon's poetry. The poem avoids bathos and ends beautifully, with the reflection that the speaker is "watching and waiting for" one "who would break the laws of time and stay". There is hope here for permanence and meaning, one that has often saved Muldoon from claims that he lacks feeling, that he is all whimsy and verbal dexterity. A similar desire for deep feeling graces "Kate Whiskey". Not that one is precisely sure of what Muldoon is saying here, but the reflective mood to be taught love is right, as is the gesture ("I sold the water, the whiskey I would give") that is made without recompense. "Vespers" likewise contains a prayer to be saved from the world's harshness. "Leaving an Island" carefully contemplates what sexuality teaches, the macrocosm of creation in the microcosm of the act, while "The Cure for Warts" and "The Radio Horse" are riddle poems, in which intimate experience provides our best cures and codes.

The poem "Good Friday, 1971, Driving Westward", is a postmodern rendition of John Donne's famous poem "Good-Friday, 1613, Riding Westward", and as such provides the central statement of the relationship between landscape, nature and family in *New Weather*. Donne's poem was famously cited as an example of an outdoor poem that made no reference to natural scenery.[8] It is meant to show how the view of nature changed from the seventeenth century Donne inhabited to the eighteenth-century birth of Sensibility and Romanticism, and their celebrations of nature. For Muldoon, it seems that we haven't taken many strides from Donne's times, even if we are now "Driving" instead of "Riding". The landscape is a text, a scripture, to be interpreted: "Doves" are making "offerings" and the poet is reading "the first edition of truth" in the landscape, the faces of waking souls and that of the girl he gives a "lift to ... out of love". Our poet is crossing the border between Derry and Donegal, that is, between Northern Ireland and the Republic on the day that celebrates Christ's crossing of the border between life and death. The sublime mountain landscapes celebrated by Romantic poets return to their roots in terror and danger. Muldoon is a metaphysical poet like Donne: the "road" puts its "thin brown arm round / A hill and held on tight out of pure fear". The underlying joke is that it is crucifixion either way.

During the drive, the girl claims that the driver has hit something in the road, the truth of which is never proved. He sees nothing "but a heap of stones", while she is "convinced" that he has killed a "lamb or herring". The Biblical note may be too ponderous but even without it that sense of original sin interrupting the view of the land is very sensible. It is the result of the fear and tension that once surrounded crossing the political border between North and South, and it is the arbitrary death that attends every journey, every border crossing, for human and animal alike, and which must be redeemed by the blood of the lamb. It is therefore historical and Biblical: implicit in the nature of humankind and explicitly the result of political events. Children, or innocence, must be protected from both:

> She stood up there and then, face full of drink,
> And announced that she and I were to blame
> For something killed along the way we came.
> Children were warned that it was rude to stare,
> Left with their parents for a breath of air.

In this poem, like the poem entitled "Behold the Lamb", we understand why nature has not been romanticised in Ireland quite as successfully as it has been in England, despite the tourist view of the landscape. As Glenn Hooper shows in his collections of travel writing on Ireland, entitled *The Tourist's Gaze*, even tourists have had trouble seeing the landscape in quite as innocent a way as they might elsewhere.[9] History converges with the subconscious and floods the consciousness of the poet.

In "Seanchas" (meaning in Irish "lore", "history", or "gossiping"), we see how this consciousness depends upon the story that the landscape tells. It is the same story the poet or storyteller ("seanchaí") must retell repeatedly, and yet repeat each time with a new slant, however slight. First he starts with epic lusts and wars, taking us back to the era of the Ulster sagas, to which the listeners (contemporary readers and those speakers within the poem) feel themselves falsely superior. He then moves towards the dilemma of the present, a version of the pastoral that seems pregnant with meaning, but which is difficult to record:

> … And no heroes people this landscape
> Through which he sees us off.
> The lifted wondering faces of his sheep
> Stare back at us like nimble rain clouds, their bellies
> Accumulate and are anonymous again. But having shape,
> Separate and memorable.

The story is yet to be told, but the landscape seems ready to tell it. In "Hedgehog", it is a strange version of Christ's sacrifice, concluding "never again / Will a god trust in the world", while in "Lives of the Saints" it is the paradox of St Brendan sailing off in a boat made of stone. "Easter Island" compares the collapsed culture of that South Pacific island to the pre-Christian ancients of Ireland and Britain who built Newgrange and Stonehenge. The homage they make is built in stone, but remains enigmatic to future generations.

There are other poems and themes in *New Weather*. "Vampires" shows Muldoon's taste for the gothic; "The Kissing Seat" his mixing of sex and violence; "The Field Hospital" is one of the first indications of Muldoon's interest in American history, in this case the Civil War; and "The Indians on Alcatraz" displays his lifelong sympathy for the plight of Native Americans. Two important poems are "Elizabeth" and "The Year of the Sloes, For Ishi". The first is a good example of the type of love poem for which Muldoon would justly become well known. Though not as affecting as the later "Incantata", "Elizabeth" is a beautiful rendition of Yeats's "The Wild Swans at Coole", only now the poet is not alone remembering and mourning the past and his solitude, but is with the beloved reckoning how the flight of birds reflects their lives, their efforts to move together in time, to avoid obstacles, to stay together through the journey:

> Every so often, getting thin
> As it slants, making straight for
> Us over your father's darkening fields,
> Till their barely visible wings
> Remember themselves, they are climbing again.

The family is a dark presence with a menacing, invisible pull. As these are seabirds, the sea beckons their inland consciousness. Unlike Yeats, Muldoon finds it difficult to count this flock. Number has nothing to do with their influence, which instead relies on movement. The birds are heading for the couple, and this seems to frighten the Elizabeth of the title, as though the birds were a "hurricane". She holds the "promised children" in her "hands", writes the poet and eventually returns, having "nothing to lose", to watch the birds fly away:

> We watch them hurtle, a recklessness of stars,
> Into the acre that has not cooled
> From my daylong ploughings and harrowings,
> Their greys flecking the brown,
> Till one, and then two, and now four
> Sway back across your father's patchwork quilt,
> Into your favorite elm. They will stay long
> Enough to underline how soon they will be gone,
> As you seem thinner than you were before.

Though the ending doesn't fulfill the promise of the beginning of the poem, it remains an effective evocation of how the natural world contains our longing and fears, with phrases like "recklessness of stars" reminding us of Muldoon's lyric gift. That she seems thinner than before is too convenient and not probing enough of a metaphor for the much deeper significance of this flight of birds and their reactions to it. The clue to the pain of the poem lies in the sense that the birds will soon be gone, in the father's house, his patchwork quilt of the fields, and in the acre that

"has not cooled" from the poet's "daylong ploughings" and "har-
rowings". The sexual motif is obvious. The play on "harrow" contains the most meaning of all; in this instance it means to draw a
harrow over; to break up, crush, or pulverise. Its other meaning is
to "harry, rob, spoil".[10] That the birds sit in her "favorite elm"
(trees have come to represent human suffering) completes the
poem's dark message. What seems to be missing from the word-
play is Christ's harrowing of hell, an action which would redeem
the land; however, transmigration of the soul gives way to simple
migration.

In the concluding poem of the volume, "The Year of the Sloes,
for Ishi", many of these themes come together: it is a poem of Native American experience that Muldoon wrote in response to
Bloody Sunday in Northern Ireland, which contemplates the relationship of history, landscape and aesthetics. There are twelve
stanzas for each moon of the year. We begin with an image of the
winter sky ("two stars"), a transcendent realm that contains the essential image of violence that haunts this poem of colonisation. In
the next stanza, "the Moon / Of the Dark Red Calf", the star tracks
itself by following the "dashes of its blood", while in the third
stanza, "the Moon / Of the Snowblind", the other star has a dream
of the hunt and of the acquisition of knowledge. We are moving
through the seasons; "in the Moon / Of the Red Grass Appearing" it
seems that the second star discovers the first, who is female, "Lying
under a bush". He finds that it is "harder / To live at the edge of the
earth / Than its centre" until by the middle of the poem, and the
year, he kills his first "bison", that ceremonial victim of the war-
rior's initiation, and "offer[s] the heart / To the sky" – to the lands
of his birth. The first female star now prepares the meal and saves
the leftovers; the etiology is complete. Native American culture has
been formed of nature, out of a divine wish to be human, to sum-
mer in the world ("In the Moon / Of the Red Cherries").

This desire, however, must be tested; and colonisation by a
European culture more antagonistic to nature than the Native
American is there to test it. Soon the couple finds evidence of
European civilisation. Their natural, circular civilisation is

matched by those "in blue shirts / Felling trees for a square". Apocalyptically, an eagle flies "Out of her side" and the man ceremoniously prepares for death. In the final stanza (which is missing from the Faber *Poems 1968–1998*)[11] the landscape is threatened by the Indian wars that the natives are fated to lose:

> In the Moon
> Of the Trees Popping, two snails
> Glittered over a dead Indian.
> I realized that if his brothers
> Could be persuaded to lie still,
> One beside the other
> Right across the Great Plains,
> Then perhaps something of this original
> Beauty would be retained.

The hope is that the Indians might survive; from our perspective this hope is impossible. The original beauty is marred by the colonial incarnation of the original sin. It seems that the landscape could have provided absolution if history had allowed it – but unfortunately it hasn't. The Romantic preference for the primitive endeavours to redeem history by looking for redemption in the very landscape its own culture has altered. To achieve redemption, however, it must be "persuaded to lie still". This appeal to an original premodern, precolonial world also recognises how the concern with "origins" and "authenticity" is dependent on a sense that they are gone, that the world is full of copies, translations, adaptations at best. Muldoon's first volume, *New Weather*, is organised around themes of landscape, nature and the question of family/community/nation. It is also haunted by the dialectical tensions between culture and nature, universal and local, modern and primitive, among others, which underlie these themes. Muldoon is ambiguous about these oppositions because he is ambivalent, not preferring one to another, recognising that the forces which make their relationship so volatile are what make them so meaningful as binaries; in later volumes he will learn to make that volatility his métier.

Endnotes

[1] Tim Kendall, *Paul Muldoon* (Chester Springs: Dufour, 1996), 33.

[2] Muldoon is perhaps playing on the idea that a combination of animal and divine characteristics underlies human experience, a concept made famous in Apuleius' ancient satire, *The Golden Ass*.

[3] Paul Muldoon, *To Ireland, I* (Oxford : Oxford UP, 2000), 7.

[4] Thomas Kinsella, *The Táin* (Dublin: Dolmen, 1969).

[5] Kendall, *Muldoon*, 37.

[6] From Louis MacNeice, *Varieties of Parable* (Cambridge: Cambridge University Press, 1965), 76, quoted by Edna Longley, in *Poetry in the Wars* (Newcastle upon Tyne: Bloodaxe, 1986); and by Kendall, *Muldoon*, 38.

[7] Quoted in Neil Corcoran, *Seamus Heaney* (London: Faber, 1986), 87.

[8] See Marjorie Hope Nicolson, *Mountain Gloom and Mountain Glory* (Ithaca: Cornell, UP, 1959), 120–35.

[9] See Glenn Hooper, *The Tourist's Gaze: Travellers to Ireland 1800–2000* (Cork: Cork UP, 2001).

[10] See "harrow" in *Oxford English Dictionary* (Oxford: Oxford UP, 2006); referred forthwith as *O.E.D.* unless otherwise noted.

[11] This stanza is, however, in the original volume (London: Faber, 1973) and in *New Selected* (London: Faber, 1994).

2

Mules (1977)

ALONG WITH LOUIS MACNEICE and W. H. Auden, Byron and Frost are most often cited as primary influences on Muldoon's poetry, and for good reason: one for his Romantic spleen, worldly wit and Neo-Augustan satirical sense, and the other for his ability to make simple, playful but profound comments on our place in nature. These influences remain throughout Muldoon's career and should not be underestimated. Nevertheless, Muldoon's satirical emphasis, especially in *Mules*, on the place of natural instincts in human relationships reminds one of Jonathan Swift. Like Swift's fury, Muldoon's sardonic wit is guided by the following aims: he wishes to argue against the abstract, theoretical tendencies of rationalism; he doubts the capacity of human reason to attain metaphysical and theological truth; he contests the attitudes of experimental and theoretical science; he opposes the Romantic conception of man, which was the result of both rationalism and science, and which taught the essential goodness of human nature; he questions the increasing power of centralised government and the corruption of English colonialism, whether in Ireland, Britain or America.[1]

All of this has been said of the author of *Gulliver's Travels* and might well be said of Paul Muldoon. Both writers create fables of social and political experience that uncover dark truths of human nature. Behind their complex political position is a sovereign intellectual satire of humanity which seeks to uncover the most primitive transgressions of power, cruelty, and lust. Both Swift and Muldoon stage a confrontation between our animal and ra-

tional characteristics. Parodying works of logic that had con-
trasted human reason with the irrationality of brute horses[2] in "A
Voyage to the Houyhnhnms" of *Gulliver's Travels*, Swift with considerable dexterity unveils the opposing designs which God and
Nature have on our moral and physical being. Muldoon does
much the same in many poems of *Mules*, which itself is a type of
bestiary of human aspirations, and, as a result, a meditation on
various types of mixtures: human and animal, poetry and politics,
truth and art. It is a lineage that in post-colonial terms is called
hybrid, but which, in Muldoon's world, is better termed mongrel
or mulish.

There also is a strong element of the anti-pastoral in this volume, meant to counter the first volume's emphasis on the landscape. It is very much a part of Muldoon's reckoning of human
endeavours entangled in the net of nature's designs. In the first
poem in the volume, "Lunch with Pancho Villa", the revolutionary leader critiques Muldoon's obsession with the pastoral conventions of poetry in light of the Troubles in the North:

'Look, son. Just look around you.
People are getting themselves killed
Left, right and centre
While you do what? Write rondeaux?
There's more to living in this country
Than stars and horses, pigs and trees,
Not that you'd guess it from your poems.
Do you never listen to the news?
You want to get down to something true,
Something a little nearer home.'

Though these lines are self-explanatory, by the end of the
poem we realise that Muldoon is caught between the lyric poet's
tendency not to tell it "true" but rather to opt for the music of language (the poetic form of the rondeaux) over the pamphleteer's
grubby descent into truth. He will have to establish a balance,
which is precisely what he does in the next poem, "The Cen-
taurs", in which landscape and history mesh. The poem begins

with a meditation on William of Orange, the Dutchman who was brought to occupy the English throne to save it from the Papist James the Second. He is often pictured in the murals of Loyalist Belfast riding triumphantly on horseback after the Battle of the Boyne, which is where we find him in this poem:

> I can think of William of Orange,
> Prince of gasworks-wall and gable-end.
> A plodding, snow-white charger
> On the green, grassy slopes of the Boyne,
> The milk-cart swimming against the current.

Then there is Hernan Cortes, dreaming of Aztec silver, and finally St Paul on the way to Damascus and his conversion to Christianity. All three men seem indistinguishable from the horses they ride. Cortes "whinnies" and the "stone" Saul (or St Paul) "picked up once has grown into a hoof". The revelation that the poem alludes to by the end is an undoing of the colonial, occupying credo of the first two stanzas. Paul is a Roman who sees the light. Spaniard and Dutchman do not. That revelation on the road to Damascus hovers over the volume, ready to exalt it, or dash its hopes to the ground.

In "Epona", the mulish or equine meditation of the volume brings the speaker more centrally into the discussion. Some background to the title is needed. In Gaulish and (later) Roman and Gallo-Roman mythology, Epona was the goddess of horses, donkeys, mules. Her name means "Divine Horse" or "Horse Goddess".[3] She was a Celtic horse goddess whose "authority extended even beyond death, accompanying the soul on its final journey",[4] and was worshipped throughout the entirety of Gaul, and as far as the Danube and Rome. Her cult was eventually adopted by the Roman army and they in turn established her worship wherever they went. She was the only Celtic Goddess to be honored by the Romans with a temple in their capital city. Among the Gaulish Celts themselves, she was worshipped as goddess of horses, asses, mules, oxen, and, to an extent, springs and rivers. Epona is depicted sitting side-saddle, lying on a horse, or standing with multiple horses around her. Her symbol is the Cornucopia ("horn of plenty") which suggests that she could (originally) have been a fertility goddess. She is also identified with the Celtic goddess Edain. Muldoon doesn't use all these references, but fertility and transmigration figure in the poem, which moves from the voice of the goddess to the need of the speaker to bring the force the jackass embodies back into his control, and with it all the forces it represents:

> I have no heart, she cries. I am driving her madder,
> Out of her depth, almost, in the tall grass
> Of Parsons' triangular meadow.
> Because I straddle some old jackass
>
> Whose every hoof curves like the blade
> Of a scythe. It staggers over
> Towards a whitethorn hedge, meaning to rid
> Itself of me. Just in time, I slither
>
> Off the sagging, flabbergasted back.
> To calm a jackass, they say, you take its ear like a snaffle
> Between your teeth. I bite her ear and shoo her back
> Into the middle of my life.

From the sexual image of the triangular meadow, through the image of reaping ("blade / Of a scythe"), to the struggle between beast of burden and rider, the theme of fertility is obvious. He is both master of the beast and devotee of the goddess, but what does it mean to be in this intermediary position, caught between irreconcilables? It seems to be the point of the conclusion (not a horse and not an ass).

Between the Yahoo moment of "Cass and Me" ("Whose were those eyes at my groin?"), the Oedipal confrontation with the taboo of the maternal body in "Cheesecake", and the brutal meditation of "Ned Skinner", in which the visit of a travelling butcher takes on a decidedly sexual air ("We heard the whiskey-jug / Tinkle, his boots diminish in the yard. / Aunt Sarah put on a fresh apron."), there are the subtle reflections on desire and form in

"How to Play Championship Tennis". This poem attempts to determine how the goddess of fertility and desire may be served without perverse enslavement. In this poem, the speaker tells how, when other boys were playing various games ("penny poker" and tennis), he became friends with the "school caretaker", who was also from the country and had a mutual regard for nature ("We seemed to speak the same language. // He knew the names of all the trees,") as well as for books. The caretaker gives him a gift of a book entitled *How to Play Championship Tennis*, but when the boy reaches for it, the caretaker makes a play for his "pecker". Escaping hurriedly, the boy sees his friends "Joe and Cyril" playing tennis outside, and notices "Their fluent lobs, their deft volleys, // As if they had found some other level". This sublimation of desire is juxtaposed with the harsh incarnation he had run away from, an incarnation which the word "pecker" both embodies and distances him from (as all profanations for the body do); so perhaps now the speaker understands better than ever *How to Play Championship Tennis*, knows how to mediate between the goddess of fertility and the beast she rides – or, if not, at least he understands the dangers of that mediation.

In the poem "Ma", we have a very autobiographical reflection on Muldoon's mother, her dilettantism, her strange love of the quintessential English World War I poet Rupert Brooke (strange for an Irish Catholic), her memory of an affair with a soldier (American, perhaps) amidst the "orchards and the cannery" of their town. In a sleight of hand, Muldoon says that this is "story-telling". Is he fictionalising the affair in order to project his desire for his mother? Or merely setting up this desire as a narrative entry to the end of the poem in which desire is as dangerous as entering into the bowels of the earth, the bowels of the mother. For quite unexpectedly, he writes: "Old miners at Coal-island / Going into the ground. Swinging, for the fear of the gas, / The soft flame of canary". The canary's soft flame is the figure of poetry itself, a beautiful singer that is sensitive to poisonous gas. This is another version of poetry's mediation of the harshness of desire. The beautiful free translation entitled "Keen" of Eibhlín Ní Chonaill's

"Lament for Art O'Leary", a famous eighteenth-century poem follows "Ma". Muldoon's version of the poem presents an elegiac
version of the same mediation between the sacred and profane
emanations of desire. Again, the theme is equine. The horse of the
women's dead husband returns to her covered in his blood. She
finds him "without pope or bishop", without cleric to perform the
sacred rites of extreme unction and so must perform them herself,
though she seems to do so unconsciously when she finds

> ... some withered old woman
> Who had wrapped you in her mantle.
> Your blood was flowing still,
> I knew of no way to staunch it.
> I cupped my hands and drank it.

The profane and sacred merge in an image that is neither specifically Christian nor Dionysian, but which contains elements of
each.

Often the line between pagan and Christian imagery is very
thin in Irish culture, for, as Muldoon writes in "Our Lady of Ard-
boe",

> Who's to know what's knowable?
> Milk from the Virgin Mother's breast,
> A feather off the Holy Ghost?
> The fairy thorn? The holy well?

If even Muldoon cannot answer these questions (and who
can?), he always returns to what, in "Big Liz", is called "the inevitability of earth". The "diamond in the navel" of the title's stripper
refracts all the meaning he needs to impart; however, such a symbol of desire and beauty is easily perverted because it often exists
in the moral ambiguity of the demimonde. "The Ducking Stool" is
a poem of perversion, of incest between grandfather and grand-
daughter in the confines of an "ancient, three-storey rectory". The
poem has an uncanny whimsical energy, considering its theme.
Partially, one must think it is because Muldoon feels comfortable

in its dark suffocating interiors, believing he has found some truth about human nature there. There is an unsettling sense of discovery at the end of the poem, when grandfather finds his female offspring in her hiding place:

> Through the ancient, three-storey rectory
> He knows like the back of his hand.
> She would crouch in some narrow wardrobe
> Among stinking, mildewed foxes
> While his steps faltered at the door,
> Which, opening, might throw light on her.

The discovery contains both the fear and the desire of the primal scene. The linking of hunting and sexual taboos, the vivid animal imagery ("stinking, mildewed foxes"), have become familiar to readers of Muldoon.

There follows a series of riddle-like poems, "The Girls in the Poolroom", "Boon", "The Wood", before we reach the historical meditation of "At Master McGrath's Grave", a poem about a famous greyhound in the sport of hare coursing. Muldoon was moved to visit his grave possibly because the dog was born small, a weak pup who went on to become the most celebrated and successful Irish racer of his time. "He won the Waterloo Cup on three occasions, 1868, 1869 and 1871, and was the first greyhound to do so. He became such a celebrity that his owner Lord Lurgan was requested to take him to be seen by Queen Victoria and the Royal Family."[5] The poem includes a variety of colonial markers ("Lord Lurgan's demesne", "the Waterloo Cup") before ending with the intriguing poignant reflection on the way McGrath (the national champion who surprised the English sportsmen) and the landscape have become inseparable. Nature and McGrath's grave make the speaker surrender to grief:

> The overhanging elm-trees
> And the knee-high grass
> Are freshly tinged
> By this last sun-shower.

I'm not beside myself with grief,
Not even so taken by McGrath,

It's just the way these elm-trees
Do more and more impinge,
The knee-high grass
Has brought me to my knees.

The landscape has become the marker of significance, of insights ("freshly tinged / By the last sun-shower"), of neglect ("knee-high grass") of rootedness becoming a burden (the impinging "elm-trees"). Nature has enveloped him, and shrouded the human dimension of the great racer. McGrath, even though the greyhound is at the centre of the poem, is hidden from the poet, making the latter ask "Should he not still smoulder, / Our shooting star / That claimed the Waterloo Cup / In eighteen sixty-nine?"

In "The Merman", another hybrid like the mule, the farming of landscape by the speaker and seascape by the merman are compared:

He was ploughing his single furrow
Through the green, heavy sward
Of water. I was sowing winter wheat
At the shoreline, when our farms met.

Though nothing will grow of the merman's hard work, and he may know nothing of the "qualities" of "friendship" and "love", he also will not be subject to the sufferings of those who cut "swathes" through "fields of corn and hay". Landscape is a marker of our fate as human beings, bringing suffering as well as relief, roots as well as burdens. We find the same marker in the short poem "Blemish":

Were it indeed an accident of birth
That she looks on the gentle earth
And the seemingly gentle sky
Through one brown and one blue eye.

It is as if our modes of perception, ways of seeing, must be adapted to all aspects of the view, brown eye for earth, blue one for sky. We must keep an eye to the ideal, another to the real. The word "seemingly" is foreboding, of course, and looks back to the "accident of birth", or the hand of fate, for its meaning. This is Muldoon beating around the bush, so to speak; in other poems he is more direct.

In "The Bearded Woman, by Ribera", for example, we return to a crossbred image of the female and male, which specifically brings together the quotidian and the transcendent, the sacred and profane, the ugly and the beautiful. This ekphrastic[6] poem is inspired by the painting of Jusepe di Ribera, when the Spaniard was working in Naples, drawn there by the presence of Caravaggio. It contains all the grime and human pathos of the master, looking for sacred presence in the face of reality. The bearded woman reminds Muldoon of both an outcast and of the Madonna. She has a preternaturally old looking baby at her breast, but Muldoon is particularly drawn to a "willowy clean-shaven" man "in the shadows", caught between his morning tasks. They seem to share a surprising and strange interest in the "bearded woman". The poem is a farrago, a brood of opposites. In "The Mixed Marriage", Muldoon reflects on his parent's mixed marriage, his father from the landless working class, his mother a "schoolmistress". Their mixed union comes out of the books she reads, in particular *Gulliver's Travels* and *Aesop's Fables*, where animal and human nature interlink for our moral edification. This interlinking underlies *Mules*. We see it in "Vacquero" and the title poem, among many others. The body is fertile with meaning, that is the secret of women (see "De Secretis Mulierum"), because of its roots in the natural world.

In "Largesse", this fertility is something to be celebrated as it gives rise to so many figures of thought, so many avenues for our appetites, and so many types of craving:

A body would think
The world was its meat and drink.

It fits like a dream!
What's the fish-pond to the fish,
Avocado and avocado-dish,
But things shaped by their names?

Muldoon is convinced that the living world is more important than the artistic precisely because of its organic movement:

For only by embroidery
Will a star take root in the sky,
A flower have a pillow for ground.
How many angels stand on a pinhead?

Not only is the natural and physical the source of all meta-physical speculation, they provide the texture for all Zen-like meditation (and anticipate the recent use of haiku by Muldoon), outliving in seed all future versions in culture:

Twelve o'clock. We climb to bed.
A trout leaps in the far pond.
The sound of one hand clapping.

And the avocado-stone is mapping
Its future through the wreck
Of dinner-table and dining-room.

Finally Muldoon must recognise the source of the inevitability of earth in his own body, his own trope of desire:

Numberless cherubim and seraphim.
Alleluia on my prick!

The tension between the transcendent world of stars and angels and the earthbound world of the mulish sexual member is tested throughout the rest of the volume; and though Muldoon certainly realises the power of the latter, especially in our neo-pagan age, he also insists on the necessity of the former.

The last three poems of the volume, "Duffy's Circus", "Mules", and the long sonnet sequence "Armageddon, Armageddon" establish the terms of the relationship. In "Duffy's Circus", we are presented with a godless version of our contemporary carnival world, where the wonders of nature appear grotesque during a performance Muldoon attended as a child. It is a world in which all the themes of the volume, dwarfs and bearded women (who don't appear but might have), are implied. The carnival itself is a mixed celebration, bidding farewell to the very flesh it indulges, during a performance in which all pretension of wisdom looks ridiculous:

> Once Duffy's Circus had shaken out its tent
> In the big field near the Moy
> God may as well have left Ireland
> And gone up a tree. My father had said so.
>
> There was no such thing as the five-legged calf,
> The God of Creation
> Was the God of Love.
> My father chose to share such Nuts of Wisdom.

The circus deflates its own expectations and with it all hopes of metaphysical significance, mocking human aspirations (in this case wealth):

> ... Nor did it matter
> When Wild Bill's Rain Dance
> Fell flat. Some clown emptied a bucket of stars
>
> Over the swankiest part of the crowd.

Muldoon loses track of his father, while the dwarfs enter the stage and a man saws a woman in half. The sexual violence, which is so central to the volume, ends the poem on centre stage. Could this not be sawing sexual intercourse, seen from a child's point of view? It is difficult to determine, but the profane emphasis is apparent.

This is not to diminish the place of the Platonic values in Muldoon's world. He must always come back to them. In the next poem, "Mules", the first sentence plaintively brings this to mind:

Should they not have the best of both worlds?

Her feet of clay gave the lie
To the star burned in our mare's brow.
Would Parsons' jackass not rest more assured
That cross wrenched from his shoulders?

The stanza that follows the solitary first interrogation carries the tensions between clay (earth) and star (sky) in answer to its question. The transcendent is in fact burned in the mare's brow. Just as we cannot escape our animal natures, we cannot remove the mark of the divine. That is the cross we and the jackass have to bear, even though we might rest "more assured" without it. Either way we have to be prepared for violent reminders ("Tense for the punch below their belts") from both worlds as Muldoon's father and Sam Parsons know, when they prepare for the birth of an infertile mule, born of mare and jackass:

For what was neither one thing or the other.

It was as though they had shuddered
To think, of their gaunt, sexless foal
Dropped tonight in the cowshed.

And then, just when you think Muldoon has decided to plant his allegiance in earth and all that it represents – the sex, violence, the energy, the perversion – he realises that there is something else, that it has come from somewhere else, even though Wordsworth's immortality "trailing clouds of glory" is now a sticky placenta:

We might yet claim that it sprang from earth
Were it not for the afterbirth
Trailed like some fine, silk parachute,
That we would know from what heights it fell.

This poem is a beautiful demonstration of how we are caught in an epistemological bind; we don't really know the origins of truth or being, but we want to, even need to. This desire underlies the apocalyptic tenor of the closing sonnet sequence, "Armageddon, Armageddon".

The poem begins with the "purity of light" around Lawrence Durrell's house in California. It is a land of plenty, a "dazzling" fairy land with a "Snow-White Villa"; one, however, that is quickly weighed down with darkness, with an image of a kneeling woman, kneeling close to earth and "spitting the stars" as though they had been knocked loose from her mouth. The return to earth is not a welcome one, as we can see; it is not celebratory as it is in "Largesse". In the second sonnet sequence of "Armageddon, Armageddon", Muldoon reflects on the mythological figure Oisin's return to Ireland after three hundred years in the Irish faery world with the goddess Niamh. Oisin becomes one with the land on his return, but quickly ages and dies, following the judgement that he would die once his feet touched mortal ground. Muldoon concludes: "And I know something of how he felt." In the third stanza, we understand his reluctance to return to Ireland. Muldoon comes from the land of "No Surrenders", the heart of virulent Orangeism, and the tide of violence is rising in the North from the early 1970s after the Provisional IRA began its campaign to oust British troops from Ireland. The conflict between reason and blood-and-soil politics has become impossible to reconcile. Here Muldoon mentions Swift directly:

> We could always go closer if you wanted,
> To where Macha had challenged the charioteer
> And Swift the Houyhnhnm,
> The open field where her twins were whelped.
> Then, the scene of the Armagh Rail Disaster.
> Why not brave the Planetarium?

Macha, the image of the power of earth and yahoo-glory, challenges the charioteer, while Swift challenges the Horses of Reason; and with these confrontations come that between rooted interests and international culture. In an earlier poem "Paris", Muldoon seems happy to be associated with the latter, and here we see why: Armagh is too etymologically and historically close to the world-ending battle of Armageddon.

The fourth sonnet's sexual dream is captured helplessly on the train as it crosses blockades and the border. Now we know why Muldoon is anxious to brave the theoretical imperatives of the planetarium, the stars that rule our destiny here on earth and which also offer promise of escape. The fifth sonnet presents a longing image of the mythological denizens (Archer, Hunter, Twins) and fabled lands of the sky:

> I knew these fields. How long were they fallow?
> Those had been Archer's sixty yellow acres,
> These Hunter's forty green and grey.
> Had Hunter and Archer got into their heads
> That they would take the stars in their strides?

The figures of the constellations think they can escape the inexorable battlefield the lands must become, but the sixth sonnet makes it clear that the wrongs that have been done are familial ones and therefore will reverberate through the heavenly society. Some violence has been done to "Grace", which must be answered. With this injury, the allegorical nature of the volume is apparent. For "Grace" joins "Mercy" and "Will" as an emblem of our virtues and faculties, which are caught in the tension between earthly drives and heavenly aspirations. In the final sonnet of the sequence, this injury will turn the hand into stone, one ready to be thrown at one's enemy as Armageddon begins:

> A summer night in Keenaghan
> So dark my light had lingered near its lamp
> For fear of it. Nor was I less afraid.
> For the Mustard Seed Mission all was darkness.
>
> I had gone out with the kettle
> To a little stream that lay down in itself
> And breathed through a hollow reed
> When yon black beetle lighted on my palm
> Like a blood-blister with a mind of its own.

My hand might well have been some flat stone
The way it made for the underside.
I had to turn my wrist against its wont
To have it walk in the paths of uprightness.

The darkness envelopes light so profoundly that no light seems to enter it, while the dark forces of nature ("black beetle") and the hurts of the subconscious body ("blood-blister") usurp the sovereignty of reason. Having a mind of their own, they force the hand to become their instrument. The hand, our sensitive tactile rejoinder to the world, is seemingly no longer at the will of Grace or Mercy. Our only hope is to turn this force against its unaccustomed path and seek virtue and the stars, but the hope is dim indeed. Mules rule this volume, and set the stage for the escape of the next volume *Why Brownlee Left* (1980) and for the harshness of the succeeding volume *Quoof* (1983), as the history of Northern Ireland itself grows increasingly bitter.

Endnotes

---

[1] I am beholden to Samuel Holt Monk's "The Pride of Gulliver", *A Norton Critical Edition*, 315–7 for much of the preceding outline.

[2] R. S. Crane, "The Houyhnhnms, the Yahoos, and the History of Ideas", *Norton*, 405. Crane specifically mentions the writings of the Neoplatonist Porphyry as an example of the logical opposition between rational man and irrational horse.

[3] "Celtic religion." *Encyclopædia Britannica*, 2006. *Encyclopædia Britannica Online.* 5 November 2006 http://search.eb.com/eb/article-65541>

[4] "Epona". *Encyclopedia Mythica* from *Encyclopedia Mythica Online*, http://www.pantheon.org/articles/e/epona.html.

[5] See "Master Mcgrath", *Wikipedia*, http://en.wikipedia.org/wiki/Master_McGrath.

[6] Alternately spelled ecphrasis, ekphrasis is a term used to denote poetry or poetic writing concerning itself with the visual arts, artistic objects and/or highly visual scenes.

3

Why Brownlee Left (1980)

SINCE THE IRISH LITERARY RENAISSANCE, Irish literature has been a testament to twentieth-century experience: the land wars, the religious and ethnic strife, the woes of colonisation and decolonisation. Questions of identity and place have been paramount and not easily answered. In the introduction to their anthology of Irish poetry, Peter Fallon and Derek Mahon state: "The word most frequently dwelt on in this selection is probably 'home', as if an uncertainty exists as to where that actually is."[1] In a move indicative of Modernist and postmodernist writing, contemporary Irish writers confront the vagaries of their own experience and history, whatever their regional identities. Home in Paul Muldoon's poetry is a place one wants to leave and can never leave. It is an identity, in fact, rather than a place. It can't be left behind, no matter how many personas one puts on. Personal reflections inevitably have public resonance, and aesthetic choices have political implications. The position of the contemporary Irish writer continues to be troublesome, to be divided, as Thomas Kinsella famously laments in his essay "The Divided Mind":

> I recognise that I stand on one side of a great rift, and can feel the discontinuity in myself. It is a matter of people and places as well as writing – of coming from a broken and uprooted family, of being drawn to those who share my origins and finding that we cannot share our lives.[2]

Kinsella captures the familial, political as well as the poetic ramifications of this idea of division from the past. In *Why Brown-*

lee Left, the family is investigated in very close terms and seen to have inevitable and perhaps regrettable public demonstrations. In the aesthetics and politics of Irishness there is constant endeavour to find a way of recreating the familiar, of healing the wounds of history with images of shared reality, one which Paul Muldoon engages throughout his career. *Why Brownlee Left* explores Ireland's history of colonisation and decolonisation, and presents a postcolonial critique of family and civility that is torn by the uneasy relationship between aesthetics and politics.

Politicising aesthetics is a familiar act now in literary criticism, but the force of the aesthetic, indeed the idea of aesthetic autonomy is not often even parried in much recent scholarship. This may be the result of the political contents of much contemporary criticism, but the implications of the relationship between politics and aesthetics must be elaborated beyond the working assumption that they inevitably collapse into one another. Behind many political readings of postmodernist writers like Muldoon is Walter Benjamin's critique of how Modernist writers had applied aesthetics to politics, as well as his contention that aesthetics must be politicised. One can easily forget that the two categories, aesthetics and politics, sometimes have different functions, however interconnected they may be. Theodor Adorno makes this point in a letter to Benjamin:

> ... you now casually transfer the concept of magical aura to the 'autonomous work of art' and flatly assign to the latter a counter-revolutionary function [...] However, it seems to me that the centre of the autonomous work of art does not itself belong on the side of myth – excuse my topic parlance – but is inherently dialectical; within itself it juxtaposes the magical and the mark of freedom.[3]

The effort to politicise the aesthetic should not simplify its inner workings or its literary heritage. This chapter attempts to show how this may be accomplished, and how we may juxtapose "the magical and the mark of freedom". It also offers a reading of the dynamic relations between the rational and irrational, the intellectual and the physical, as they unfold in Muldoon's creative articulations of self and other within as well as outside the confines of a contested region. Successful forms of this articulation rely on the retrieval of both morality and freedom (formerly opposed for the colonised within the conventions of the colonial order), and occur during that time when the violent struggle finds its reflection in the self's romances, in the forgiveness between opposites, however brief, that is necessary for the inevitable combinations of future life.

In *Why Brownlee Left* (1980), the struggle to articulate haunts the text. The move to escape, or at least voyage, is evident in the titles of the poems (from the title poem to "Making the Move"). The Troubles in the North were reaching crisis point and Muldoon's own personal life, a divorce, the death of his mother from cancer, mirrors public problems. That he would crave departure is no surprise, but as much as the poems reflect this desire, there is a contrary pull back to the old dilemmas. In the first poem, "Whim", the poet cannot escape his obsessions. Sexuality and violence, human and animal, history and private lives, myth and reality, merge inextricably until one of the central motifs of Muldoon's early work, sex and desire, is locked into the image of a couple who get "stuck" while having sex and who have to be carried away in an ambulance. The capriciousness of this image is aimed as much at the poet himself as it is at the subject. The poem begins in the Europa Hotel, one of the most bombed sites of Northern Ireland, where the woman is reading an old Legend, "Cu Chulainn and the Birds of Appetite". The man observes that this translation by Standish O'Grady from the original Irish is old-fashioned and recommends that she reads Kuno Meyer's translation. O'Grady is very much connected to the national myth-making that occurred at the inception of the Irish Literary Revival, and so this advice has political, as well as artistic, resonances. On their way toward his house, where Meyer's translation awaits, the couple walk into the Botanic Gardens in Belfast, situated near The Queen's University, where passion takes over. Muldoon is playing the self-parodying storyteller as he concludes the poem:

To cut not a very long story short,
Once he got stuck into her he got stuck
Full stop.

     They lay there quietly until dusk
When an attendant found them out.
He called an ambulance, and gently but firmly
They were manhandled onto a stretcher
Like the last of an endangered species.

It doesn't require much interpretation at this point to see how the themes of sexuality and violence, human and animal, history and private lives, myth and reality, are coupled. It is indeed an Oedipal nightmare from which Muldoon, like Joyce, is trying to awaken.

In "October 1950", the second poem in the volume, Muldoon contemplates the night of his conception, looking for the talisman that will lift him to consciousness, awaken him from the bad dream in which the lovers locked ridiculously in their embrace look like an "endangered species":

Whatever it is, it all comes down to this:
My father's cock
Between my mother's thighs.

Muldoon proceeds to see that the whole political process is the result of this act. "Cookers and eaters" (in the eat-or-be-eaten taxonomy of Northern sectarian violence), the Protestant oath of "Fuck the Pope", the drinking and mixed children that result from drunken passion (the "sly quadroon"), "Anything wild or wonderful" comes down to "this night". Again the tension between the earth and stars is apparent. The parents have sex in "an open field, as like as not / Under the little stars", but Muldoon is left "in the dark". He is left without a verifiable epistemology for either his conception or the cause of the Troubles; he only knows that they come from the same dark place of desire. Transcendence for Muldoon, as he makes clear in the poem "Bran", is innocence; knowledge is the highly sexualised fall of his imagination:

> While he looks into the eyes of women
> Who have let themselves go,
> While they sigh and they moan
> For pure joy,
>
> He weeps for the boy on that small farm
> Who takes an oatmeal Labrador
> In his arms,
> Who knows all there is of rapture.

This is the cause of all his sadness. Does the aesthetic redeem this? Partially.

In the boyhood memory of film viewing, "The Weepies", the potently named Will Hunter is a leader of a gang who "in a single, fluent gesture" can "peel an orange". Before the images of "Hippodrome", of the "crippled girl / Who wanted to be a dancer" meeting the "married man ... dying of cancer", even Will Hunter is undone with the rest of the audience:

> Our hankies unfurled
> Like flags of surrender.
> I believe something fell asunder
> In even Will Hunter's hands.

So the aesthetic, the performative act, is cherished, but doesn't stand up to reality. It does, however, have its place, as in "The Geography Lesson":

> You should have seen them, small and wild
> Against a map of the known world,
>
> The back row of the class of '61.
> Internal exiles at thirteen or fourteen [...]
>
> Who knew it all. Where to listen for the cuckoo
> When she touched down from Africa.
>
> Why bananas were harvested while green
> But would hanker after where they'd grown,
>
> Their sighing from the depths of a ship

Or from under the counter in Lightbody's shop,

How all that greenness turned to gold
Through unremembering darkness, an unsteady hold.

In the postcolonial nature of this geography lesson and its
dark encounter with the other, there is a type of sublime firmly
rooted in the abject, with little enough of the transcendent about
it. And it has the same sense of "the Fall" as Frost's poem "Nothing Gold Can Stay", to which the second to last line alludes. Even
in poems such as the quixotically titled "Cuba" there is something
defiled, something foreign. Is the otherness of the title the damned
sensuality and sexual trepidation of a girl's night out? At the end
of that poem we hear a very uninteresting confession from the sister named "May":

... Father, a boy touched me once.'
'Tell me, child. Was this touch immodest?
Did he touch your breast, for example?'
'He brushed against me, Father. Very gently.'

Everything is immodest in this poem: the Father's questions,
the girl's teasing answer, the confession itself, which contains the
dark secrets and abject lessons of "Cuba" – both historical tropical
island and imaginary realm of the poem.

This type of truth is what drives the bishop crazy in the poem
of that name ("The Bishop"), even though he travels the world to
escape it, until he cannot tell the difference between what is inter-
nal or external, until the boundaries of his mind are blurred. In
"The Boundary Commission", there is a similar blurring of
boundaries, one which plays on the arbitrariness of the boundary
that was drawn between Northern Ireland and the Free State, and
which divided villages in the process:

You remember that village where the border ran
Down the middle of the street,
With the butcher and baker in different states?

The division between the butcher and baker is like that between Cain and Abel. On one side, we have the slaughterer and on the other the bread of life, with the mark of the beast, the border, running between them. For Muldoon, who wants to tread lightly like Golightly, it is a difficult question, both politically and aesthetically.

"Lull" is a quietly argued but serious poem of interstices, of intervening spaces in time and place. The lull might be in the violence in the North; or the longer one that constitutes the slow pace of country life. At first it seems a pastoral lull:

> I've heard it argued in some quarters
> That in Armagh they mow the hay
> With only a week to go to Christmas,
> That no one's in a hurry ...

This notion quickly broadens out to religious suffering and redemption:

> To save it, or their own sweet selves.
> Tomorrow is another day
> As your man said on the Mount of Olives.
> The same is held of Country Derry.

The Mount of Olives calls to mind both Jesus' passion in the Garden, situated at the base of the Mount of Olives, and the Jewish belief that God will redeem the dead at the end of days on the Mount. There is no rush, no rush to solve the problems, no rush because tomorrow means suffering and/or redemption – and if both are coming what does it matter which or when, especially when redemption only comes through suffering. This is the "eternal interim" with which the poem closes. Is that what "they're waiting for / In Tyrone, Fermanagh, Down and Antrim"? Is that why there are "houses where the fire / Hasn't gone out in a century"? Is the fire religious fervour, commitment to home and family, or a more divisive sectarian fire? With Muldoon, it is sometimes better to leave the questions hanging. These are rich ambiguities that highlight the ambivalences of the poem and poet. The roots of this consciousness are showing, but they extend underground where it is difficult to follow.

In "Remember Sir Alfred", the dirt itself has political and social significance:

> The gardens of Buckingham Palace
> Were strewn once with Irish loam
> So those English moles that knew their place
> Would have no sense of home.

The joke is that there are no moles in Ireland; Irish loam would feel unwelcoming to the moles. Home would seem to be a racial construction, one made out of blood and soil, but for Muldoon this is a form of idealisation. He is quizzical about the straight-thinking Sir Alfred McAlpine, an English engineer who believes that "the shortest distance between to points is a straight line", and whose gaze is fixed on "something beyond the horizon, / Love, or fidelity". Truth is more mixed, as we have seen. In the next stanza, the truth of a situation must hold disparate objects together; it must contain nationalist Protestants like Parnell and the "I.R.A.", as well as the racial stereotype of "Red-headed women". Truth is often unexpected, and is best understood in a complex imaginative way. Muldoon closes that stanza with this reflection upon a reflection:

> The Irish squire
> Who trained his spy-glass
> On a distant spire
> And imagined himself to be attending Mass.

Home is more likely to be understood in this way. Sir Alfred then dislodges a hare and finds that nature's lines are never straight as the hare "goes by leaps and bounds" by "singleminded swervings". The implication is that singlemindedness which doesn't swerve becomes too rigid.

In "Anseo" we see that that is precisely what happens. The military roll-call of the IRA parallels the roll-call at Muldoon's boyhood school in Collegelands. The boy, Joseph Mary Plunkett Ward, has the appropriate Irish martyr's name.[4] The disciplined punishment he receives for not being present at roll-call ("Anseo" being the Irish for the answer "here") leads to an obsession with discipline itself:

> I remember the first time he came back
> The Master had sent him out
> Along the hedges
> To weigh up for himself and cut
> A stick with which he would be beaten.
> After a while, nothing was spoken;
> He would arrive as a matter of course
> With an ash-plant, a salley-rod.
> Or, finally, the hazel wand
> He had whittled down to a whip-lash,
> Its twist of red and yellow lacquers
> Sanded and polished,
> And altogether so delicately wrought
> That he had engraved his initials on it.

The weapon of his punishment becomes an artifact, one which he would carry him to his fight for Ireland, living in a "secret camp". The reification of secrets is what all this martial rhetoric has been about; it gives shape to our irrational desires just as Ward whittles and polishes the cane with which he is beaten. If the volume is about escape and exotic places, half of them apocryphal, as Muldoon's father never did go to the places he is imagined to have gone, "Anseo" tells us why. If that is what it means to be here, one would rather be elsewhere.

It is no surprise that the next poem is the famous and beautiful title poem, "Why Brownlee Left". Robert Frost is considered to be a formative influence on Muldoon. The harsh sexual terms of a poem like Frost's "The Subverted Flower" is one that would seem very important to Muldoon, but, to the present writer, the connec-

tion had always seemed somewhat difficult to follow. If one examines this sonnet closely, however, Frost's marks are increasingly evident in style and tone:

> Why Brownlee left, and where he went,
> Is a mystery even now.
> For if a man should have been content
> It was him; two acres of barley,
> One of potatoes, four bullocks,
> A milker, a slated farmhouse.
> He was last seen going out to plough
> On a March morning, bright and early.
>
> By noon Brownlee was famous;
> They had found all abandoned, with
> The last rig unbroken, his pair of black
> Horses, like man and wife,
> Shifting their weight from foot to
> Foot, and gazing into the future.

There is the sly indirect question of the beginning that ends in
a mystery (for Frost a poem "begins in delight and ends in wisdom").[5] There is then a Frostian list of rural possessions, and the
last sighting of the man; and how his leaving has made him famous (one asks, was he famous before?). Rural legends are the
stuff of Frost's poetry. The closing image of the horses, "like man
and wife" shifting their weight, is most Frostian of all. They shift
as if deciding whether to stay or go, gazing into the future, as if to
see where Brownlee has gone. Perhaps they are considering the
lack of any prospects on the horizon and so represent the married
life one wonders whether Brownlee enjoyed, as no wife is mentioned. All these questions and items are put forth in a decep-
tively simple way so like Robert Frost. Think of the lines of "The
Road not Taken": "Two roads diverged in a wood, and I – / I took
the one less traveled by, / And that has made all the difference."[6]
For both Frost and Muldoon departures raise as many questions
as they settle. Notice also the light rhyme dwindling away as we
see the evidence of what he left behind, and feel his departure. By

this stage in the volume, we know why he left, or at least we can guess.

Poems like "Immrama" (the Irish for voyage poems) and "Truce" are poems of travels, dark secrets (the Nazi connections of the former poem) and the familiar connection between love and war (the truce between lovers and sectarian divides of the latter poem). In "History", these connections include the making of poetry:

> Where and when exactly did we first have sex?
> Do you remember? Was it Fitzroy Avenue,
> Or Cromwell Road, or Notting Hill?
> Your place or mine? Marseilles or Aix?
> Or as long ago as that Thursday evening
> When you and I climbed through the bay window
> On the ground floor of Aquinas Hall
> And into the room where MacNeice wrote 'Snow'.
> Or the room where they say he wrote 'Snow'.

The various names of streets bring together English, Irish, Catholic and Protestant consciousness (from the British Isles and the continent) as possible places for their first act of sex. Clearly, if the question is purely rhetorical it would be better, more fitting, to have had sex where MacNeice wrote his sensual apostrophe to plurality: "Snow", the poem of the "drunkenness of things being various". That it only might have been the room accentuates the fictive strategy of the poem. If there must be a place and a time for their first sex, what better time and place than in this poem. It celebrates life's plurality more successfully than many other places and times might have done. Again, we look to escape place, time and home, and must rely on aesthetics to do so. This is where victory really lies, at least in the imaginative realm of poetry, the land of aesthetic play; but just as soon as Muldoon asserts this, he craves the opposite.

In "Palm Sunday", the poem of Christ's victorious entry into Jerusalem, Muldoon considers victories such as the English victory at Agincourt, or the Normans in Ireland. Being Irish, he also must consider that these victories depend on others' defeat, that longbows are made out of wood like that of the yew (the tree of mourning), which chimes in well with the Victor-Victim Christ's journey towards his own defeat upon the cross and his subsequent conquest of death. The complicated figures ("the coffin-board that yearns to be a tree / Goes on to bear no small, sweet gourds / As might be trampled by another Christ") lead Muldoon to ask for "a world where everything stands / For itself and carries / just as much weight as me on you". This world where the object is self-contained cherishes the object, just as lover on lover does, at least in the ideal world. Once the object stands for more than itself, or when something disrupts that perfect assessment where "everything stands ... for itself", then secrets are unlocked, identity disrupted. And those moments are to be feared, as we see in "Holy Thursday":

> We know, you and I, that it's over,
> That something or other has come between
> Us, whatever we are, or were.

This last supper mirrors the Last Supper; a lie has been told, a kiss is not a kiss. The symbol abounds; and the lovers must suffer a different type of passion. What's left behind is made meaningful by the absence of those sharing the meal and by the simple gestures they made to share it:

> The waiter swabs his plate with bread
> And drains what's left of his wine,
> Then rearranges, one by one,
> The knife, the fork, the spoon, the napkin,
> The table itself, the chair he's simply borrowed,
> And smiles, and bows to his own absence.

After this melancholy, though beautiful scenario, we again move to a poem of departure, "Making the Move", about Ulysses braving the "wine-dark sea". Muldoon peoples his myths with modern characters.

On his odyssey, literary influences like Lord Byron, Raymond Chandler appear, as does the French philosopher Blaise Pascal. On his journey, personal crutches fall away and accentuate the distances between us:

> Such books as one may think one owns
> Unloose themselves like stones
>
> And clatter down into this wider gulf
> Between myself and my good wife ...

The bow is the identifying feature of Ulysses when he returns home, for only he is strong enough to bend it. Muldoon rather shyly notes that his bow is a "boyish length of maple upon maple" that is "Unseasoned and unsupple". With its almost boyish closing end-rhyme (Were I embarking on that wine-dark sea / I would bring my bow with me") the poem is innocently hurt and youthful, for he is not yet departing ("Were I"), he is fearful (so he needs the bow), and, one thinks, needful of reasons to stay. Instead all he finds is dark secrets to trouble him and his beloved, driven by the spectre of divorce. In Muldoon's poetic rendition of a fairytale of the same name, "The Princess and the Pea", the niggling pea is revealed to be something much worse and more personal. It is the "stir / Of someone still alive. / Then a cry, far down. It is your own". The final assertion is like a death-knell of any hope of wanting to remain in Ireland. In "Grief", about his mother's death, Muldoon bitterly notes that "there's nothing left of our black horse / But the plume of his ornamental harness". In "Come into the Parlour", a poem mocking the consolatory gesture that the bereaved family makes, he ends with an image of the "wreckage of bath-tubs and bedsteads, / Of couches and mangles, / That was scattered for miles around." Before his long journey poem, "Immram", that ends the volume, Muldoon gives way to one image of transcendence, but, as always, it is a complicated one.

The poem "The One Desire" follows the image of one surviving desire. It is a transcendent desire, despite our neglect. A palm tree is ascending through the palm house that has been left to decay. Even though its architectural genius was ahead of its time, this has not been enough to keep it intact:

> The palm-house in Belfast's Botanic Gardens
> Was built before Kew.
> In the spirit that means to outdo
> The modern by the more modern,
>
> That iron be beaten, and glass
> Bent to our will,
> That heaven be brought closer still
> And we converse with the angels.
>
> The palm-house has now run to seed;
> Rusting girders, a missing pane
> Through which some delicate tree
> Let by kindly light
> Would seem at last to have broken through.
> We have excelled ourselves again.

It is an extraordinary sonnet that meditates on aesthetic choices, the peripheral (Belfast) culture's relationship to the centre (Kew, London), and religious inspiration, the ascending palm, the "kindly light" of God (it is a play on a famous hymn by Cardinal Newman, "Lead, Kindly Light", 1833). In Newman's hymn, the light leads him "amidst the tumult and gloom" even though he is "far from home". Muldoon's allusion makes it clear that leaving home for him implies homesickness, however strong the desire to leave might be. Perhaps this is merely true of human nature. He will have to break through the glass ceiling of his own limitations to make this transcendent gesture, but the excellence he may attain is not uncritically celebrated here. Have we excelled ourselves again because of the beauty of the image, or merely because we have left town and left the building to rot. It seems more likely that it is the latter, and Muldoon's destructive desire to leave must leave this destruction behind. Though Muldoon will not leave Ireland until after the next volume *Quoof* (1983) is written, his sense of place is expanding, and he is journeying in mind and body, beginning to take temporary positions in the States and elsewhere, and reflecting on the parallels and differences between places and histories.

"Promises, Promises" comes at the middle of the volume, but it is discussed here because its look at America nicely introduces the volume's final poem "Immram". In "Promises, Promises", Muldoon is in the tobacco country of North Carolina. He is there because he had begun to be published by Dillon Johnston of Wake Forest University Press (WFU is in that double-barrelled cigarette-city, Winston-Salem, NC). Like Derek Mahon's "A Globe in Carolina", Medbh McGuckian's "Cape Fear", and Michael Longley's "The Shack", Muldoon's poem is a product of this early connection with Wake Forest University Press and the surrounding area. The poem is composed of three sonnet structures, begins in the foothills, the Piedmont of the Blue Ridge, which is where Wake Forest University is located, and then moves east to the coast line where Raleigh landed with a band of eighty whom he then left behind when he sailed for England. This group became the famous 'lost colony' at Roanoke. The disappearance of this colony has always haunted the American imagination, and it becomes a big part of Muldoon's cosmology in his subsequent poetry. When Raleigh returns, the colony is gone, but he does see "one fair hair in her braid" and "blue in an Indian girl's dead eye". The image of a mixed breed, even if it is anticipated (for surely a birth couldn't have taken place yet), has already been important to Muldoon for metaphysical as well as cultural reasons. For Muldoon this dream of racial mixing contains various hopes and parallels: a hope to transcend the conflicts that would engulf the Indians and whites as the United States formed and moved westward, and the parallel he feels between the Irish and American Indian experience. The final stanza is literally and figuratively ghosted by such a parallel and hope:

> I am stretched out under the lean-to
> Of an old tobacco-shed
> On a farm in North Carolina,

When someone or other, warm, naked,
Stirs within my own skeleton
And stands on tip-toe to look out
Over the horizon,
Through the zones, across the ocean.
The cardinal sings from a redbud
For the love of one slender and shy,
The flight after flight of stairs
To her room in Bayswater,
The damson freckle on her throat
That I kissed when we kissed Goodbye.

The image of happiness in this new landscape, embodied by the cardinal's song, goes over the head of the poet, who feels bereft amid the rolling hills in the first stanza. Now, after the image of racial mixing, Muldoon feels the presence of the "other" stirring within him. The cardinal's song, instead of being in praise of marijuana or being an overly Romanticised version of splendour in the grass, as it was in the first stanza, now is given very specific reference. The ecstatic song is placed on the redbud, a luxuriant flowering purple tree that grows wild and is common in North Carolina. It is an image a native might have and emphasises the importance of the indigenous. With this specific image comes a specific memory of one "slender and shy" whom Muldoon or merely the speaker left behind in Bayswater. A balance between places is struck, but one doubts whether the promise, of love, of the new world, will be fulfilled. The tone of the poem, like its title, is ironic, but it forms an important poetic model for Muldoon upon which he will transform his poetic. It also gives him some respite from the stark situation at home.

The harsh tone of the long final poem of the volume, "Immram", drums this self-assessment home, as Muldoon takes a trip throughout the world (or at least with global associations) and then returns where he started in "Foster's pool-hall". The poem begins with a direct assault on Muldoon's fictionalised, part Native American, American lineage:

I was fairly and squarely behind the eight
That morning in Foster's pool-hall
When it came to me out of the blue
In the shape of a sixteen-ounce billiard cue
That lent what he said some little weight.
'Your old man was an ass-hole.
That makes an ass-hole out of you.'
My grandfather hailed from New York State.
My grandmother was part Cree.
This must be some new strain in my pedigree.

"Immram" has a Byronic stanza and Chandleresque tone as Muldoon narrates this rough confrontation and this "new strain" in his pedigree. The word Immram means "voyaging". The poem has parallels with the *Immram Mael Duin*, the most obvious one being that the ancient text translates as the 'Voyaging of Muldoon", a correspondence our poet must have liked. How many parallels exist is a subject of some debate.[7] What concerns us here is the imaginative landscape Muldoon creates, full of places, characters and situations out of American mythology. The history we encounter therein is cyclical, popular and/or fictional, drawn from the mythical method, but with a postmodern sense of pastiche: there are the recurring figures of Suzanne or Susan, Mr and Mrs Alfred Tennyson (the English poet wrote a version of "The Voyage of Muldoon", which the Irish poet dislikes), King Kong, and Blind Lemon, just to name a few. Muldoon's sense of play is never more in evidence: *"The Lord is my surf-board. I shall not want."* There is fate, repetition and a seeming randomness that increasingly defines Muldoon's poetry. What it all means is beyond an easy reckoning; the energy of the journey itself is apparent as are certain half-mocked mystical associations experienced in the cinematic reality of the twentieth century:

He went on to explain to O'Leary and myself
How only that morning he had acquired the lease
On the old Baptist mission,
Though his was a wholly new religion.

He called it *The Way of the One Wave.*
This one wave was sky-high, like a wall of glass,
And had come to him in a vision.
You could ride it forever, effortlessly …

This is the energy of the new millennium and New World, which Muldoon has harnessed in his efforts to understand why Brownlee left, where he went, and what he left behind.

Endnotes

---

[1] Peter Fallon and Derek Mahon, *The Penguin Book of Contemporary Irish Poetry* (London: Penguin, 1990), xxii.

[2] Thomas Kinsella, "The Divided Mind", *Irish Poets in English*, ed. Sean Lucy (Cork: Mercier, 1972), 208–9.

[3] Theodor W. Adorno, "Letters to Walter Benjamin", *Aesthetics and Politics*, ed. Ronald Taylor with an afterword by Fredric Jameson (London: Verso, 1980), 121.

[4] Joseph Mary Plunkett (1887–1916) was an Irish nationalist, poet and leader of the 1916 Easter Rising; he was executed by the British for his role in this rebellion. He was also a poet, which makes him important for Muldoon.

[5] Robert Frost, "The Figure a Poem Makes", *Selected Poems of Robert Frost* (New York: Holt, Rinehart, and Winston, 1963), 104.

[6] Robert Frost, *Collected Poems* (New York: Holt, 1969), 105.

[7] Kendall, *Paul Muldoon*, 83.

4

Quoof (1983)

MULDOON'S PENCHANT FOR VIOLENCE in his poetry reaches its height in this fourth collection of poetry, which was published in 1983 right after the hunger strikes in Ireland. A brief discussion of the preceding three years gives a sense of the tumult of the period. "In Northern Ireland the withdrawal of 'special category' status from the IRA prisoners convicted after March 1976 provoked an immediate 'dirty protest'." The prisoners, angry that they were treated as criminals rather than as political prisoners, covered their prison walls with faeces and then in 1980 went on hunger strike in H-Blocks, a maximum security prison in Northern Ireland. On December 15–16, thirty more Republicans joined the hunger strike. "The election to parliament of the strike's leader, Bobby Sands, initiated Sinn Fein's entry into electoral politics, while nationalist outrage at the death of Sands [from the hunger strike] and nine others [Francis Hughes, Raymond McCreesh, Patsy O'Hara, among their number] helped to ensure some dramatic early successes at the polls."[1] The era was defined death by death, bomb by bomb with violence flourishing and politics weakening. On December 6 in 1982 seventeen people were killed in the INLA (Irish National Liberation Army) bombing of the Droppin' Well disco in Ballykelly, Co. Derry. Three elders were later shot dead during service in Darkley Pentecostal Church, Co. Armagh; the shooting claimed by Catholic Reaction Force. In December 1983, Harrods was bombed by IRA. The list of murders committed on both sides grew longer as the decade progressed.

It is no surprise then that *Quoof* (1983) is a troubling volume for a troubling time, juxtaposing and confusing poems of violence with nostalgic celebrations of childhood and home. The poet's father figures largely in *Quoof*. His presence in Muldoon's imagination and his absence, following his death, form a leitmotif throughout the volume; perhaps the misogynistic tone of many of the poems results from his mother's role in this relationship, as Muldoon's mother appears to have consistently disrupted the affections between father and son. Psychoanalysis is always tricky for the literary critic, but the formulations cannot simply be avoided; it's best to keep them fluid, keeping the family romance, the nation, culture and landscape as components of his poetic. This family romance is settled in different ways and raises various questions. Is the depiction of home liberating or confining? Is the father's influence corrupting or benign? Muldoon is seeking a solution, but dubious as ever regarding the curative abilities of poetry. As Clair Wills notes of the various familial, aesthetic/ religious and political themes:

> *Quoof* reveals Muldoon to be as suspicious as ever about poetry's transformative, healing properties, but also more than ever in need of a cure. The sickness in this volume is in part the violence and brutality in Northern Ireland, as the images of violated women and the fragmented body parts suggests, it is represented above all in physical terms. *Quoof* places tremendous emphasis on the physical body and its appetites (nutritional and sexual). The body is of course the most personal of properties, and therefore perhaps the logical extension of Muldoon's autobiographical concerns. In part Muldoon is exploring here the problem of communicating that which is most personal and corporeal, of how to overcome the individual's confinement within the body. But the insistent emphasis on bodies and body parts in *Quoof* also has to do with entrapment in a very specific sense – with imprisonment and with the spectacle of the body then being enacted in Northern Irish prisons.[2]

This interconnection of themes, especially of the body politic and the personal body, has always been important to Muldoon, as to many Irish poets, but now it has taken on a real, often surreal, urgency. It is difficult to separate the volume from the political context: each body part calls forth a bombing, each act of oppression an army or police assault, and yet the volume does seek to both mirror political reality and to transform it. One of the ways Muldoon does this is to enlarge the scope of the action, historically and geographically.

The influence of time spent in the US is also evident on Muldoon's poetry: there is a sense of exaggerated geography, intensified experience, and the monolithic modernity that strikes most Europeans when they come to live in the States. One of Muldoon's great strengths as a poet is his ability to give familial resonance to historical and social conditions; the idea of "America", "Britain" or "Ireland" is parried in poems that question what place might mean and where home might be found. From the psychedelic reflections of "Gathering Mushrooms", the aesthetic rendering of "Mary Farl Powers", the myths and visions of "Yggdrasill", "Sky-woman", "The Unicorn Defends Himself", and "Aisling", to the surreal wanderings in "The More a Man Has the More a Man Wants", one sees how expansive Muldoon's poetic is, although his obsessions have become harsh, almost restrictive. It is the strange contradictory pull of the volume that gives it great power, even as it makes it discomforting to read. And this is the first volume, at least as far as the Faber *Poems 1968–1998* is concerned, in which Muldoon no longer uses the traditional capitalisation of the left-hand margin. It is as if his ways of seeing have changed, have been influenced by American practice and experience.

The hallucinogenic "Gathering Mushrooms" reflects Muldoon's father's working career as a mushroom picker and the poet's own drug use. Psychedelic means "soul or mind imagining ... to make the soul/mind manifest", it is important to remember, and if the soul is both reflected in our visions and our racial roots then this poem is perfectly psychedelic. There is a wire-service article in this morning's paper entitled "Hallucinogen opens gateway to the mystical, new study says". It concerns the studied benefits and hazards of psilocybin, the mushrooms at the centre of Muldoon's poem. Some of the conclusions and observations make a good introduction:

> People who took an illegal drug made from mushrooms reported profound mystical experiences that led to behavioral changes lasting for weeks – all part of an experiment that recalls the psychedelic 1960s. Many of the thirty-six volunteers rated their reaction to a single dose of the drug, called psilocybin, as one of the most meaningful or spiritually important experiences of their lives. Some compared it to the birth of a child or the death of a parent ... Almost a third of the research participants found the drug experience frightening even in the controlled setting. That suggests that people experimenting with the illicit drug on their own could be harmed ... The researchers suggest that the drug someday may help drug addicts kick their habit or aid terminally ill patients struggling with anxiety or depression. It may also provide a way to study what happens in the brain during intense spiritual experiences ... Psilocybin has been used for centuries in religious practices, and its ability to produce a mystical experience is no surprise. But the new work demonstrates it more clearly than before ... Even two months after taking the drug, most of the volunteers said that the experience had changed them in beneficial ways, such as making them more compassionate, loving, optimistic and patient. Family members and friends said they noticed a difference, too ... Twenty-two of the thirty-six volunteers reported having a 'complete' mystical experience ... That experience included such things as a sense of pure awareness and a merging with ultimate reality, a feeling of sacredness or awe, and deeply felt positive moods such as joy, peace and love.[3]

The poem takes many of these themes and looks at them askance. It starts with an image of his father labouring at mushroom picking and then moves to a memory of Muldoon and friends thinking of taking psilocybin mushrooms, while they might have been "thinking of the fire-bomb / that sent Malone House sky-high". Already the tension between public reality and private vision is established. The first is too real and the second seems escapist in its light; the poem will endeavor to resolve this tension. To do this, it has to allow the vision, the mystical experience to take place in all its aesthetic finery:

> We followed the overgrown tow-path by the Lagan.
> The sunset would deepen through cinnamon
> to aubergine,
> the wood-pigeon's concerto for oboe and strings,
> allegro, blowing your mind.
> And you were suddenly out of my ken, hurtling
> towards the ever-receding ground,
> into the maw
> of a shimmering green-gold dragon.
> You discovered yourself in some outbuilding
> with your long-lost companion, me,
> though my head had grown into the head of a horse
> that shook its dirty-fair mane ...

We begin with images from the pastoral tradition, a bit baroque, even rococo, but not drug-inspired as yet. The visionary and the aesthetic have the same basis of experience. Once the dragon enters the scene, we are entering a new creative space. As drug-induced as the vision is, it is in keeping with Muldoon's poetic preoccupations. Muldoon has the head of one of the horses from *Mules*, and the wisdom he will speak is based in the mixed blessings of animal and human, instinct and reason. This combination is the matrix of "pure awareness and a merging with ultimate reality, a feeling of sacredness or awe" that characterised the participants in the study. The vision that horse-Muldoon describes contains peace and joy, but also the fear that haunted those who partook of the drug:

> *Come back to us. However cold and raw, your feet*
> *were always meant*
> *to negotiate terms with bare cement.*

Beyond this concrete wall is a wall of concrete
and barbed wire. Your only hope
is to come back. If sing you must, let your song
tell of treading your own dung,
let straw and dung give a spring to your step.
If we never live to see the day we leap
into our true domain,
lie down with us now and wrap
yourself in the soiled grey blanket of Irish rain
that will, one day, bleach itself white.
Lie down with us and wait.

The scene is meant to reconcile the public and private, the aesthetic and political, the divine and the animal, and contains echoes of Isaiah and *The Golden Ass* in the last imperative. The first is an echo of sacred reconciliation between the lion and the lamb, the second a profane image of sexual union between human and beast. Both are valuable here, though the latter is also to be feared. Here is a wish to make the vision restorative, to solve the problems that drove Muldoon and his friends to take the drug, to leap "into our true domain", to transcend reality, though it remains doubtful whether the "soiled grey blanket of Irish rain" and everything it represents (the bomb in Malone house in particular) will ever be "bleached white". For can we "negotiate terms with bare cement" and can the "dung give a spring" to our step? Yes and no. Ambivalence reigns and wreaks violence upon us. As the most tellingly realistic line declares, the fear is that "Beyond this concrete wall is a wall of concrete / and barbed wire", that nothing will change. The only hope is to come back and sing. The rest of the volume makes that return and that gesture.

In poems such as "Trance", "The Right Arm", "The Mirror", Muldoon looks at the family romance as a nexus of political and artistic associations. These are subtle poems that depend in many ways on associations that the poet has already established. The trance of the first poem is that which centres round his mother's harsh presence and that which results from drug taking, the "Fly-Agaric" and "mind-expanding urine". The visions are again rooted in earthly reality: the star-clusters of the tea his mother has thrown outside on the snow brings us back to the star/earth duality at the close of *Mules*. The rocking horse, appearing later, is "unsteady on its legs": it is both symbol of aesthetic play and of the animal basis of our being. In "The Right Arm", stealing candy is symbolic of the fall; the town's name (Eglish) is caught orthographically between "ecclesia and église", that is between the assembly, or the people (the hierarchy perhaps most of all), and the church, or the spiritualised place. His act of stealing candy becomes the aestheticised profane act around which this sacred space moves:

> The Eglish sky was its own stained-glass vault
> and my right arm was sleeved in glass
> that has yet to shatter.

The poem is what keeps the glass round his arm from shattering, being an aesthetic object itself, being the sleeve of glass. In "The Mirror", from the Irish of Michael Davitt, the death of Muldoon's father is a source of guilt. Muldoon's inability to help him in life left a mirror of remorse; and his father's death of a heart attack shortly thereafter merely intensified the reflection. The poem shows how universal guilt is the reigning principle of consciousness. In a dream, Muldoon envisions driving home the nails that set the mirror in place, but the nails are those that crucify his father, while the mirror is where he sees his own identity reflected through the terms of his guilt.

In "The Hands", "The Sightseers" and "My Father and I and Billy Two Rivers", there are various acts of violence and interrogation. The amputated hands come back beating the windows of home; the Catholic father and uncle are treated as sightseers in their own land, especially the uncle who is made to sing a Protestant song, and curse the Pope of Rome before he returns home with the O of the mark of a gun held to his forehead still visible. Homecoming mirrors the violence of the land around it. The house in Ireland is always such a heavy signifier in Irish literature that it often collapses under the weight of its own meaning. In the third poem, "My Father and I and Billy Two Rivers", the sectarianism of the North finds its parallels first in the racism of North America and then in their shared colonial roots. The Americans who dressed like Mohawk Indians in order to inflict the Boston Tea Party, during which they threw the contested taxed tea overboard, enacted a ritual confrontation between the self and other: the other as self, the self as other. This confrontation, whether between Catholic or Protestant, white or black, Indian or white, woman or man, animal or human, is as the heart of Muldoon's poetic model of experience. This Swiftian moment of reflection on the self and other is a paradigm of the Irish experience of family, place, religion, politics, and gender. Allegories and aesthetics unfold in its mirror. As Muldoon writes in "Quoof", the title poem of the volume, the dark force of family secrets are connected to the uncanny recognition of our animal nature:

> How often I carried our family word
> for the hot water bottle
> to a strange bed,
> as my father would juggle a red-hot half-brick
> in an old sock
> to his childhood settle.
> I have taken it into so many lovely heads
> or laid it between us like a sword.
>
> A hotel room in New York City
> with a girl who spoke hardly any English,
> my hand on her breast
> like the smouldering one-off spoor of the yeti
> or some other shy beast.
> that has yet to enter the language.

Like Gulliver, Muldoon's own hand bares traces of the yeti, abominable snowman, or yahoo that resides in the landscape within and without. Is it his family inheritance or has he been infected by the woman? Or, finally, is the spore in the sonnet's loose simile caught between his hand and her breast? As Clair Wills notes: "It is precisely because the two are so alien (like the yeti), because their association has yet to enter the language, that the burdens of the tribe can be sloughed off."[4] Again, we wonder whether nature can provide absolution.

"Bigfoot" and "Beaver" have similar themes. "Bigfoot" is of course based on the legend of Sasquatch. Muldoon gives it the marriage theme of *Frankenstein*, as he captures the image of the legendary half-man, half-animal crossing "a clearing" and passing the "cabin" where a man "mourn[s]" his wife. We don't know whether she has died or merely left. As the monster of Mary Shelley's novel promises to visit the hero on his marriage night and to reek revenge for the Doctor's refusal to create a mate for him, here the "fur coat" of Bigfoot becomes a symbol of the promised fur coat, which the subject of the poem had promised his mourned-for wife. In "Beaver", one feels that the American usage of that word for woman's genitalia is at play in this image of tracking "beaver", making the poem both a tale of animal life and slang for women. Importantly, the search takes him indoors into a house and before a scene of passion. The eternal recurrence of desire and of the human/animal theme provides the turn, and return, of the poem. This eternal recurrence, this repetition, becomes the source of a postmodern play of signifiers in later volumes, one that has metaphysical significance: we can never do more than point beyond the physical world and its fixed referents. Transcendence is only that, a perspective from within the boundaries of experience.

"Beaver" signals the inability to escape from the primal scene, which we flee only to discover it again through another door. The only escape, or transit to a new place of bliss with sublimated energies, is through art. The poem provides the objectivity on our predicaments, and allows us to look at them with the right perspective, to laugh, perhaps, or to cry; it is the purgative force of what the French theorists call *jouissance*. In "Mary Farl Powers: *Pink Spotted Torso*", a poem Muldoon wrote for the artist Mary Powers, and based on her art work, we begin with a natural image, a Kerr's Pink potato which "answer[s] her knife / with hieroglyph". It is body ("Pink Spotted Torso"), art work and nature in one. In the second stanza, Muldoon seems affectionately to mock

Powers' open Midwestern personality ("the open book of Minnesota"), out of which came a story of "midnight swims with the Baumgartner boy". The third stanza descends into the depths of nature and consciousness, "a flooded granite quarry", where it seems that the Baumgartner boy may have drowned. In this dream memory, he almost gets free, having "unmanacle[d] / himself from buckled steel, from the weight of symbol / only to be fettered by an ankle". The notion that we are fettered to nature, and unable to rise to the pure breathable surface of consciousness, is central to this scene. Could it also be an imagined revenge because of Baumgartner's youthful shared passion with Powers, in the vein of Joyce's "The Dead" where the author/speaker is jealous of a past love?

Similar inabilities, similar recurrences appear in poems like "Edward Kienholz: The State Hospital", in which the strange plaster cast of a mentally disturbed man is naked, asleep and strapped to a bed. He seems to be abused by "an orderly" and has "trouble / with his bowels". In the last stanza Muldoon takes us to the upper bunk in this bunkbed, where another identical plaster cast is encircled by a neon "dream bubble" from a "comic strip". Muldoon would like to include "Hope, Idaho" in the picture, but is forced to admit that the neon light "takes in only the upper bunk of the bed / where a naked man, asleep, is strapped". This doubled image of human suffering is inescapable. The physical nature of this truth is what Muldoon beats mercilessly home in many of the poems that follow. In "The Salmon of Knowledge", wisdom seems the result of a sadomasochistic ritual, while in "From Strength to Strength" and "Cherish The Ladies", woman as heifer finds a strange place in the slaughterhouse, or abbatoir, of the poet's eye. A poem later in the volume, "Blewits", makes this profound misogyny all too real:

> And later in the wee, small hours,
> you will lie on the bed
> of your own entrails,
>
> to be fist-fucked all night

by blewits, or by chanterelles,
until the morning that never comes.

The image is so ferocious that it makes readers stop in their tracks. As Clair Wills notes, the volume is "full of women represented as sexualised objects, variously fantasised, discarded, raped, murdered, or violently punished", and she thinks "it is a mistake to dismiss criticism of *Quoof*'s misogyny in the name of ... unsentimental realism". She concludes: "What's distressing about it is not simply that Muldoon describes unpleasant events, acts, thoughts and fantasies, but that he acknowledges them as his own."[5] This is valid. If we remember that "blewits" and "chanterelles" are mushrooms or fungus, we see the source of this poetic fantasy. Without making excuses for the violence, we might add that women as objects of desire in Muldoon's poetry represent the larger objective world; perhaps this is true for the male imagination in general. It is also important to remember that desire reifies, or objectifies by its very nature, unless it is tempered by love, the sacred, or some higher human faculty. Muldoon is disillusioned with the world and he can find no faculty to temper the objectification he feels and which he violently extends to others. That much is plain. Our descent into fungal parasitic nature is final and harrowing. All projection is futile. Even fantasy is infected by the mushrooming truth of our substance. We are no more than the earth out of which we are made. In "Yggdrasill", this unbearable rootedness is given mythological basis.

In Norse mythology, Yggdrasill is the great tree of the world. Its branches and roots extended through all the universe – the heavens, the earth, and the underworld. At its top sat an eagle, at its bottom twined a serpent, and between them ran a squirrel breeding discord. It was prophesied that at the doom of the gods the tree would be destroyed. In the poem, Muldoon is the squirrel who finds on the tree various signs of his lover's betrayal. The tree itself, made up of various trees, is like a body: "waist-thick pine", "birch / perhaps". The last two stanzas contain the inevitability and necessity of myth ("people yearn / for a legend") and the leg-

end of apocalypse associated with it; in the 1980s Armageddon is
linked to the Russians:

> Yet the lichened
> tree trunk will taper
> to a point where one scrape of paper
> is spiked, and my people yearn
> for a legend:

> *It may not be today*
> *or tomorrow, but sooner or later*
> *the Russians will water*
> *their horses on the shore of Lough Erne*
> *and Lough Neagh.*

The Russians will have taken over Ireland and that will be the
death of the gods. The allusions to Laurence Sterne's *Tristram
Shandy* elsewhere in the poem are meant to cement the associations between creativity and sexual potency; Muldoon has often
followed Sterne in this. Here the sexual significance has political
as well as personal relevance. "The Frog" takes a similarly self-
conscious but nastier look at this theme. In this poem, the "entire
population of Ireland" is said to spring from a pair of frogs. Muldoon ends ironically, saying there is "surely" a "moral for our
times" in this story. And then contemplates squeezing the life out
of the frog in his hand, "like the juice of freshly squeezed limes, /
or a lemon sorbet?" The twist of course is that another Ireland,
with similarly long and brutal history of political troubles might
be born from this frog, so he had better be killed. We soon see
why he is so bitter. In the next poem, "A Trifle", whose title is
aimed on the poem itself, Muldoon remembers one of a number
of bomb scares. In this he passes a woman holding trifle as he
hurriedly descends the stairs. The image of the dessert, "blue-pink
... jelly sponge", calls to mind the carnage of bombs that go off.
The trifle is the bomb itself as well as the poem.

The mythos of "Yggdrasill" becomes increasingly prominent
in the poems that precede another long final journey poem, "The
More a Man Has the More a Man Wants". In the poems "Sky-

Woman", "The Unicorn Defends Himself", "The Destroying Angel" and "Aisling" we see that at some deep level this volume
charts the failure of the imagination, even as it is remarkably
imaginative. "The Unicorn Defends Himself" is a poem of imagination's last stand. The unicorn, symbol of both sexual power and
purity, as his horn is aphrodisiac and the ferocious unicorn can
only be tamed by a virgin, is placed in various historical scenes.
First he is on the tapestries from Flanders, defending himself
against hunters, then amidst the drug-taking and sexual promis-
cuities of the Lower East Side. In the last stanza, he is about to be
killed in a sexual manner:

> Everything centres
> on that spear tip poised to squander
> the cleft
> of his 'innocent behind'.
> At Houston Street and Lafayette
>
> the unicorn defends himself.

The imagination is doomed. In the other poems, the fate is set
in more specifically historical terms.

"Sky-Woman" is based on the *speirbhean*, which means sky-
woman, and is closely connected to the *aisling* tradition. She is
both a figure of poetic inspiration and of national sovereignty.
Aisling means vision in the Irish language. The tradition of the *aisling* dates back to the Irish language Jacobite poetry of the seventeenth and eighteenth centuries; the tradition has been interpreted
by contemporary writers in a variety of ways and, most importantly, by female authors who have interrogated a passive icon of
femininity and nationality until it has yielded a more positive
model for Irish women. The *aisling*'s image of a woman waiting to
be rescued by the men of Ireland because she is being forced to
marry a 'foreigner' (a representation of Ireland under English
colonisation) has been recuperated for cultural uses, especially by
Nuala Ní Dhomhnaill, the foremost Irish language poet in Ireland
and among the best of any poet writing in Ireland. Ní Dhomhnaill

is a poet whom Muldoon has translated extensively. Muldoon's take on this tradition is very consistent with his poetic. She is either the unfaithful lover in "Sky-Woman", who is more interested in undoing Orion's belt (Orion is a Greek figure of huge, insatiable male desire) than in inspiring our poet, or else she is a more complex figure of health and disease in "Aisling". In the later poem, she, who once was comparable to Aurora, Flora, or Venus, is now like Anorexia, because this is the Ireland of the hunger strikes and that is the trope she inspires amongst her followers.

These female muses are dangerous. In "The Destroying Angel", the muse is one of battle, a sort of female Mars, haunting the imagination of a military man. Her promises are false ones, as the culture and aesthetics with which the muse is associated seems to have no lasting power on the "eve of battle". The final stanza contains many of the images we have come to associate with Muldoon's poetry:

> The destroying angel wants to drink
> to your campaign.
> A gin and tonic, this time.
> You will unbutton your tunic
> and raise a glass. She raises hers.
> Try as you may,
> You cannot make them chink or chime.

The closing image is deeply foreboding. It is sensible that a toast with such an angel would not be easy to complete, as she destroys even that. The closing poem's meditation on the insatiability of desire makes this destroying angel an image of desire's destructiveness. In the *Poetry Book Society Bulletin*, which was published alongside *Quoof* in 1983, Muldoon said that the book was an attempt to "purge" himself "of the very public vocabulary it employs, the kennings of the hourly news bulletin". [6] One of the main characters in the last poem, Gallogly, is the image of what Muldoon wants to purge. He is a figure of instinctual drive and appetite, forever hungry.

"The More a Man has the More a Man Wants" records the journey of Gallogly, a terrorist mercenary on the run, and his alter-ego and nemesis, Mangas Jones, an American Indian in Northern Ireland seeking revenge. At the beginning of the poem, Gallogly is connected to animal imagery; he "squats in his own pelt" amidst the detritus of the sexual act ("froth" of bra and panties), and then prepares to make off like the fox he is "among hen runs and pigeon lofts". He flies on a charter flight from Florida to Aldergrove airport outside Belfast, and finds Mangas Jones with him. He makes his way into the city, through industrial wastelands, steals a milkvan, beating up the driver and causing general mayhem. Gallogly is a hardman. He sees the police waiting outside his last address, and meets a milkman who has taken *his* clothes and watches as he takes *his* Cortina. All of this description not only plays with the identity of the characters but plays with the reader's identity as well ("He's sporting your / Sunday clothes …). The question of whether the milkman (who always rings twice in a typical Muldoon spin on a cliché) has made love to his/your wife remains to be answered. This sense of sexual malfeasance leads to the punishment of the girl in the street, whose head is shaven and who is tarred and feathered. She becomes a sacrificial victim:

> Someone on their way to early Mass
> will find her hog-tied
> to the chapel gates –
> O Child of Prague –
> big-eyed, anorexic.

Of course, we are brought back to the image of the nation in "Aisling" – sacred image of destruction that stands in contrast to the tone of the poem, and its whimsical violence. Now it is attached to the Catholic icon of Prague. The poem then moves through a series of associative images of sectarian violence. Sometimes it is difficult to tell who is who. This metamorphosis is central to the poem's theme of the mythical violence of change:

In Ovid's conspicuously tongue-in-cheek
account of an eyeball
to eyeball
between the goddess Leto
and a shower of Lycian reed cutters
who refuse her a cup of cloudy
water
from their churned-up lake,
Live then forever in that lake of yours,
she cries, and has them
bubble
and squeak
and plunk themselves down as bullfrogs
in their icy jissom.

Leto is the mother of Apollo and Artemis, impregnated by Zeus, and shunned by all in her travels through fear of Hera's wrath and of having so great a god as Apollo born in their lands. Punished unfairly, she is one of Muldoon's outsiders; in this instance, it is understandable why she is quick to punish those who do not offer her simple human hospitality. The idea that one is cursed to suffer in a place because one has failed to perform the essential duties of humanity is at the root of Northern problems and the poem's meditations. It is also, of course, the root and mechanism of Greek tragedy.

The importance of myth for Muldoon is important but so is that of modern art. In one stanza, Gallogly – who travels from continent to continent in this poem with little warning – enters into Picasso's famous work on the bombing of the city Guernica during the Spanish civil war. He specifically enters the horse in the painting, when it was still in New York and before it had been given back to Spain following Franco's death (obedient to Picasso's request):

Gallogly has only to part the veil
of its stomach wall
to get right under the skin,
the spluttering heart

and collapsed lung,
of the horse in *Guernica*.
He flees the Museum of Modern Art
with its bit between his teeth.

This "hoarde of destructions" is what Wallace Steven calls "a picture of ourselves",[7] and mirrors the life of Gallogly, who is everyman. His departure from the Museum of Modern Art is almost a parody of everyman's escape from high culture, as he is being reminded of his failings, his animal nature, rather than his abilities, reminded he'd rather watch sports, have sex, kill a man. That's the joke that runs through this fast-paced shape-changing difficult poem. Along with art works, artists (from Picasso through Edward Hopper to Jackson Pollock) there are an assortment of Irish heroes (Wolfe Tone, Napper Tandy) as the poem breaks down into outright pastiche. First there is the pastiche of lines and themes from earlier poem in this volume (from "Gathering Mushrooms" and "Aisling"):

Was she Aurora, or the goddess Flora,
Artemidora, or Venus bright,
or Helen fair beyond compare
that Priam stole from the Grecian sight?
Quite modestly she answered me
and she gave me her head one fetch up
and she said I am gathering musheroons
to make my mammy ketchup.
The dunt and dunder
of a culvert-bomb
wakes him
as it might have woke Leander.
And she said I am gathering musheroons
to make my mammy ketchup O.

At this stage in the poem it is less important what the poem tells us—the voyage really is to nowhere, the action is all action (sex, violence, travelling) and therefore static – than how it says it.

Hence, we have the pastiche, like the songs sung in a Las Vegas revue.

Once we get to the title line of the poem, we find that its imperative, which seems all powerful and undeniable (the more we have the more we want), is not necessarily true, and we find ourselves in a "Las Vegas Lounge and Cabaret" with a decidedly Irish twist:

> *The more a man has the more a man wants,*
> *the same I don't think true.*
> *For I never met a man with one black eye*
> *who ever wanted two.*
> In the Las Vegas Lounge and Cabaret
> the resident group –
> pot bellies, Aran knits –
> have you eating out of their hands.
> *Never throw a brick at a drowning man*
> *when you're near to a grocer's store.*
> *Just throw him a cake of Sunlight soap,*
> *let him wash himself ashore.*
> You will act the galoot, and gallivant,
> and call for another encore.

Gallogly finally seems like a lizard lounge himself, working "a gobbet of Brylcreem / into his quiff". A later stanza takes a line from that quoted above to capture the general movement of the poem itself in a fourteen-word stanza, one word per line. It is as if the purgation that Muldoon sought in all these travels, battles and sex washed down to this:

> *Just*
> *throw*
> *him*
> *a*
> *cake*
> *of*
> *Sunlight*
> *soap,*

> *let*
> *him*
> *wash*
> *him-*
> *self*
> *ashore.*

The poem then becomes a series of depictions, drawn according to the aesthetic of various artists, and from their distinctive
perspectives (first, Hopper's then the woodcuts of Derricke), until
the poem ends with Gallogly's and/or Mangas Jones' death – a
quartz stone, the weapon of choice. Who dies is a matter of critical
dispute, for while some critics have argued that Gallogly dies,
others have presumed it to be Jones.[8] The quartz is a stone that
Jones brought with him from America. Quartz is an ambivalent
symbol. It is of the earth and luminous as stars in the sky. Again,
we have a mixed marriage between earth and sky. Like the word
"quoof", quartz is a byword for all that is inexpressible in human
nature – corruption, desire, and transcendence – but in the end it
is a symbol of destruction.

Endnotes

---

[1] S. J. Connolly, *The Oxford Companion to Irish History* (Oxford: Oxford UP, 1998),
265.

[2] Clair Wills, *Reading Paul Muldoon*, 87.

[3] "Hallucinogen opens gateway to the mystical, new study says", *Winston-Salem
Journal*, 11 July 2006.

[4] Clair Wills, *Reading Paul Muldoon*, 104.

[5] Wills, *Reading Paul Muldoon*, 87.

[6] Wills, *Reading Paul Muldoon*, 96.

[7] Wallace Stevens, *Collected Poems* (New York: Vintage, 1990), 173.

[8] See Kendall, *Paul Muldoon*, 115. In "Fluid disjunction in Paul Muldoon's
'Immram' and 'The More a Man Has the More a Man Wants'", Steven D. Putzel
writes: "During a poetry reading a few years ago, Muldoon warned his audience
not to expect his poems to have conclusions, final chords or the snap of a lid, and
if we are to reach any conclusion here, to get beyond the poem's last word –
'huh' – it has to be with Muldoon's warning firmly in mind. 'Immram' and 'The

More a Man Has the More a Man Wants' are clearly complex and difficult works, but it is just as clear that Muldoon, like Joyce before him, expects us to be somewhat baffled and to revel in and play with that bafflement." *Papers on Language and Literature*: Winter 1996.

5

Meeting the British (1987)

F ROM THE EIGHTEENTH TO THE TWENTIETH century, the idea of
family remained a ruling aesthetic and political concept in Irish
writing. Though this is obviously true of many Irish writers, it is
particularly true of Muldoon. Among his predecessors, Louis
MacNeice figures largely in the long poem "7, Middagh Street" that
ends this volume. MacNeice's sublimation of the family romance
onto the landscape in his lyric poems, alongside *Autumn Journal*,
serves as evidence of his national consciousness. Family feeling is
the solving ambiguity between the longer poem's panorama of a
society preparing for war and the particular landscape of its confession of faith after the collapse of his marriage. In many of
MacNeice's poems, the poet's father and mother seem to fuse with
natural forces of the landscape. His father, a minister in the Church
of Ireland who believed in Home Rule, exudes something "solitary
and wild" ("The Strand"), while his mother, dying early in his life,
becomes "the pre-natal mountain" ("Carrick Revisited").[1]

Importantly for Muldoon, MacNeice's aestheticisation is not
mere escapism or retreat, but another starting point for considerations of history and nature within Ireland, Britain, and Europe,
which have deep philosophical implications. Muldoon himself
establishes a similar starting point for these considerations. One
difference between these two poets may be that Muldoon's family
is written into the landscape and nature rather than sublimated as
they are in MacNeice. Muldoon is more like Montague or Heaney
in this respect. He places himself and his ancestors on the land
and considers how history, nature, politics and personal/familial

life have shaped them in very specific ways. Whether one can un-falteringly say that Protestants sublimate while Catholics person-alise family and history onto nature is perhaps not easily ascer-tainable, but it does seem safe to say that there is a noticeable ten-dency in these directions. For all of this difference, it is MacNeice's urbanity, his resistance of racially or sectarian in-spired politics, his complicated take on poetry and politics, that provide an important example for Muldoon. His is not the only example; there are Auden, Frost, and others, but as for many Northern Irish writers (Mahon, Longley and Muldoon among them) MacNeice is exemplary.

The other aspect of Muldoon's poetic that is worth mentioning is the American influence, particularly that of the New York School of Poets, a group of experimental writers including John Ashbery, Frank O'Hara, James Schuyler, Kenneth Koch and Bar-bara Guest, who are linked by friendship, shared place and time – New York City in the early 1950s – and close connections to the New York School of abstract expressionist painters, whose work transformed New York City into the capital of the art world (and whose most famous painter was Jackson Pollock). The poets were influenced by the experiments in the arts, as Muldoon is ("My Grandfather's Wake", "Christo's", and "Paul Klee: *They're Bit-ing*"). From their cosmopolitan and avant-garde perspective, they challenged repressive provincial values as well as the prevailing formalist verse associated with the academy. Though there were vast differences between any two of the American poets, they were all committed to vanguardism and experimentation, they all resisted symbolism and moralising, and emphasised surfaces, play, process, improvisation and chance. Without putting enor-mous weight on the American influence, Muldoon has increas-ingly become American in certain aspects of his writing as well as citizenship (he has become a citizen and even won the Pulitzer Prize). It is safe to say that he is committed to vanguardism and experimentation; he resists moralising while emphasising sur-faces, play, process, improvisation and chance as no Irish poet has done before him. He also has a very postmodern sense of the role and uses of popular culture, for he often employs high and low forms of art together with little sense of conflict between the two. In this light, he appears very American indeed.

John Ashbery's poem "But What is the Reader to Make of This?" provides an excellent introduction to some of the aesthetic concerns of the New York School and of Muldoon's poetry as well, even if Muldoon has a different take from Ashbery. The latter's poem also makes clear the personal nature of an avant-garde poetic. Politics and history, though important to literature, are not its truest domain. Poetry is at least partially born from politics, but it is not where it lives. Muldoon himself makes this point in "7, Middagh Street", as we shall see. Poetry tells us more about the interior life, and the principles behind the brutal facts that surround us, than it does about the facts themselves. It all depends on how one perceives the world outside, how one interacts emotionally with what and whom one meets, how nature is unveiled in the moment of perception. This is one of the great lessons poetry teaches. Ashbery follows the line of vision within a type of sacred landscape to show that history itself is concentrated in the perception of the moment:

> A lake of pain, an absence
> Leading to a flowering sea? Give it a quarter-turn
> And watch the centuries begin to collapse
> Through each other, like floors in a burning building,
> Until we get to this afternoon.

Then he turns to celebrate the senses, disregarding all that interrupts their full display, avoiding the hurts of history ("We have lived blasphemously in history / And nothing has hurt us or can"), and depending on the force of the interior life for their significance ("Still, it is the personal, / Interior life that gives us something to think about").

The senses are shadowed by pain, and live blasphemously because they avoid the "blunt archives" of the real. Facts are the enemy of the sensual web of perception that Ashbery defends. He makes the dominance of the interior life his battle cry, inverting

the old order that said the personal life is melodrama, the public is
history. For Ashbery, the real lies in wait within the interior
world. The personal life contains the essential dynamics of the
world: "At the edge of a forest a battle rages in and out of / For a
whole day. It's not the background, we're the background." In
this instance the background is where the important things hap-
pen; it is also where we are forced to dwell in the moment, as the
moment is impossible to foreground, however much we struggle
to do so. Yet, Ashbery does not claim that the interior and personal life is without suffering or is in any way transcendent, except in the way it leads to artistic insight. In fact, he makes the
opposite claim, while invoking the need for the senses to be
sweetly and imaginatively fulfilled as the imperative of the poetic
mood, a mood that survives both life and death:

> The surprises history has
> For us are nothing compared to the shock we get
> From each other, though time still wears
> The colors of meanness and melancholy, and the general life
> Is still many sizes too big, yet
> Has style, woven of things that never happened
> With those that did, so that a mood survives
> Where life and death never could. Make it sweet again!

The fictive imperative of the imagination (to make things up,
to fit us in a world too big for us, to weave those clothes of lies
and truth) is an age-old theme of art and poetry. "Art is a lie that
makes us realize the truth," says Picasso.[2] Muldoon makes similar
statements and, as in the poem "The Wishbone", he has some of
the same desires, particularly at this moment of his career when
he is moving from his early to middle period and moving from
Europe to America.

The movement from *Quoof* to *Meeting the British* was a difficult
one for Muldoon. He was aware that in *Quoof* he had achieved the
pinnacle of his early style. *Meeting the British* then is a transitional
volume, in which he worked in a format he had perfected and
through which he tried to prepare another for his future develop-

ment. The very first poem of the volume, the prose poem "Ontario", illustrates both an American influence and attempt to establish a new poetic. For though Baudelaire and other French and English poets wrote prose poems, the style of Muldoon's prose poem and conversations that occur in it are definably American. The landscape of "My Grandfather's Wake" is similarly American, though it also mixes figures from Ireland. The poem begins with an invocation of Wyeth's famous painting "Christina's World" (1948), in which a teen-aged girl, who is stricken with polio, sits in the foreground looking across an autumn field at crows in flight around a distant barn in Maine.[3] The original painting is displayed in the New York Museum of Modern Art. For Muldoon, the image is a gothic dream of the family, the Maine house near the barn was in fact the house in which Christina lived, one which he compares to the houses in Terence Malick's film *Days of Heaven* (1978). He sees the houses as triremes, ancient galleys, ships of war "riding the 'sea of grain'", and insists that "each has a little barge / in tow – a freshly-dug grave." The gothic is a particularly potent convention of colonial and post-colonial societies, such as the American and Irish, containing, as it does, the nightmare scenarios of their turbulent histories.

If the American influence is present in this volume and will become even more apparent in later ones, while Muldoon settles into the country and culture, Irish history, landscape, nature and culture never cease to be as important. Muldoon's take on them may become more innovatively heuristic, more playfully self-conscious, however. In "The Coney", for instance, the familiar image of the hunt as palimpsest of intellectual and personal discovery is portrayed with a type of cartoon savagery and boyish wistfulness, which, though not out of keeping with earlier volumes, is more pronouncedly playful than before and perhaps less inventive, less effective. Muldoon remembers that he and his late father had sharpened the scythes they used on the farm. "This past winter he had been too ill / to work. The scythe would dull." Finally a coney, or rabbit, makes its home inside the whetstone. The poem ends with a surreal image of the rabbit taking a swim and being torn apart by, but miraculously surviving, a pack of dogs. The closing couplet's wish to follow the rabbit and by extension his father ("And although I have never learned to swim / I would willingly have followed him") reminds us of the final couplet of "Making the Move". For Muldoon the aesthetic sometimes rehearses various wish fulfillments, whether personal or political, and sometimes recapitulates the pain of disappointment.

In "The Marriage of Strongbow and Aoife", the historical disappointment of the first wedding between native (the Irish princess Aoife) and coloniser (the Norman Strongbow) is felt personally by Muldoon. Strongbow's coming to Ireland (he was invited to fight on behalf of Aoife's father) is seen as the beginning of English colonisation, even though, of course, the Normans would become "more Irish than the Irish themselves" and the true conquest would begin when religion became a defining factor, for the Spanish and French cultural threats to the English aligned with the native Irish. This marriage, the first among many imagined to settle historical wrongs of colonisation (from Edmund Burke, through Lady Morgan and William Carleton, and on to Seamus Heaney), contains the hopes of generations. For Muldoon, hope remains in the "creative pause", but not very forcefully, as the "invisible waitress", a figure for history, threateningly appears at the margins of the table with the famous drink of Normandy (Calvados):

> I might as well be another guest
> at the wedding-feast
> of Strongbow and Aoife MacMurrough
> as watch you, Mary,
>
> try to get to grips [...]
> A creative pause before the second course
>
> of Ireland's whole ox on a spit;
> the invisible waitress
> brings us each a Calvados and water-ice.
>
> It's as if someone had slipped
> a double-edged knife between my ribs
> and hit the spot exactly.

The pain is almost Adamic, as this is the source of his own historical dilemma, the birth of his Eve (unredeemed by his Mary) and the cause of his rejection from Eden. The post-colonial idyll of an ideal pre-conquest society is an important myth even if it is only a myth.

Muldoon has to find something in the world that is redemptive and, in *Meeting the British*, he finds it most convincingly in bones, that is in "The Wishbone" and in "The Lass of Aughrim". In the first poem, a eulogy to his father, Muldoon begins by noting that sister and brother are away from home and the mother is dead ("Maureen in England, Joseph in Guelph / my mother in her grave"). Father and son alone watch the Queen's message to the Commonwealth with "the sound turned off". They eat some chicken and then share a wish over a wishbone, imagining it to be the fibula of an English peer. It is the opposite symbol from the marriage as union. It is a breaking up, a separation as wish for the future over the corpse of the past. In the beautiful second poem on human bones, "The Lass of Aughrim", this image is given a more fabled landscape:

> On a tributary of the Amazon
> an Indian boy
> steps out of the forest
> and strikes up on a flute.
>
> Imagine my delight
> when we cut the outboard motor
> and I recognize the strains
> of *The Lass of Aughrim*.
>
> 'He hopes,' Jesus explains
> 'to charm
> fish from the water
>
> on what was the tibia
> of a priest
> from a long-abandoned Mission.'

We're back to Muldoon's lyric mastery in this poem. We also
see how much better his work is when, as in this case, the parody
is more lightly placed and nuanced. Jesus is merely a Spanish
name, used commonly in the Latin American New World. It also
works as the Saviour's name, when we think of the boy's desire to
charm fish out of water. The joining of pagan and Christian magic
seems an accurate reflection of New-World thinking. And the
"long-abandoned Mission" has legs yet, only moving in directions
hitherto unconsidered.

Poems like the title poem "Meeting the British", "Crossing the
Line" and "Bechbretha" attempt similar historical considerations
and reclamations. In the first, the importation of "small pox" into
the New World, which was one of the main reasons for the deci-
mation of the native population, is recorded as a gift. The second
poem portrays gifts as harbingers of destruction. "Bechbretha",
which according to the poem means "the Brehon judgements /
on every conceivable form / of bee-dispute", is an allegory of bee-
keeping as cultural signifier. Each of these poems suffer from a
lack of emotional force, at least in terms of other Muldoon poems.
"Meeting the British" may be the most successful in that it vividly
portrays this deadly meeting, and "Bechbretha" is funny in its
parody of the bigoted British politician Enoch Powell (who represented Ulster), but Muldoon's searching poetic is missing here.
What one doesn't understand, and comes to with some effort, is
not matched in poetic intensity, as compared to poems such as
"The Fox", "The Soap-Pig", and "The Toe-Tag", which are powerful poems of the personal and cultural significance of nature, family and politics, three of Muldoon's standard themes.

In "The Fox", predation is the subject; this time a fox among
the geese, who are raising the alarm while Muldoon is thinking of
his father in the grave in Collegelands (the town of his youth,
named after Trinity College Dublin, which owned the land and
traditionally collected rents from tenants). To Muldoon, his buried
father seems to have been drowned by history, being buried "in
ground / so wet you weren't so much / buried there as drowned".
Muldoon then remembers his father during the wake ("your face /

above its bib / pumped full of formaldehyde"), thinking that his features looked engrossed as though he were writing his name on a box of mushrooms (that he'd picked). The notion that he was preserved by the spirits of formaldehyde and is seen to be writing mirrors the act of the poem itself. The father's spiritual admonition to *"Go back to bed"*, however, marks the difference between father and son. The father is accustomed to such scenes as the fox raid, while the poet-son is not. This difference is like that between Heaney and his father; the typical divide between those connected to the land and those who write about it. Writing is a sign of division, which paradoxically it tries to overcome. The attributes of the fox come into play here. If poet can be like fox, can "raid ... the inarticulate"[4] and give it utterance, then something has been achieved. This is another mixed marriage. Paul Muldoon is still using the language and themes from the first four volumes. He has perfected them, so why shouldn't he employ them, even as he seeks newer themes and styles for future writing.

In "The Soap-Pig" we see an even grander demonstration of Muldoon's ability at this stage. The first stanza is a bravura performance of how the knowledge of his friend's death entered his consciousness:

> I must have been dozing in the tub
> when the telephone
> rang and a small white grub
> crawled along the line
> and into my head:
> Michael Heffernan was dead.

The second stanza introduces the title image, and thereby sets up the themes of physical corruption and purging on which the poem moves:

> All I could think of
> was his Christmas present
> from what must have been 1975.
> It squatted there on the wash-stand,

an amber, pig-shaped
bar of soap.

The rest of the poem is a memory of their friendship, of Muldoon's "stink" which Heffernan mocked, of Heffernan's bad heart and operations, and his love for *quidditas*, or whatness, for the world of objects, a love which must have moved the poet. Heffernan's imminent death and love of the world parallel the themes of corruption and purging. In the poem their respective mates articulate the poem's affectionate attempt to hold corruption in check. The last stanza returns us to the bar of soap, the cleansing device, only now it is given the setting of Muldoon's own parents, his own familial context, with the poem taking on the idea of original sin that must be redeemed or reconciled:

And the soap-pig? It's a bar of soap,

now the soap-sliver
in a flowered dish
that I work each morning into a lather
with my father's wobbling-brush,
then reconcile to its pool of glop
on my mother's wash-stand's marble top.

The soap-pig is a talisman to ward off the evil; it is like mule and horse, earth and stars, all those antinomies Muldoon has tried, with varying degrees of success, finally to reconcile—only now there's not much left: the pig is a "sliver".

"The Toe-Tag" presents us with another, more morbid talisman. The poem begins with two material images of the self-made whole. The first, which becomes the beloved, is a pair of her "kid gloves … folded into the halves / of a walnut-shell". The second is a Rolls-Royce Silver Shadow. Muldoon is playing on cliché-driven images: she should have been treated with "kid gloves", but wasn't, and the silver shadow is ominous of early death (upholstered with "hides of stillborn calves"). The final stanza of the poem shows the items that they are choosing, rooted in family:

> The intricate, salt-stiff
> family motif
> in a month-drowned Aranman's *geansaí*
> becomes you. Your ecstasy
> at having found
> among the orangery's body-bags
> of peat one pot of sand
> and one untimely, indigo-flowering cactus
> like a big toe with its tag.

One must remember that the family motif is sewn into the Aranman's jumper in order to make identification easier if he has drowned. Not a good omen, among other bad ones: the bags of peat are like "body-bags"; and the cactus, that prickly image of phallic desire, is "untimely" in its flowering. Finally, the flowering cactus looks like the toe of the drowned fisherman who in more modern times has an identity tag on his toe. All signs point towards death in other words. The next poem "Gone" makes this explicit.

In "Paul Klee: *They're Biting*", "Something Else", and "Sushi", the avant-garde and philosophical concerns of Muldoon's subsequent poetry come into play. This is not to say that he did not have these concerns before *Meeting the British*. "The More a Man has the More a Man Wants" is a case in point, as are other poems from previous volumes, but it is merely to point out that now these interests are becoming more central. A painting composed of graphite and oil by Paul Klee (1879–1940) is the basis of Muldoon's meditation in "Paul Klee: *They're Biting*". His description aptly captures the tone and look of a fishing-boat scene:

> The lake supports some kind of bathysphere,
> an Arab dhow
>
> and a fishing-boat
> complete with languorous net.
>
> Two caricature anglers
> have fallen hook, line and sinker

for the goitered
spiny fish-caricatures

with which the lake is stocked.

When Muldoon receives this image on a postcard, he looks up
and sees "a plane sky-writing // *I LOVE YOU* over Hyde Park".
There is "an exclamation mark / at the painting's heart" which
makes Muldoon feel that whoever is biting, it is not him being
caught or doing the fishing. Muldoon is finding inspiration in art
now in a way that reflects his maturity as an artist. Life is going to
have to enter in different ways from those more physical avenues
he found in the past. In "Something Else", Muldoon reflects on
the romantic agony of Nerval, how it led first to madness ("Nerval / was given to promenade / a lobster on a gossamer thread"),
and then to his suicide ("he hanged himself from a lamp-post").
The lobster on a gossamer thread becomes the hanging poet in
Muldoon's mind. Muldoon might also be thinking of Samuel
Beckett's early story "Dante and the Lobster" in which boiling the
lobster takes on the religious significance of pitying those con-
demned by God's judgement. Muldoon is writing associatively
and concludes that this "made me think / of something else, then
something else again". This critique of the mind's processes is the
mark of a mature artist.

In "Sushi", we also see a surrealist interest in the illusionary
aspects of reality, art and perception. The poet is in a Japanese restaurant, watching how the master chefs make one thing seem like
another. The subject, sushi, being raw is itself between the live
and the cooked. Their fictive genius is much to be admired and
sets Muldoon to noticing similar blurring of reality around him.
He looks outside the restaurant and sees

On the sidewalk
a woman in a leotard
with a real leopard
in tow.
For an instant I saw beyond the roe
of sea-urchins,

the erogenous
zones of shad and sea-bream ...

Muldoon immediately plays on the closeness of the word leotard and leopard, a visual pun that unveils the felineness of the
feminine. This reflection moves him to a sexual contemplation of
the source of creative couplings like the woman and leopard, to
that of the creation of art itself, of how one might make the end of a
carrot seem like wood or stone. It becomes a symbol of the Far
Eastern aesthetic (alabaster or jade) to Muldoon. The visual pun on
Irish philosophers' names at the end of the poem has metaphysical
significance.

Since the seventeenth century, it has become usual to refer to
one Irish philosopher as Scotus Eriugena so to distinguish him
from the thirteenth-century John Duns Scotus. The first, Johannes
(*c.*800–*c.*877), who signed himself as "Eriugena" in one manu-
script, and who was referred to by his contemporaries as "the
Irishman" (or scottus – in the ninth century, Ireland was referred
to as "Scotia Maior" and its inhabitants as "scotti") is the most significant Irish intellectual of the early monastic period. Eriugena's
thought is best understood as a sustained attempt to create a consistent, systematic, Christian Neoplatonism from diverse but primarily Christian sources. The second, John Duns Scotus (1265/66–
1308) was one of the most important and influential philosopher-
theologians of the High Middle Ages. His brilliantly complex and
nuanced thought, which earned him the nickname "the Subtle
Doctor", left a mark on discussions of such disparate topics as the
semantics of religious language, the problem of universals, divine
illumination, and the nature of human freedom.[5] Obviously the
stances of these philosophers are different, but both are concerned
with the relationship of the material world with the transcendent
values, or metaphysical values, that lay behind them, which is
precisely what the poem "Sushi" discusses. And the poet's work
must be informed by these arguments.

Whatever one might say about Muldoon's falling off in this
volume, there is also proof of maturity, of growth, which would

lead to the philosophical musings of *Madoc: A Mystery* (1990). The final long poem of this volume, even if it does not measure up to the final poems of *Why Brownlee Left* and *Quoof*, does anticipate many of the techniques and themes that appear in subsequent volumes. It is also concerned with the unstable nature of reality, and examines how perception shapes it. The poem likewise makes some important points about the relationship between poetry and politics, a relationship that Muldoon has been considering through much of his career. "7, Middagh Street" is a collection of sequences listed under the names of various artists of the 1930s and '40s and continues Muldoon's preoccupation with the inter-sections of art, history (particularly during wartime), and the personal life. "The poem is constructed as a sequence of seven linked monologues spoken on Thanksgiving Day, 1940, by the inhabitants of a house in Brooklyn, New York, which was rented at the time by the poet W. H. Auden. The monologues are spoken by Auden, his lover Chester Kallman, the novelist Carson McCullers, the striptease artist Gypsy Rose Lee, Benjamin Britten, Salvador Dali, and Louis MacNeiece."[6] One of the most quoted passages in the poem is the critique of W. B. Yeats's politics, placed on Auden's lips:

> As for his crass, rhetorical
>
> posturing, 'Did that play of mine
> send out certain men (*certain* men?)
>
> the English shot ... ?'
> the answer is 'Certainly not'.
>
> If Yeats had saved his pencil-lead
> would certain men have stayed in bed?
>
> For history's a twisted root
> with art its small, translucent fruit
>
> and never the other way round.

The play referred to is *Cathleen Ní Houlihan* (1902), which Yeats believed (and feared) helped foment the Easter Rebellion of 1916.

The rhetorical question "Did that play of mine ..." is asked in "The Man and the Echo", one of Yeats's last poems in which he too wonders on the moral effects of art and literature ("the spiritual intellect's great work" is to clean "man's dirty slate").[7] Before considering whether we think that Muldoon himself actually agrees with this beautiful, but ultimately limited statement, we must remember that Muldoon has MacNeice say almost the opposite when discussing the murder of the poet Federico García Lorca by Franco's forces during the Spanish Civil War:

> In dreams begin responsibilities
> it was on account of just such an allegory
> that Lorca
> was riddled with bullets
>
> and lay mouth-down
> in the fickle shadow of his own blood.
> As the drunken soldiers of the *Gypsy Ballads*
> started back for town
>
> they heard him calling through the mist
> 'When I die leave the balcony shutters open.'
> For poetry *can* make things happen –
> not only can, but *must* –
>
> and the very painting of that oyster
> is in itself a political gesture.

Muldoon begins with a quote that W. B. Yeats used as an epigraph for the pivotal volume *Responsibilities* (1914), in which Yeats first began to discuss the political and social situation around him in detail and then developed a philosophy accordingly. Lorca's philosophy is notably more leftist, democratic, *gypsy* – that's for certain. This takes us back to some of the discussion at the beginning of this chapter. Poetry and politics are intermixed, but separate. Poetry tells us more about the interior life than it does about the facts themselves. It all depends on how one perceives the world outside, how nature is unveiled in the moment of perception. If we look at a passage in "7, Middagh Street" on art and morality from the monologue written for the surrealist artist Salvador Dalí, we come closer to Muldoon's own violent aesthetic, and his opinion of the relationship between politics and art. For him they both have the same dynamic in bloodshed (the Biblical first murder of Abel by Cain), ritual sacrifice, sexual predation ("boudoir in the abbatoir"). They have the same earthly basis and starry hopes for redemption, but they speak differently and have different ends or purposes:

> We cannot gormandize upon
>
> the flesh of Cain and Abel
> without some melancholic vegetable
>
> bringing us back to earth, to the boudoir
> in the abbatoir.
>
> Our civil wars, the crumbling of empires,
> the starry nights without number
>
> safely under our belts,
> have only slightly modified the tilt
>
> of the acanthus leaf,
> its spiky puce-and-alabaster an end in itself.

We might almost read the end of this passage as a return for "art for art's sake", an art that is an end in itself and has no roots in the world or history; however, the inner workings themselves are too politicised, too brutal for us to make that surmise. Art may be an end in itself, an acanthus flower grown only for ornamental purposes and put on the capitals of Corinthian columns, but does not begin in itself. It is not autotelic. It may be separate from politics, but can never be divorced. Like many an artist, Muldoon continues to struggle with the makings of the unhappy marriage of aesthetics and politics which distinguishes the poetry of the twentieth century. If the idea of family remained a ruling principle of aesthetics and politics since eighteenth-century Ireland, it is not surprising that spectres of marriage or union would haunt the Cain-and-Abel-like relationship between aesthetics and politics.

Family feeling is the solving ambiguity in considerations of history, aesthetics and nature within Ireland, Britain, and, indeed, within America, as we soon shall see in *Madoc: A Mystery* (1990).

Endnotes

---

1 For a biographical discussion of the importance of this figure, see Jon Stallworthy, *Louis MacNeice* (London: Faber, 1995), 1–13. For a discussion of family and landscape, see Jefferson Holdridge, "Solving Ambiguities: Family Feeling in Louis MacNeice's *Autumn Journal*", *Studi Irlandese*, ed. Carlo Bigazzi (Latina, Italy: Yorick Libri, 2004).

2 Simpson, James B., comp. Simpson's Contemporary Quotations. Boston: Houghton Mifflin, 1988. www.bartleby.com/63/. [Feb. 7, 2007].

3 See www.ott.zynet.co.uk/polio/lincolnshire/library/drhenry/christinasworld.html

4 T.S. Eliot, "Burnt Norton", *The Four Quartets* (London: Faber, 1963).

5 Dermot Moran, "John Scottus Eriugena", *The Stanford Encyclopedia of Philosophy (Winter 2004 Edition)*, Edward N. Zalta (ed.), URL = http://plato.stanford.edu/archives/win2004/entries/scottus-eriugena/; Williams, Thomas, "John Duns Scotus", *The Stanford Encyclopedia of Philosophy (Fall 2005 Edition)*, Edward N. Zalta (ed.), URL = <http://plato.stanford.edu/archives/fall2005/entries/duns-scotus/.

6 Wills, *Reading Paul Muldoon*, 130.

7 W.B. Yeats, *The Complete Poems*, ed. Daniel J. Albright (London: Dent, 1990), 393.

Madoc: A Mystery (1990)

FOLLOWING HIS MOVE TO THE US in 1987, Paul Muldoon published the complex amalgam of puzzles that is *Madoc: A Mystery*. The volume consists of seven short lyrics and one long poem of the same title as the volume. The title poem is a weird narrative stretching over one hundred and twenty pages in the Faber *Poems 1968–1998*, and is comprised of two hundred and thirty-three lyrics, each titled in brackets with the name of a Western philosopher, moving from the Pre-Socratics (580 B.C.E.) to contemporary philosophers.[1] "Madoc" is a philosophical poem with no consistent credo, whose set of beliefs is difficult to trace from beginning to end. It is a poem in which certain congeries of ideas are apparent, however. Kendall believes that each of the poem's sections "reflects, or is in some way shaped by, the presiding philosopher",[2] though not every critic agrees. Kendall does give some good examples, however, which will be duly noted, and expanded upon.

This long baffling but alluring poem is a strange combination of ontogeny recapitulating phylogeny, that is the birth of the individual recapitulating or summarizing the development of the species (from reptile to human, or in this case from wilderness to civilisation), and the history of philosophy condensing the history of colonisation. It makes sense, however, to combine these two recapitulations. For one, in reading the poem we chart the development of various characters who have come to America from Britain, and see how their trials and tribulations mirror the developing colony. Also, the birth of a nation almost presupposes the return to a primitive state of mind. That we go through many centuries of philosophy so quickly says something about the accelerated pace of development in the New World. Nearly every poem in the sequence endeavours to prove that sensual experience is the only kernel of truth that we have. Philosophy falls short of the poetry of that knowledge. How do we measure man but through perception, scanning the eyeball and what it has perceived? "Madoc" thereby measures the philosophical quandary and diseased body politic of Western civilisation as it appears in the New World. We may say that the senses war with reason as do the ruled and the ruler in this nightmare vision of the utopian spirit.

Before we move on to the historical and literary background of the epic poem, and then to the critical responses to it, one of the best introductions to what takes place is given by Muldoon himself. In an interview with Lynn Keller, Muldoon comments on the narrative of "Madoc":

> There is a narrative in *Madoc*. To use the Hollywood producer analogy again, if you went in to a Hollywood producer and said, 'In two or three sentences, this is a story of two youthful poets who set up a little colony in North America and, for various reasons, went their separate ways. One turned into a bit of a demagogue, or worse, a despot – as Frost says, "I never dared be radical when young for fear of being conservative when old" – and the other subsided into drug abuse, and this is the story of their lives.' That is the narrative, their various adventures along the way. One of them, Samuel Taylor Coleridge, joins, briefly, the Lewis and Clark Expedition, then finds himself in the western part of the United States moving from tribe to tribe, while the other, Robert Southey, embarks on this disastrous course of self-aggrandizement and increasing self-delusion. Actually, one might say that in fact this is very much like what happened to them in their actual lives. However, this is just a story. And this is the poem's story. Then one can add, "All of that is told within the framework of a descendant, we think, of Southey's. It's set a little bit in the future, and it's all retrieved from the back of his eye by some remarkable device, which will probably be available to us very

shortly, and this guy has a strange vision of the world. He's some kind of a Sunday philosophy buff, and he's really weird. It's as if his whole way of ordering the world – and we all have a way of ordering the world, somehow, of making sense of it – is very strange. The way he's made sense of the story about where he comes from and who he is, is to filter it through a totally madcap history of Western thought. And that's what happens in the story." When you put it like that, it's very, very simple. I hope it's comparatively simple.[3]

Though there is nothing simple about reading this poem, the summary of the action is very helpful.

On a directly narrative level, "Madoc" *is* a strange tale containing, among other things, the imaginary exploits of two Romantic poets, Robert Southey and Samuel Taylor Coleridge, as they arrive in America to fulfill their dream of establishing a utopian community in the newly established country. The two poets actually never left Europe, so he is describing the road not taken as if it had been taken. Robert Frost's poem, "The Road Not Taken" seems to have always haunted Muldoon, as he consistently imagined where that other road might have led. In the poem "Madoc", he becomes that self "ages and ages hence" whom Frost envisions telling the tale of the decision to take one path over another:

> I shall be telling this with a sigh
> Somewhere ages and ages hence:
> Two roads diverged in a wood, and I –
> I took the one less travelled by,
> And that has made all the difference.[4]

Muldoon's epic poem is about a history that might have been, if the Romantic poets had taken the road to America that they only contemplated taking. Muldoon borrows the actual historical events in the lives of the two poets (their publication of poems, their letters, journal entries, familial lives, the deaths of Coleridge's children, etc.) and combines them with a history of colonisation and expansion in early nineteenth-century America, one which includes murder, rape and revenge.

The title of the poem is taken from Southey's own *Madoc* (1805), which tells the story of Madoc, a Welsh prince who has come to America and who never returns. Madoc, also spelled Madog, is a legendary voyager to America, a son (if he existed at all) of Owain Gwynedd (d. 1170), prince of Gwynedd, in North Wales. A quarrel among Owain's sons over the distribution of their late father's estate led Madog to sail to Ireland and then westward. In a year or so he returned to Wales and assembled a group to colonise the land he had discovered. The party sailed west in ten ships and was not seen again. Richard Hakluyt's *Voyages* (1582) and David Powell's *The Historie of Cambria* (1584) are the oldest extant accounts. There is a tradition of a "white Indian" settlement at Louisville, Kentucky, and several seventeenth- and eighteenth-century reports were published concerning encounters of frontiersmen with Welsh-speaking Indians. "Most anthropologists reject the idea of pre-Columbian European contacts with American Indians, but the evidence is not conclusive."[5] Such pre-Columbian contacts have been important to Muldoon since the poem "Promises, Promises" in *Why Brownlee Left* (1980). They also allow him to contemplate the meeting of two peoples, one colonised and one the coloniser, so that he can better understand the history of Northern Ireland.

Most critics feel that there are few resemblances between Southey's and Muldoon's "Madoc", except for the fact that Southey himself is a character in the poem and a few quotes from the original that are in this text. Yet, Beshero-Bondar, a critic of Southey's, outlines preoccupations that are remarkably similar to Muldoon's. "Southey's Madoc is the poem in which he attempted to rewrite the Spanish conquest of Mexico in British terms [...] Southey attempted to model a complex cultural confrontation of medieval Welsh immigrants with the Aztec empire and its subject peoples. Hybrid horror emerges from the poem's effort to build upon yet supersede the imperial authority of Spanish Catholic history [...] Southey's efforts to create a distinctly British attack on the foundations of the Spanish empire spectacularly backfired." Beshero-Bondar concludes:

> Yet I would also suggest that Southey's failure is much less
> important than the processes of imperial construction and de-
> struction that Madoc illuminates. The poem's investigation of
> world cultures presents a provocative model of colliding
> worldviews and the hybridizing results of their impact.[6]

As the reader must be aware by now, "hybrid horror" is certainly Muldoon's concern as well, and his "Madoc" may be the
height of his expression. His long poem on the hybrid horror of
colonisation has earned both considerable fame and opprobrium,
because it is a poem that attracts strong supporters and creates
equally strong detractors. Let us begin with a look at some of the
supportive critical reckonings. Andrew J. Auge makes these pertinent observations:

> Muldoon's bizarre masterpiece [...] incorporates such disparate
> materials as snippets from the poetry, journals, and letters of the
> Romantic poets Samuel Taylor Coleridge, Robert Southey,
> Thomas Moore, and Byron; ... passages from the journals of the
> American explorers Meriwether Lewis and William Clark, and
> shorter ones from the journals of George Catlin, the American
> painter of western indigenes; and speeches from Native Ameri-
> can chieftains [...] All of this heterogeneous material is gathered
> together in a desultory narrative structure that interweaves an
> imagined account of the Pantisocracy, the utopian community
> that Coleridge and Southey envisioned creating in early nine-
> teenth-century America ... What is less apparent and more in-
> teresting is the way in which seemingly extraneous features of
> this strange text – its frame narrative and subtitles – deepen the
> poem's critique of imperialism by locating it within the context
> of the age-old quarrel between philosophy and poetry.[7]

John Goodby sees the poem as "a savage critique of Western
imperialism and its metaphysical foundations".[8]

Clair Wills introduces her analysis of the poem with a discussion of Muldoon's "exploration of states of movement and suspension ... as a way of resolving the post-romantic dilemma concerning the relation between poetic language (with its formal pat-

terning) and the particularities of experience. In his poetry the conflict between the generalizing and abstract aspects of poetic form – sequence, lineation, rhyme, temporal duration, and connections of all kinds – and the unique moment of experience is, as it were, 'resolved' on another plane, that of the imagination."[9] All the supporters believe that the poem is a celebration of language and of poetry. The problem with the poem is that it is difficult to follow the lines of the celebration. The violence of the poem moves one to consider more than just pure philosophy, but history as well. This points to the complex nature of the work, which has distinguished reactions to it since its publication.

Now we move to the detractors, for whom, more often than not, the difficulty proves insurmountable or is deemed unnecessary. Upon its publication, the Irish novelist John Banville complained:

> I cannot help feeling that this time (Muldoon) has gone too far
> – so far, at least, that I can hardly make him out at all, off there
> in the distance, dancing by himself. Yes, art *should* be resistant,
> poetry *should* hold back something of its essential self. The
> trouble is, *Madoc* demands that the reader work in ways that
> seem inappropriate to the occasion: one pictures work details
> of Ph.D. students already setting to, tracking down the refer-
> ences, preparing glosses, grinding keys. [...] *Madoc* is a little
> too playful in its profundities, and many of its jokes are
> weighed down with leaden solemnity.[10]

And Michael Hoffman simply said that he felt tempted to "throw the whole thing at the computer and say: 'Here you do it'".[11] More recently, David Masson writes frustratedly and somewhat patronisingly:

> The book-length sequence *Madoc: A Mystery* (1990) might be a
> watershed in Muldoon's career so far. It's like popcorn for the
> intellect; reading it goes at a fast clip, and when you're done
> you wonder what you've ingested. Muldoon's two subsequent
> collections represent some sort of maturation.[12]

David Wheatley writes with some skepticism, but apprecia-
tively, in what is the proper balanced assessment of Muldoon's
achievement:

> For all its preposterousness, *Madoc* represented an important
> development for Muldoon. Its bold attempt to engage with
> American history is unmatched by other Irish poets who have
> taught in the U.S., while even in eighteenth-century America
> the poem finds suggestive parallels with present-day Ireland
> (for example, the town of Ulster, Pennsylvania features promi-
> nently). The autobiographical dimension to the poem too is
> hard to miss [...] Muldoon's poem has been read by some critics
> as a veiled commentary on Northern Irish politics. [13]

Perhaps most instructively in terms of Muldoon's critical reception, Ivan Phillips sees the volume as

> a direct and provocative response to some of the criticism that
> its predecessor had received, not least from John Carey in the
> *Sunday Times*, who described it as "tricky, clever, tickled by its
> own knowingness", "a pantomime horse" in comparison to
> Seamus Heaney's "Derby winner", *The Haw Lantern*.

Phillips concludes:

> Tellingly, the opium-addicted hero of "Madoc – A Mystery"
> (identified by some critics as a cypher for Muldoon) is first en-
> countered riding "a young ass or hinny" – a reference to Col-
> eridge's ode "To a Young Ass", but also, surely, to what the
> unpublished poem "Triad" refers to as "the curse of Carey".
> (Southey – seen by some as a Heaney figure – is accompanied
> throughout the poem by a talking horse named after Alexan-
> der the Great's mount, Bucephalus.) [14]

What then is the general reader to do? The following discussion will be an attempt to find a starting point for making sense of
the bloody history of the colonial world, which is what the poem
is really setting out to do in the first place.

Though there are stories to be told here of Samuel Taylor Coleridge, Robert Southey, Cinnamond, Bucephalus, Red Jacket, and many others, the real story here is that it matters less what happens to those involved than the fact that the various characters are only half aware of what happens and what it means. This is especially true of Coleridge, who loses Sara, thinks he finds Mary Evans in the person of an Indian woman, but who ultimately is left ignorant. The other characters suffer a similar, if less evocative, fate. Their ignorance is the source of conflict, one suspects, and the various philosophical frames provided merely show that no matter what intellectual tack one takes the most lasting impression is of the disappearance of truth and reality among the fantastic display of historical circumstance.

The overriding metaphor is that of CROATAN, the lost colony which, as we saw in "Promises, Promises", Raleigh left behind and never discovered on his return to the Americas. The lost colony, specifically its disappearance into the world of Native America, which itself would be lost in large measure, broods over our understanding of reality. In South, Southey's imagined son, or an injured version of the father (critics disagree), we have an image of the mixed breed that results from the colonial world, the blurring of boundaries, coming back to Ireland by the end of the poem, coming home to roost, as it were. South could be symbolic of the New Ireland, the South of Ireland. This is difficult to prove, but insinuation is rife in the poem, as metaphysical truths seem to disappear as soon as they appear. Almost every poem in this sequence illustrates that sensual experience is the only kernel of truth that we have. All our philosophy falls short of the poetry of that knowledge. Yet postmodernist philosophical play is not sufficient if it does not inflect history. Stan Smith believes that "'Madoc' squanders its noble impulse to recovery in a display of postmodern cleverness", [15] but Omaar Hena answers this effectively: "Muldoon's multilayered narratives, ironic humor and language games, far from an evasion of history and suffering, signify his way of confronting the pain and complexity of history, giving voice to those excluded from or nearly wiped out by Amer-

European modernity."[16] It could be that Muldoon translates the philosophical paradigm of mind and sense into coloniser and colonised. In that case, we are left with the colonised senses finally being given central place.

In his essay on the relationship of reason and the senses, Schrödinger recounts Democritus's famous demonstration:

> Democritus realized that the naked intellectual construction which in his world-picture had supplanted the actual world of light and colour, sound and fragrance, sweetness, bitterness and beauty, was actually based on nothing but the sense perceptions themselves which had ostensibly vanished from it. In fragment D 125, taken from Galen and discovered only about fifty years ago, he introduces intellect in a contest with the sense. The former says: 'Ostensibly there is colour, ostensibly sweetness, ostensibly bitterness, actually only atoms and the void'; to which the senses retort: 'Poor intellect, do you hope to defeat us while from us you borrow your evidence? Your victory is your defeat.'

Schrödinger concludes of this dialogue: "You simply cannot put it more briefly."[17] This insistence on the role of the senses becomes a political statement for Muldoon. "Mon is the mezjur of all thungs" in Muldoon's Scots-Irish version of Protagoras's famous saying ("Man is the measure of all things"). And how do we measure man but through perception, scanning the eyeball and what it has perceived. "Madoc" thereby measures the philosophical quandary and diseased body politic of Western civilisation, as it appears in the New World. We may say that the senses war with reason as do the ruled and the ruler in this critique of the utopian spirit.

If we look at the series of poems in very specific terms we see this disappearance of metaphysical terms of engagement in stark historical settings. As an imminent metaphysician, Coleridge is of prime interest, but not the only one. The search for a Utopia that underlies the hoped-for creation of the Romantic pantisocracy is the metaphysical illusion that Muldoon wants most to undermine; for it is what drove American expansion, the plantations of

Northern Ireland, the destruction of the Native Americans, as well as the paradigms of great thought that drive this poem, and which are undermined by the philosophical CROATAN that stands ready to disappear into the hybrid reality of the New World (remember that CROATAN was both an Indian tribe and the name carved on a gate post of the abandoned "Cittie of Ralegh" on Roanoke Island to indicate a possible refuge for the "lost" colony of 1587).[18] In the end "Madoc" is not an easy sequence of poems by any stretch, no matter how far you extend the imagination, because experience always pulls against any attempt at intellectual coherence we might make – and yet we must make the attempt.

If we follow a line through the poem, we can establish a system for establishing the failure of systems. Even the system of philosophers' names, as titles for the lyrics, is both helpful and misleading. Muldoon himself has regrets about this catalogue of philosophers, comparing it to the schema of names taken from the chapters of the Homeric original that James Joyce used for *Ulysses*, but which the latter decided not to include in the text.[19] First we must look briefly at the seven lyrics that precede the long poem. The first, "The Key", doesn't really provide a key, though it does contain certain embedded legends to unlock the key. We want to establish a system based on a general reading. We may then say that the poem establishes the American context of the volume, introducing criminal elements, as well as elements from Native American culture, mixed, as always, with an Irish ingredient. In "Tea" it helps to know that Muldoon is playing on the idea of the Boston Tea Party, in which American colonists dressed as Mohawks boarded a British vessel in Boston Harbor and threw tea chests overboard in protest against British taxes. In the poem, Muldoon imagines himself in Key West, off the tip of the Florida peninsula, "rooting through tea-chest after tea-chest". The poem is a meditation on American myth-making, but importantly shows how symbolic this exercise must be. The close of the poem is a type of Eucharistic entry into the volume: "Take it. Drink."

"Carpercailles" is an exuberant display of wit and formal skill. It is an acrostic; that is, if you read down the left-hand margin, the first letter of each line combines to make a sentence. In this case the letters read: "Is this a New Yorker poem, or what?" Without trying to answer that question, we may say that the poem exhibits many of Muldoon's typical concerns; it is a mixture of the mystical, the martial, the sexual, the animal and human. We must also note that Muldoon has recently been made Poetry Editor for that magazine, so he must now know the answer to that question himself. The subject is a bird with a name that comes from the Gaelic, meaning "horse of the woods". In "Madoc: A Mystery", the club-footed Byron appears stamping "his cloven hoof". As in Swift's *Gulliver's Travels*, horse-imagery remains central to Muldoon's vision of humanity struggling with its own animal nature. Shape-changing again is important to Muldoon, as is a type of international and transhistorical consciousness that juxtaposes St Joan, a "straggler from Hadrian's sixth legion", commercial items from Harrods, the American poet Elizabeth Bishop, among other figures and things. The poem gives us a foretaste of the long title poem. Like "Capercaillies", "Asra" combines the sexual and martial as well, while "The Panther" and "Cauliflowers" present the violence of the new world in a jocular and surreal way respectively. The last introductory poem, "The Briefcase", is a wistful sonnet dedicated to Seamus Heaney, that seems almost to want to escape back to Ireland, however imagined, before the farrago of bloodletting, sex and philosophical dissolution of "Madoc: A Mystery" begins.

The first section, entitled "[Thales]", describes a scene in a high-tech, high-security facility named "Unitel", where, it seems, evidence of Coleridge's time in America is stored:

> When he ventured forth from the smallroom
> he activated a sensor-tile
> that set off the first in a series of alarms
> and sent a ripple through Unitel.

By the end of the section, this character has become "just another twist in the plot". We see such twists throughout the rest of the poem. At the close of the next section, South weighs more when he left the "crapper" than when he went in. How much more? "Exactly as much as the scrap of paper ..." This type of scientific precision about nothing marks the poem, in very Swiftian fashion. We are among the "Projectors" of the Third Voyage of *Gulliver's Travels*. We are told that CROATAN, in the section "[Pythagoras]" stands for a "C[oleridge] RO[bert Southey The S]ATAN[ic School]", mocking this detective work in the process. The closest we come to reality is in admitting it is in flux, as in this section entitled "[Heraclitus]":

> So that, though it may seem somewhat improbable,
> all that follows
> flickers and flows
> from the back of his right eyeball.

Reality is indistinguishable from perception. The river that flows outside us and which is never the same twice, as the Pre-Socratic philosopher famously said, flows in us as well. The despair of the philosopher Empedocles, who threw himself into the volcano Mt Aetna, is apparent in the section under his name. Empedocles becomes a symbol of the despair of Native American culture, a parallel for its Ghost Dance: "The woodchuck has had occasion / to turn into a moccasin." In the preceding section we saw that the woodchuck, or groundhog (two different names for the same animal), numbers among the inaugural animals of North America. Groundhog Day, February 2, is the day that if the Groundhog sees his shadow it means a short winter and if he doesn't it means a long one. This prophecy is linked to the poem itself. Again, it is sensual experience that determines reality. In the section "[Anaxagoras]", the woodchuck is joined by the Beaver, another "emissary from the Great Spirit" of Native American culture. The beaver, caught in a trap, has "gnawed both drubs / to the bone". Animals become signs of the future, which, like them, will come to a bad end.

Many of the sections that follow come to similarly bad ends in terms of knowledge, things, animals or persons. The domestic items in a house "go smattering into the void" ("[Democritus]"). The watchdog Cerebus lies with her throat slashed and her eyes "wide-open, world-weary and oddly wise" ("[Zeno]"). Southey rams "goose-quills" into Cinnamond's eyes ("[Scotus Eriugena]"). All attempts to find meaning, especially original meaning such as the Welsh or Irish roots of certain Indians, wind up sounding false: "Yet his own people, the Mohegan, / are the seed of the Celtic chieftain, Eoghan" ("[Duns Scotus]"). Efforts at securing origins usually end thus:

> he'll dilly-dally
> and dawdle and dither
> until he's utterly
> at a loss
>
> as to the whys and wherefores
> of either or either or either or either. [Buridan]

Through one source of meaning springs another symbol, in an unending flow of signification. Perhaps the best thought behind this is the fact that Coleridge and Southey were supposed to build their Utopia by the Susquehanna River. The flow of the river dominates meaning by dispersing it. Even Bacon's experiential method, that one should not merely consult the Ancients or the Bible, that beliefs must be tested by experience, a method which has proved so influential to modern consciousness, stumbles before the real identity of the white woman about whom the town wonders. "I know / only that her name is Sybil / and that she belongs to Red Jacket / I know nothing of her origins. / This I swear to you, as God is my witness." Her name is significant: the identity, if not the name, of the keeper of the oracle (the Sybil) remains unknown. The most concrete thing we are presented with in this section is the "boiled ham" that puns on Bacon's name. Behind this search for origins is the search for racial purity amidst the mongrelisation of the New World. Cornelius Stugeon "stuffs himself with whiteness", while the white woman belongs to the Indian Red Jacket. The poem in one way tries to prove a Pre-Colombian settlement in the Americas through evidence of racial mixing, but, like any metaphysical enquiry, it is lost in the confusion of the physical world.

The attempt to find original sources is paralleled in the poem with an attempt to bring the Old World to the New. In "[Campanella]", Harman Blennerhassett is "building a Roman / villa / complete with mosaics / and frescoes / and a modest cupola". This arrogance, of course, reflects one of the chief problems of colonisation. Not that it is so bad in and of itself. Weren't the Italians of the Renaissance mimicking Greece? No, it merely reflects a way of thinking that led to the removal and replacement of native culture, but for that, at least, it shares responsibility: "That rather unsightly / stand / of birch / and sugar-maple / is destined / soon to become a lawn." The Cherokee trail of tears runs alongside this type of removal. This is the dangerous outcome of Utopian thinking; and so the section ends: "This is the New Atlantis. / The City of the Sun."

Perhaps one must face the gritty truth of the new reality that all these cultures are intermixed anyway. In "[Hobbes]", this Hobbesian view is unsurprisingly expressed. Coleridge, looking for Sara, doesn't know if he has seen her, but thinks he has:

> The white woman is being rogered
> by one Seneca tipped with chert
> she sap-
> sips
>
> a second.
> Coleridge turns away, sickened,
>
> snaps shut the telescope
> And fumbles for his pony's halter-rope.

Is Coleridge sickened because he suspects that Sara has met a similar end, or it is because he has come across an Indian ritual that mixes sacred and profane, and doesn't know what to make of it? Or finally do all metaphysical illusions break down to this image of procreation, which includes us all. Perhaps he can only ascribe to it the basest of human motives. Such reasons run "parallel to the parallel / realm to which it is itself the only clue" ("[Jefferson]"). In other words, we can't be sure; our search for the lost self is like the "copperplate" recording of the "whippoorwill" — a bird's song that cannot be deciphered, only recognised. In "[Boyle]", a horse-fart shakes the "rafters / of the metaphysical long-house" and in "[Locke]" Southey's mind is a "total blank", a tabula rasa, until the experience of "the great cloud-eddy / renewing itself in a pond", or until he hears the "sobbing of a resinous plank". In this version of philosophical and cultural relativism, experiences shape us. We bring no innate way of understanding the world that isn't reflected in the world itself. The river in the eye and the river outside; we haven't gotten beyond Heraclitus. One of the most central sections is "[Seneca]", important partly because of the play on the name of the Indian tribe and the Roman Stoic philosopher, which itself works off the association between the stoicism of the Romans and the stoicism of Native Americans, but also important because it is an etiological poem whose Indian cosmogony contains all the harsh sexuality in brief that the poem itself considers as a whole:

> A woman falls to earth, onto the muddy turtle-back of the earth.
>
> There Wind has his way with her ...
>
> Her sons are Flint and Sapling ...
>
> Sapling makes two-way rivers for easy canoe-journeys. But Flint undoes the work, causing rivers to flow, like this, in one direction only.
>
> And the river flows into Handsome Lake.

Again, there is an image of the river, flowing one way when it might have flowed both ways, when past and present might have flowed into one another, along with time and space, and all the dualities that divide up reality. The river itself seems to seek the aesthetic object, the dreamed of release and mingling into a larger sphere.

Philosophical and cultural relativism is a ubiquitous and complex theme in Modernism, and Modernists struggled with the relationship of form and flux, with the relationship between a permanent rational order and the changing nature of sensory experience. The preoccupation with the unity of immediate experience is merely a vestige of metaphysical thinking. Insofar as we find unity in the chaotic stream of sensations, it is we who have introduced it. In the section entitled "[Nietzsche]", Southey holds the horse Bucephalus "in a fast embrace", as the German philosopher felt we had to confront the sexual/animal basis of thought itself, that is, we must face what drove the stream of sensation. Culturally, as well as philosophically, most Modernist writers lamented the loss of national and religious myths which accompanied relativism. In postmodernism, there is supposed to be a celebration of relativism. Rather than lamenting the loss of religious and national myths, postmodernists celebrate it as freedom from their constraints. This, after inspection, becomes somewhat troubling, especially when we examine it in terms of the stability and freedom of the subject, and in terms of cultural norms that rule behaviour. In Modernism, there is artistic awareness, self-determination; that is, the idea of free will against society. Almost all Modernist artists feel that they, as artists, must confront various repressive aspects of social convention, such as sexual taboos, religious fundamentalism, crass materialism, or more subtly masked forms of philistinism, in order to move towards individual freedom. In postmodernism, there is the loss of self-determination; the "end of Man". The lack of individual freedom and the instability of the self are highlighted in order either to show the necessity for rebellion, or else its impossibility. Here, as Ihab Hassan writes, we move "in nihilistic play or mystic transcendence, toward the vanishing point".[20] This is not entirely sufficient, however, and one knows for certain that many postmodern critics and writers, Muldoon included, believe that there is an ethical imperative and a need to express freedom of will.

An example of these distinctions between the two movements will help to extricate some systematic understanding from their thorny interactions. There are two sides to Paul Muldoon's poetry;

for, while displaying a postmodern suspicion of the aesthetic, he is nevertheless attuned to the traditional reflexes of Romanticism and that side of Modernism, and so believes that the monuments of poetry may still offer some solace. Two examples from his poetry make this dichotomy clear. One presents a traditionally Romantic vision of the redemptive possibilities of art, while the other displays a more sceptical postmodern view. The latter side of the dichotomy, "[Vico]", is from *Madoc: A Mystery* (1990) and portrays the philosopher of history, Giambattista Vico (1668–1744), trapped in a system of copies that, for all its complexity, has no origin or purpose and reduces the Italian philosopher's conception of historical cycles to the ridiculous:

> A hand-wringing, small grey squirrel
> plods
> along a wicker
>
> treadmill that's attached
> by an elaborate
> system of levers
>
> and cogs and cranks
> and pulleys
> and gears [...]
>
> and the whole palaver
> of rods
> and ratchets
>
> to a wicker
> treadmill in which there plods
> a hand-wringing, small grey squirrel.

It is a picture of the closed postmodern aesthetic – elaborate, but repetitive – a baroque frame around an absurdity. The example of a redemptive image is from "Incantata", which comes in the next volume, *The Annals of Chile* (1994), and will be discussed in the next chapter. Let us say that such a concern is not at the heart of this long poem. The uncontrollably shape-changing mystery of experience and history is its subject. After being blinded by Southey,

Cinnamond rapes Southey's wife Edith (sister of Sara) in revenge, and Southey finds her "dazed / wearing only a crumpled, blood-spattered smock". In this condition, the only truth lies in that suffering and confusion. In the section on "[Kant]", "reason" is undone and only "sow[s] the seeds of treason / in the 'fertile mind' of Aaron Burr". In the section entitled "[Newman]", the Cardinal's famous conversion from Anglicanism to Catholicism is inscribed in the image of following someone's trail and then losing it. Changes in belief are not easy to follow. Soon, Coleridge is "resigned to the fact that Sara / could be anywhere west of the Missouri". The key word in this section, "[Boole]", is "assimilation". Assimilation means shape-changing and that sort of constant metamorphosis is what metaphysical enquiry, seeking permanent forms behind the shifting veil of reality, endeavours to avoid.

In "Madoc: A Mystery", the shifting veil, the shape-changing is connected to Indian rituals, which Southey, representing the Western drive for metaphysical purity, believes must be suppressed:

> The truth is that the phantom hound
> was a coyote
>
> the Cayuga women had killed with their bare hands
> and tied by its brush to the postern-gate.
>
> Southey interprets this as a revival
> of the white dog ceremony
>
> and inaugurates a witch-hunt.
> [Tarski]

It isn't until the section entitled "[Lévi-Straus]" that Coleridge is introduced to his familiar, "a coyote made of snow". He has already slept with the Indian woman who reminded him of Mary Evans, an early love he forsook for Sara, and now Coleridge, like the abducted Sara, is entering a new realm of natural symbolism, of primitive, psychedelic awareness, of raw rather than cooked knowledge. The penultimate section, "[Kristeva]", which according to Auge is spoken by Sara, reads: "Signifump. Signifump. Signifump." Auge observes: "Among other things, the poststructuralist theorist Julia

Kristeva is renowned for her assertion that all human discourse is irrevocably marked by both semiotic and semantic processes, by unintelligible bodily resonances as well as by cognitive significance. Signifump serves, then, as a kind of Kristevan shibboleth, a reminder of the anarchic corporeality intrinsic to language that prohibits the word from being reduced to a mere signifier."[21] This physical type of knowledge threatens the whole system of Western thought, just as Nietzsche believed. In the last section entitled "[Hawking]", after the scientist Stephen Hawking, the evidence is gathered for the dismantling of the metaphysical structures that this experience in the New World suggests. The last lines read:

> It will all be over, de dum,
> in next to no time –
>
> long before 'The fluted cypresses
> rear'd up their living obelisks'
>
> has sent a shiver, de dum, de dum,
> through Unitel, its iridescent Dome.

The Platonic or metaphysical structure of knowledge that Unitel's dome represents is undone by the physical force of experience, represented by de dum, or Signifump. The totemic power of the "fluted cypresses" as "living obelisks" returns us to a primitive awareness of the world. In this, we postmoderns are Pre-Socratic pagans looking to the elements for meaning and finding only change, as well as twined experiences of pain and pleasure, violence and beauty. What meaning Muldoon finds in later volumes, and how the "iridescent Dome" becomes a golden "monument to the human heart", is the subject of the next chapter.

Endnotes

---

[1] Two hundred and thirty-three is also, as Tim Kendall has noted (Kendall, *Muldoon*, 161), the number of native tribes thought to have existed in America at the time of Columbus, though this figure is contentious.

[2] Kendall, *Muldoon*, 157.

[3] Lynn Keller, "An Interview with Paul Muldoon" *Contemporary Literature* 35: 1 (1994), 11.

[4] Robert Frost, *Collected Poems* (New York: Holt, 1969), 105.

[5] "Madog Ab Owain Gwynedd." *Encyclopædia Britannica.* 2006. *Encyclopædia Britannica Online.* 18 July 2006 <http://search.eb.com/eb/article-9049911>

[6] Elisa E. Beshero-Bondar, "British conquistadors and Aztec priests: the horror of Southey's *Madoc,*" *Philological Quarterly (Univ. of Iowa, Iowa City)* (82:1) [Winter 2003], 87–113.

[7] Andrew J. Auge, "To Send a Shiver through Unitel", *Contemporary Literature* 46.4 (2005) 636–7.

[8] John Goodby, *Irish Poetry Since 1950: From Stillness into History* (New York: St. Martin's Press, 2000), 299.

[9] Wills, *Reading Paul Muldoon*, 136.

[10] John Banville, "Slouching Toward Bethlehem", *New York Review of Books*, 30 May 1991, 37–9.

[11] Michael Hoffman, "Muldoon: A Mystery", *London Review of Books*, 20 December 1990, 18–9.

[12] Mason, David: "In praise of artifice", *Hudson Review* (54:4) Winter 2002, 687.

[13] David Wheatley, "Books and Issues: An Irish Poet in America", *Raritan: A Quarterly Review* (Rutgers University, New Brunswick, NJ) (18:4) [Spring 1999], 145–57.

[14] Ivan Phillips, University of Hertfordshire. "Madoc: A Mystery." *The Literary Encyclopedia.* 29 August 2005, The Literary Dictionary Company, 18 July 2006. <http://www.litencyc.com/php/sworks.php?rec=true&UID=3776>

[15] Stan Smith, *Irish Poetry and the Construction of Modern Identity* (Dublin: Irish Academic Press, 2005), 193.

[16] Omaar Hena, "Playing Indian/Disintegrating Irishness: Globalization and Cross-Cultural Identity in Paul Muldoon's "Madoc: A Mystery". *Contemporary Literature* 49:2 (forthcoming).

[17] Erwin Schrödinger, *Nature and the Greeks* and *Science and Humanism* (Cambridge: Cambridge UP, 1996; first published 1954), 32.

[18] David S. Phelps, "The Search for Croatan", ECU Newsletter, http://www.ecu.edu/rcro/Newsletter/4-1/Search.htm

[19] Lynn Keller, "An Interview with Paul Muldoon", *Contemporary Literature* 35: 1 (1994), 12.

[20] Ihab Hassan, *The Dismemberment of Orpheus* (Madison: Wisconsin, 1982), 267-8; for a discussion of postmodernism as "a declaration of cultural independence", see Perry Anderson, *The Origins of Postmodernity* (London and New York: Verso, 1998), 3.

[21] Auge, "To Send a Shiver through Unitel", 639.

7

The Annals of Chile (1994)

IT WOULD NOT BE NEWS TO SAY that Paul Muldoon is one of the most exemplary postmodern poets of Ireland and the US. While accepting some notable differences between a modernist poet such as Yeats and the postmodern Muldoon, this chapter will discuss how conceptions of aesthetics apply to the question of the stability of the subject, to politics, history and landscape, as well as to postmodernity and postcoloniality within an Irish frame. The philosophical and aesthetic dilemmas of postmodernism and modernism are remarkably similar; no matter how "incorrigibly plural"[1] we've become, poets want to achieve some sort of stability in their subject, to clear a space in which poetry can be created, to illuminate form. Even if Muldoon seems to have delineated the ways in which this effort is interrupted in "Madoc: A Mystery", in *The Annals of Chile* (1994), for which he won the T. S. Eliot Award, he has personal reasons (the elegy for his friend Mary Powers, the birth of his daughters, the elegy for his mother) for this aesthetic illumination, and his considerations of its redemptive capacity.

In moments of highly sensory and usually sensual experience one achieves a sense of a rational order behind the chaos of "reality"; there is movement behind the veil. Yeats calls this moment "ecstasy", "tragic joy", "heroic reverie", among other epithets; Ezra Pound calls it "the luminous detail", "the great acorn of light"; Eliot, "the still point"; and Wallace Stevens, "the supreme fiction", the "revelation of reality". These moments obviously exist in Modernist novels as well: such as Virginia Woolf's "moments of being", Joyce's "epiphanies",[2] for instance. The illumination is based in the subject-object relationship, specifically in perception, and often its erotic drive. A healthy society sublimates it or gives it form. An unhealthy one thwarts it, violates it. As the Modernists saw their societies as the latter type of culture, they often reflected this fact in the violence of their art. They then sought purgation in their aesthetic, but even their catharsis is sensible of disappointment. The position here outlined is that, even with some notable differences in tone and style, a paradigmatic linking of art and violence holds for postmodernism as well as Modernism, certainly as they are practiced by Muldoon and Yeats respectively.

As we noted in the last chapter, there are two sides to Paul Muldoon's poetry: a postmodern suspicion of the aesthetic, on the one hand; and, on the other, the belief that the monuments of poetry may still offer some solace. Two examples from his poetry make this dichotomy clear. One presents a traditionally romantic vision of the redemptive possibilities of art, inherited by many Modernists, while the other displays a more sceptical postmodern view. The latter side of the dichotomy, "[Vico]", is from *Madoc: A Mystery* (1990) and was discussed in the introduction and in Chapter 6. The second example is from the elegy "Incantata", in The *Annals of Chile* (1994), and contains all the lyricism and redemptive possibilities of the old Modernists:

> I thought again of how art may be made, as it was by André
>   Derain,
> of nothing more than a turn
> in the road where a swallow dips into the mire
> or plucks a strand of bloody wool from a strand of barbed
>   wire
> in the aftermath of Chickamauga or Culloden
> and builds from pain, from misery, from a deep-seated hurt,
> a monument to the human heart
> that shines like a golden dome among roofs rain-glazed and
>   leaden.

The "golden dome" as monumental image of art and religion offers some redemptive hope for the slaughter of the Scottish at Culloden or of the soldiers at the American Civil War battle of Chickamauga. In this, the golden dome is much like the "pleasure dome" of Coleridge's "Kublai Khan", another poem in which art tries to quell the "ancestral voices prophesying war". If we take these quotations as statements of his central dual poetic, Muldoon has not moved beyond Yeats's "The Circus Animals' Desertion" – no more than had Frost, Auden, or MacNeice, poets more typically seen as Muldoon's predecessors. Art aims to assuage the pain and transform the ugliness that conceived it in "the foul rag and bone shop of the heart". Yet, if we cannot look to Muldoon for a new postmodern poetic, at least in this regard, we may yet allow his tone and technique, his witty vulnerability and elusiveness to embody our contemporary confusion. In *The Annals of Chile* (1994), we see that Muldoon, like Louis MacNeice, has no nostalgia for an idealised past, that he is eclectic and playfully baroque in style, but that when it comes to his central philosophy of the illumination of the subject, and its place in the world, he is beholden to the modernists for his poetic, that he celebrates relativism only to a point, and not to a point of no return.

The first poem of *The Annals of Chile* (1994) is a translation from Ovid's *Metamorphoses*, Book VI, lines 313–81. It tells the tale of Leto who turned the peasants of Lycia into frogs because they did not allow her to drink from their spring when she and her children were suffering from thirst; we remember this story from *Quoof*. This tale of moral and ethical values and of the consequent suffering that falls on those who fail the test is a strangely centred tale after the violently decentred narrative of "Madoc: A Mystery". This is not to say this book leaves the postmodern sense of play and the deferral of meaning entirely behind. It does not. In many ways, poems like the closing long-poem "Yarrow", one of many long closing poems in Muldoon's career, or like "Brazil", "Twice", even "Incantata", are as formally postmodern as anything before, if not more so. What we notice is that within this aesthetic, certain Modernist tendencies resurface, or even surface for the first time. Critics hailed this "seriousness" as a sign of Muldoon's maturity. In many ways this is correct, but it might be more effective and just to say that his parody of the philosophical quandary of Western metaphysics was an entangled prelude to the redemptive possibilities of his art. It also is a reflection of new personal realities. Muldoon is outside Ireland and its Troubles. He is also a newly minted parent. These changes have affected him. In Muldoon's poetry since *Meeting the British* (1987), it seems that he needs an emotional focus to his work if it is not mainly to be about language itself, philosophy, aesthetics, or a postmodern meditation on history. In poems like "Incantata", all those concerns exist, only now they revolve around the pain and sadness of the subject. As a consequence, the whimsy, the associative games for which he is famous, seem to have more of an edge in these poems, as if they themselves reflect the pain of the slippage of meaning.

In poems like "Brazil", on the other hand, Muldoon almost seems tired of the themes, especially his own family and the family romance, that have occupied his poetry from the start. It does not matter if it is Ireland or not. It could be "Brazil" and "if not Brazil, // then Uruguay […] if not Uruguay, then Ecuador". As he says in the poem "Twice", he is "Two places at one, was it, or one place twice". The maternal body follows him wherever he goes: "One nipple darkening her smock." That body is the object of veneration and requires a "shame-faced *Tantum Ergo* / struggling through thurified smoke". *Tantum Ergo* are the first two words of the penultimate stanza of the benediction, which begins *"Tantum ergo sacramentum Veneremur cernui"* (Therefore we, before him bending, This great sacrament revere). Though hardly recognisable in her flamboyance, the mother plays on the theme of mushrooms and hallucinations. The maternal body itself is one recurring dream:

> So much for the obliq-
>
> uity of leaving *What a Boy Should Know*
> under my pillow: now *vagina* and *vas*
>
> *deferens* made a holy show
> of themselves.

The family reference quickly takes on political significance. Bernardo O'Higgins says: "There is inherent vice // in everything." Chilean born, but of Irish ancestry, O'Higgins was a South American revolutionary leader and the first Chilean head of state ("supreme director", 1817–23), who commanded the military forces that won independence from Spain. Famous for his honesty, his view of existence as rife with vice is telling in this poem's conjunction of family and political life. That he expunges two Hiberno-English words ("deasil" and "widdershins") from "the annals of Chile" is a pointed reference to the need to purify this conjunction. No amount of aestheticising can release Muldoon from this dilemma; the political and the familial are often inextricable. In the playful poem "Oscar", the mythos of the son, from mythology, Oscar son of Oisin, or simultaneously Oscar Wilde, is a symbol of the inability of removing oneself from one's parentage: "... my mother's skeleton // has managed to worm / its way back on top of the old man's." Similarly, in "Milkweed and Monarch", Muldoon feels that the inheritance is so intense and so archetypal that the people, the individual characters of his mother and father matter little; even their sex isn't of importance anymore: "as he knelt by the grave of his mother and father / he could barely tell one from the other." Struck by the indecipherability of grief so great he cannot accurately describe the object of his grief, and by the decay of the body, the dissolution of all binaries in death, Muldoon is weary of his content and so takes intense comfort in his style. This intensity is the source of his artistic quest to establish how fantasy, history, myth, public and private lives, art and politics combine. This combination may give new life to his poetic, that is his hope, and such a hope is especially evident in "Yarrow", but it is partially true of many of the poems that Muldoon has written since. In "Incantata", however, Muldoon is also focused on a very particular loss, the death of the American artist Mary Farl Powers (1948–1992). In this powerful experience a new mythos is born out of the earth, like the potato in the art work by Powers. The poem has less of the world-weariness of some of the other poems in the volume, but it has the same linguistic and aesthetic playfulness.

In a loose form of *octava rima*, borrowed from Byron, without the strict rhyme scheme, but with similarly ingenuous weak-ended rhymes ("dark rums", "doldrums"), Muldoon rehearses what it was he learned from Powers. This relationship seems to present a type of conversation between certain values. In a simple way, Muldoon realises the futility of the drinking culture from which he comes. He also learns from her that those who subjugate poetry to politics want "only blood on the sand", to be aware of the "fourth estate", the revolutionary vanguard. These are some of his lessons, but there are others that make him question his own whimsical self. Powers' life and art, for instance, combine a focused Catholic belief with a scepticism worthy of Sartre or "His Nibs" Samuel Beckett:

> Again and again you'd hold forth on your own version of
>   Thomism,
> your own *Summa*
> *Theologiae* that in everything there is an order,
> that the things of the world sing out in a great oratorio:
> it was Thomism, though, tempered by *La Nausée*,
> by His Nibs Sam Bethicket,
> and by that Dublin thing, that an artist must walk down Baggot
> Street wearing a hair-shirt under the shirt of Nessus.

Perhaps, because Powers saw through him (as stanza 12 beginning "Hamm and Clov" makes clear), Muldoon knows that he was never the "centre of [her] universe". He goes on to make the following characterisation of her art, one which reflects the above combination of faith and scepticism:

> Nor should I have been, since you were there already, your
>   own *Ding*
> *an sich*, no less likely to take wing
> than the Christ you drew for a Christmas card as a pupa
> in swaddling clothes: and how resolutely you would pooh-
>   pooh
> the idea I shared with Vladimir and Estragon,
> with whom I'd been having a couple of jars,

that this image of the Christ-child swaddled and laid in the
  manger
could be traced directly to those army-worm dragoons.

Muldoon is referring to a work by Powers of a nightmarish vision of worms in the last line. He sees Powers as her own "thing-in-
itself", self sufficient, connected to the oratorio of the world. Christ
as worm in a pupa implicitly becomes Christ the butterfly. That we
don't see it in this poem is the influence of a Beckettian aesthetic in
which that type of sign is relegated to a mere leaf upon a bare tree.
Even here, that transformation is questioned, indeed threatened, by
the "army-worm dragoons". It is yet to be established whether
there is anything permanent or transfigurative.

For Muldoon's cast of mind, Powers' faith without an image of
permanence is not understandable. Powers, it seems from this
poem, had a rooted sense of the world, a natural piety, which he
does not. Without this natural piety, transcendent proof is the
only way to believe. Therefore he looks to her art, her potato
mouth (which we remember from the poem "Mary Farl Powers:
Pink Spotted Torso", *Quoof*, 1983), for prophetic powers (a pun on
her name employed throughout the poem):

I thought of you again tonight, thin as a rake, as you bent
over the copper plate of 'Emblements,'
its tidal wave of army-worms into which you all but disap-
  peared:
I wanted to catch something of its spirit
and yours, to body out your disembodied *vox*
clamantis in deserto, to let this all-too-cumbersome device
of a potato-mouth in a potato-face
speak out, unencumbered, from its long, low, mould-filled
  box.

Cancer stricken, she became a figure from her own nightmare;
Muldoon can't resist the power of the image and seeks some way
to lift her from its mouldy remains; in many ways, he looks to
heaven, and cries in the wilderness (*"clamantis in deserto"*). He is

both ashamed of his own artificiality when faced with her work and life ("which is why you called me 'Polyester' or 'Polyurethane'"), and annoyed at her own self-deprecation: "I wanted it [the potato-mouth] to speak to what seems always true of the truly great, / that you had a winningly inaccurate / sense of your own worth, that you would second-guess / yourself ..."

Muldoon then remembers her fight with cancer through images of belief and survival in the face of death that are hauntingly appropriate for our age. "I try to imagine the strain / you must have been under, pretending to be as right as rain / while hearing the bells of a church from some long-flooded valley." He sees her "death-mask / in that swallow's nest". Through her powers, Muldoon is producing one of his finest poems. He proceeds then to the discussion of the Fauvist painter André Derain and his "golden dome" as monumental image of art and religion, offering some redemptive hope for the suffering of the world. He imagines her as a ghost haunting him, and then reflects that she had no belief in ghosts. Hers was a Deist sense of the order of the world:

> You'd be aghast at the idea of your spirit hanging over this
>   vale
> of tears like a jump-suited jump-jet whose vapour trail
> unravels a sky: for there's nothing, you'd say, nothing over
> and above the sky itself, nothing but cloud-cover
> reflected in a thousand lakes: it seems that Minne-
> sota itself means 'sky-tinted water', that the sky is a great slab
> of granite or iron ore that might at any moment slip
> back into the worked-out sky-quarry, into the worked-out sky-
>   mines.

The natural imagery of the state of ten-thousand lakes reminds Muldoon of the transcendental, but that never lasts long unchallenged. Here it is challenged by the "worked-out sky quarry" and "sky-mines". Soon the force of association, which is the force of *his* art, takes over. The potato mouth is all that's left of a number of things. Nothing, the void of grief, is the dominant mood and word of the stanza. It is the enchanted subject of "Incantata" of a narrative ("Cantata") in verse set to the recitative of this poem, of his alternate recitative and air. It is first for a single voice, then after becomes a choral work. It is either sacred (resembling an oratorio but shorter) or secular (as a lyric drama set to music): the reader and writer have yet to determine. It is like magic, but also sounds like "cantata" in "cantata" (in song). It also means something suspended. In Italian they say *"il disco si è incantato"* (when it repeats the same tune because it is scratched and keeps skipping). All of these definitions of the title come into play as Muldoon is struck by his grief, but the climax of grief is inexpressible, beyond words. Art is insufficient and yet provides the only means of signification. Caught in this paradox, Muldoon appropriately turns to the master of paradox, Samuel Beckett:

> The fact that you were determined to cut yourself off in your
>   prime
> because it was *pre*-determined has my eyes abrim:
> I crouch with Belacqua
> and Lucky and Pozzo in the Acacacac-
> ademy of Anthropopopometry, trying to make sense of the
>   *'quaquaqua'*
> of that potato-mouth; that mouth as prim
> and proper as it's full of self-opprobrium,
> with its *'quaquaqua'*, with its 'Quoiquoiquoiquoiquoiquoiquoi'.

These are allusions to Beckett's characters (from short fiction and from his drama) and to Beckett's celebration of failure to express what he wants to express, to encompass experience, or to find something worth expressing that isn't about failure. After this, Muldoon lists a series of events, people, experiences, associations and ideas to which Power's potato mouth gives utterance and stutterance. Some are merely shared artist friends, "Medbh, and Michael and Frank and Ciaran" (or Medbh McGuckian, Michael Longley, Frank Ormsby, Ciaran Carson). And some are natural images of revelation that test the limits of experience despite those limits: "where the salmon breaks through the either/or neither/nor nether / reaches despite the temple-veil." Some are more traditional images of failed revelation taken from the Greek myths: "where Orpheus was again overwhelmed by that urge to turn / back and lost not only Eurydice but his steel-strung lyre." And then there are more self-explanatory images like that "of Watt [a Beckett character] remembering the 'Krak! Krek! Krik! / of those three frogs' karaoke / like the still sad *basso continuo* of the great quotidian." The intent is to show how the everyday, the mystical, the mythical, the logical, the factual, and the fantastic are expressed by this voice crying in the wilderness. These articulations of life itself are all drawn together by the final elegy Muldoon makes to the fact of Powers' dying and her attitude toward fate:

> Of the day your father came to call, of your leaving your sick-
>   room
> in what can only have been a state of delirium,
> of how you simply wouldn't relent
> from your vision of a blind
> watch-maker, of your fatal belief that fate
> governs everything from the honey-rust of your father's ter-
>   rier's
> eyebrows to the horse that rusts and rears
> in the furrow, of the furrows from which we can no more de-
>   viate
>
> than they can from themselves, no more than the map of
>   Europe
> can be redrawn, than that Hermes might make a harp from his
>   *harpe,*
> than that we must live in a vale
> of tears on the banks of the Lagan and Foyle,
> than that the Irish Hermes,
> Lugh, might have leafed through his vast herbarium
> for the leaf that had it within it, Mary, to anoint and anneal,
>
> than that Lugh of the Long Arm might have found in the
>   midst of *lus*
> *na leac* or *lus na treatha* or *Frannc-lus,*

in the midst of eyebright, or speedwell, or tansy, and antidote,
than that this *Incantata*
might have you look up from your plate of copper or zinc
on which you've etched the row upon row
of army-worms, than that you might reach out, arrah,
and take in your ink-stained hands my own hands stained
    with ink.

Fate itself rules in the end, except for the human gesture of
those ink-stained hands meeting. The gestures towards the transcendental, seen in the image of Hermes and the Irish Hermes
Lugh, and the transmigration of souls they represent, come down
to the enchantment of Power's being on earth, which has transmi-
grated into the text as into Muldoon's life. Her artistic powers allow him to endure along the Lagan and Foyle rivers in Derry and
Belfast, help him to endure and grow, anointed and annealed
(that is, toughened in this case)[3] by the leaves in Lugh's vast herbarium, amidst the "army-worms" of Troubles that haunt their
banks.

   The poems that follow are meditations surrounding the birth
of his child Dorothy ("The Sonogram", "Footling", "The Birth"), a
paean to César Vallejo, the Peruvian poet-revolutionary ("César
Vallejo: *Testimony*") that plays on the Peruvian poet's own poem
"Black Stone on Top of a White Stone", which imagines his death,
as well as a surreal series of riffs on the metaphysics ("metaphysi-
cattle"), myths, and etymologies associated with "Cows". In the
first poem on the coming infant, the sonogram reveals that the
baby in the placenta looks like Ireland, with the feet presumably
being Kerry, the hands Connemara, and the head Ulster. The notion of the family as a republic, traceable back to the eighteenth
century is powerfully if playfully presented here. The child then
looks like she's hitching a ride, fighting a gladiatorial contest or
waving like an Emperor who has passed "judgment on the
crowd". All these possibilities are inherent in the potentiality of
birth, and only in the womb can they all exist simultaneously. In
"Footling" there is a sense that the child doesn't want to be born,
almost presaging a miscarriage, like "the phantom 'a' (in the

American spelling of) Cesarian", that she has "turned in on her-self" and now will require an operation if she is to be born natu-rally. The centre of the poem is the will not to be born, not to pass through the threshold, a wish Muldoon may take from Beckett, and which here achieves great beauty: "she shows instead her ut-ter / disregard ... for what lies behind the great sea-wall / and what knocks away at the great sea-cliff." All of this surfaces in the poem of beauty, joy and violence called "The Birth". The unset-tling combination of images takes us back to Muldoon's early preoccupation with earth and star imagery. We have entered the "realm of apple-blossoms and chanterelles and damsons ... and foxes"; in short, we have entered Muldoon's realm, for these are images he has always used. This is the natural world, the world of animals, where we learn our ethics, as Muldoon notes in his in-troduction to *The Faber Book of Beasts*.[4] This world, however, is also brutally real. The nurses therefore are the "windlass-women" who "ply their shears" and who, as Muldoon sees his child through "floods of tears", proceed to "check their staple-guns for staples" before sewing up his wife.

The final poem of the book, "Yarrow", another monumental closing work, is an elegy for Muldoon's mother, written some twenty years after her death. Yarrow is "the common name of the herb *Achillea Millefolium* (N. O. *Compositæ*), also called MILFOIL and NOSE-BLEED, frequent on roadsides, dry meadows, and waste ground, with tough greyish stem, finely-divided bipinnate leaves, and close flat clusters of flower-heads of a somewhat dull white, often varying to pink or crimson; sometimes used medici-nally as a tonic".[5] The medicinal aspect of the leaf brings us back to the annealing, anointing leaf from Lugh's "vast herbarium" in "Incantata". Achilles is said to have applied it at Troy to stanch blood; hence its botanical name, *Achillea Millefolium.* One suspects that the grief behind the poem must have been inspired by Mary Powers' death. The interconnectedness of women in Muldoon's mind is apparent in most men's minds, even if he, like others, is trying to keep this secret, like the yarrow leaf "keeping a secret / from itself, something on the tip of its own tongue". While turning inward, the poem is almost Joycean in its exuberant word-play. Never are we more reminded that contemporary Irish poetry is probably more beholden to Joyce than it is to Yeats. We should think of Irish poetry *after* Joyce, as the critic Dillon Johnston famously noted, rather than merely *after* Yeats, as the title of a previous anthology collected by Maurice Harmon had declared. Both critics are right, of course.

We have already seen Muldoon's struggle with Yeats's influence; here we see a real embracing of Joycean love of compound nouns. Like Beckett, Muldoon follows Joyce in contriving words of his own. We have words such as "expiapiaratory", "knobker-rieknout", "lillibulablies". Muldoon has done this before, but now it is becoming a prominent part of his work, and he is being taken to task for it by various critics. Tim Kendall ably and evocatively defends the poem against such criticisms:

> ... such linguistic strategies did not help endear 'Yarrow' to every critic. Jamie McKendrick in *The Independent* (London) argued that the best poems "are all in the first part of the book"; and Sean Dunne complained that "We are watching a clever poet at practiced play rather than being absorbed by the power of his poems". This could hardly be more wrong. 'Yarrow' is as emotionally charged as anything Muldoon has ever written; it is a frantic and at times painful elegy for the poet's mother which can barely bring itself to register the loss. [...] It is intriguing to wonder whether 'Yarrow' was itself begun on Brigid's Feast-day; but the poem is undoubtedly Muldoon's more generous response to an "excess of love" which seems to have taken the form of snobbery, over-protection and moralistic strictures. 'Yarrow' reads like a reluctant but overwhelming love poem. Its endless allusions to adventure stories, its intricate formal patterning, and its time-shifts and channel-hops, constitute desperate swervings away from the source of grief; but the poem still homes in agonizingly on Brigid's death-bed and the poet's subsequent desolation. This desolation is so intense, and so entwined with negative emotions, that it can apparently only now be confronted, from a distance of twenty years."[6]

The poem begins by noting that the world will be swept away in the Heraclitean flux of time. Everything is changeable: "all of us // would be overwhelmed ... All would be swept away." It is a flux perhaps more like something out of Cratylus, than Heraclitus. Truth cannot be known. The perceptible world is heaving, whatever transcendence might linger. Muldoon is again trying to find something that lasts, some immanence that will spark in its fall. Perhaps it is the energy of that effort to fix something in the powerful flux of loss and discomfort that gives this poem its charge.

The poem begins with images of family, of religious themes in the colonies (from Montezuma to Loyola), of ancient Egypt and Medieval Europe, of Muldoon's own youth in rural Ireland, a meditation of the character of yarrow, and flashes of pop culture (Michael Jackson). This heteroglossia characterises the rest of the poem. The various worlds represented all come together in the narrative as Muldoon tries to find a language and a context that will articulate his complicated feelings for his mother, and will chart his trajectory from his youth (inspired by nationalism and Irish culture, its language, myth and politics), through his flight to freedom in poetry and art, to his maturity. The most moving and consistent parallel context is that of a Christian crusader sent out to fight the Saracens. This fight is reflected in pop culture, films and rock-and-roll music, in literature and in life. The fight is an expression of the personal phantasmagoric nation of Paul Muldoon.

Muldoon's sexually repressive childhood (and his mother's fear of his masturbation) provides the context for the flight to freedom and the fight against the enemy, whoever that might be. What makes that fight so complicated is that it is his mother and his motherland that instigates the fight for national independence in the troubled counties of the North. This fuels his desire to fight, but finally his struggle is against the very terms of its inception. The countermuse to his mother, and one that constantly intermingles with her, is the figure of "S—", an unnamed female who is an artist and a drugtaker, who incites Muldoon to break out of the fold. She follows thoughts of his mother and leads to thoughts of his mother. She also is connected in the poem to Sylvia Plath, another self-destructive visionary living on the edge. Muldoon claims that the end of her poem "Edge" is confused: "Is it the woman on the funeral urn / or the moon? Are they both '"masturbating a glitter'"? The need to see his own sexuality mirrored is intense. It is the source of all the hallucinatory fantasies in the poem. It is the "expiapiatory rush / of poppies". Instructively, he is like Arthur, whose identity is proved by his ability to release the sword Excalibur from the rock. His artistic identity is also reflected in this mythology. He is like Tennyson, and dashes off a couple of sparrow- // songs" (here Muldoon is playing off Tennyson's description of "In Memoriam", and both Muldoon's and Tennyson's poems are sexually ambivalent eulogies). Thoughts of Tennyson lead to Tennyson's "The Charge of the Light Brigade" and another war between the West and the Muslim East.

A third of the way through the poem and Muldoon is caught between the mythic battles between East and West and the search for the Holy Grail, which in this poem is a real if playful allusion to a vagina. This latter search is coupled with the Oedipal complex; hence there is a reference to Synge's *The Playboy of the Western World* ("While my da studies the grain in the shaft of his rake / and I tug at the rusted blade of the loy"). Soon, perhaps because he is now living in America, or perhaps because he is remembering his youth, figures from the Wild West enter the poem (Wild Bill Hickok and Wyatt Earp). He cannot purge himself of the sense that his soul must be punished, as his reference to Yeats's "The Cold Heaven" makes clear ("as though ice burned and was but the more ice"). He then recalls his first forays into literature, when he first read Ovid's famously sexual *Amores*, while the scandal of Christine Keeler grabbed the British headlines and shocked his mother. In breaking this rule, Muldoon has a parallel memory of his father confronting a "stalwart Prod" over some contested kale. These two confrontations, one personal and one national, become inextricable in his life and art, however much he tries to separate them and however separate they in fact may be. Similarly, his own angst and the pain of the nation also merge. His mother believed "whosoever looketh on a woman to lust //

after would go the way of Charles Stewart Parnell", the Irish par-
liamentary leader who fell from grace and political power because
of an affair with a married woman. As noted before, some of
Muldoon's most furious parodies seem the result of the repeti-
tiveness of his themes, and a sense of wrong that he cannot seem
to purge. His mother then becomes "Olyve Oyl" to his Popeye. He
remembers how his mother made him think that the salacious
book by Apuleius, *The Golden Ass*, was called *The Golden Beam*. She
wants him to be a defender of the faith, but gets it backwards ("It
should be *Fidei Defensor*, by the way, not *Defensor Fidei*"), in speech
and in act. As he goes through hero after hero, from Arthur to
Aladdin to Popeye, one wonders what he is fighting. Sexual re-
pression, it seems.

Muldoon later has a dream of sexual/political freedom: "a girl
… laid her exquisite flank beside me under the covers and offered
me her breast […] she cajoled, 'must we rant and rail / against the
ermine / yoke of the House of Hanover?'" After reciting the ancient call to arms against Britain ("the House of Hanover"), she
then asks the most pertinent question of all: "When might the
roots of Freedom take hold?" This call to freedom is formative,
but is it a call to arms or a redefinition of freedom? It is not easy to
tell in this poem. One can only say that for Muldoon it is probably
more of the latter, even if it was meant as the former. Muldoon
takes flight in an automobile, much as before he sought escape in
flicking television channels, only now he is flying into the real,
whatever that might be. He hears his mother's call "O come ye
back / to Erin", and he goes. The poem then moves to the centre of
Muldoon's Dadaist art and he helps "S–" move into her apart-
ment, where he notes that "Duchamp's 'The Bride Stripped Bare
by Her Bachelors', Even / all said one thing – 'I masturbate'". This
belief becomes insistent as he goes through a series of lines by
Yeats about Maud Gonne, and points out their sexual double
meanings. "The woman that I loved … all gave tongue, gave
tongue right royally." He does this all very self-consciously:
"How dare you suggest that his 'far-off, most secret, / and invio-
late rose' is a cunt." Finally, even Popeye's "Blow me" takes on a

new meaning. Yet, when he feels he is "getting hard" never has he felt "so mortified"; in other words, the old taboos are in place. This is why he is straining to knock them off their totemic seat. Myth, fantasy and history, however, join thereon. "S– would detect the mating call of Fine Gael and Fianna Fáil," Muldoon remembers. The last time he sees her, she is taking drugs before heading back home, like Deirdre and Naoise, two mythological Irish lovers who crossed the king's power, but eventually returned home to meet their deaths.

The close of the poem presents the image of his mother's death, her very physical demise from cancer, while the flurry of associations, sexual, filmic, historical and mythological, embracing pop and high culture, had sought to evade. In the end she meets her death, cancer cutting through her like the sword of fabled Saladin, who, during his struggle against the Crusaders, was renowned in both the Christian and Muslim worlds for his leadership and military prowess tempered by his chivalry and merciful nature. In other words, she was killed by the enemy whom Muldoon had been invoked to fight. The guilt and anger over sexual transgression becomes guilt and anger over her death. While "S–" becomes a Sharon Tate-like figure moving to the murderous rule of Charles Manson and the helter-skelter of the early '70s, Muldoon finds himself like Lear carrying the body of his dead daughter, feeling that he is the one to blame for her death. At this stage, whether it is a mother, daughter, or a lover, it doesn't matter. Lear may well be lamenting for his absent mother in this confrontation of his dead daughter, as critics have suggested.[7] At the end of the poem, Muldoon is having as much difficulty interpreting his mother's death, and a series of other texts that paralleled it, as we have had interpreting his. As he states: "I can no more read between the lines ..." The ship full of signification that set sail to avoid being overwhelmed by the storm of grief at the beginning of the poem has been "lost with all hands between Ireland and Montevideo". Again, Muldoon is caught between New and Old World colonies, wondering where he fits.

Endnotes

---

[1] Louis MacNeice, "Snow", *Collected Poems*, ed. E. R. Dodds (New York: Oxford, 1967), 133; all quotations from MacNeice are taken from this volume unless otherwise stated.

[2] Most of these famous phrases don't need footnoting; however, perhaps one does. The phrase "luminous detail" is from Pound's essay "I gather the Limbs of Osiris", *Selected Prose, 1909–1963* (London: Faber, 1973), 21.

[3] See *Oxford English Dictionary* (second edition, 1989) for definition number 4 of "anneal": "To toughen anything, made brittle from the action of fire, by exposure to continuous and slowly diminished heat, or by other equivalent process."

[4] Paul Muldoon, *The Faber Book of Beasts* (London: Faber, 1997), xvii.

[5] See "Yarrow" *Oxford English Dictionary* (second edition, 1989).

[6] Kendall, *Muldoon*, 226.

[7] See, for example, Coppelia Kahn, "The Absent Mother in King Lear", *Rewriting the Renaissance* (Chicago: U of Chicago P, 1986), 47–9.

8

Hay (1998)

STYLE BECOMES A BURDEN TO A WRITER at a certain stage in his or
her career. Great writers periodically transform their styles
and often these stylistic developments reflect differing personal
realities in the lives of the authors. W. B. Yeats's transformations
are legendary: from the early transcendental mode to the hard-
edged satiric, elegiac or realistic middle period, to the visionary
anger and historical/philosophical systems of his late great style.
His defence of these changes, especially as concerns his revision of
earlier work, is famous for its linking of self and style:

> The friends that have it I do wrong
> Whenever I remake a song,
> Should know what issue is at stake:
> It is myself that I remake.[1]

The choice of style resonates from the graphic characters on
the page, their selection and arrangement, out to the personal and
social conditions of the writer. As Renato Barilli notes: "The word
'style' derives from a slight deformation and elevation of the stilo
or pen, as we should more correctly transcribe the Latin *stilus*,
which, in turn, was a technical instrument invented for the exercise of an art, but in the largest and most common sense of the
term corresponding to a practical ability." Because there were so
many physical ways of writing in ancient Roman times, he continues, the stilo opened the way to "varying degrees of elegance",
as well as "to noble and superior meanings". Thus, the "material
style became the indicator (style) of an entire system of aesthetic

choices, at first relative only to the act of writing, but then extended to any other artistic practice".[2] In other words, the physical act of writing and the crafting of aesthetic forms become sedimentary evidence of choices made within cultural spheres.

For Muldoon, changes in style have been quite apparent. We have seen how natural, political and aesthetic concerns have shaped his verse in successive ways. Themes in Muldoon have changed along with his styles. There were the pastoral meditations and linguistic openness of *New Weather* (1973), reflecting his upbringing and his poetic education. Then there was the rejection of polarities, especially human and animal, in *Mules* (1977), reflecting his attitudes towards philosophical, political and poetic issues. Later came the speculations on the nature of perception in *Why Brownlee Left* (1980), taking on violent uncanny forms in *Quoof* (1983), both of which volumes bore the burden of the Northern Troubles, and wore the mark of the beast in light of the mixed human-animal forms of the earlier volume *Mules*. If one flips through the pages of the Faber *Poems 1968–1998*, one sees that in *Quoof* (as noted previously) Muldoon ceases to capitalise the left margin. This decision may both reflect American influence and a feeling on Muldoon's part that poetry cannot be written with a capital anymore, that is must reflect a different reality. To this day, Muldoon has chosen this latter style, even if he is still very much a formal poet in some important respects. Clearly *Quoof* was a seminal volume in style and content. The Ovidian transformations of *Meeting the British* (1987) began to illustrate the complexity of Muldoon's mature craft, always complex, but now particularly so. This became apparent in the audacious cultural and philosophical linkages of *Madoc: A Mystery* (1990). Birth and death intervened, culminating finally in the elegies of *The Annals of Chile* (1994).

In *Hay* (1998), Muldoon entered what might be the later stages of his mature style. The Muldoonesque, as Clair Wills trenchantly observes, is now open to parody.[3] And a writer's greatest fear is unwilling, and unselfconscious, self-parody. Late style, as Edward Said writes, "involves a nonharmonious, nonserene tension, and,

above all, a sort of deliberately unproductive productiveness going against".[4] In this vein, Muldoon knowingly mocks himself in
Hay. He is overweight, middle-aged and suburban: Americanised
in the worst sense. Poems such as "Paunch" and "The Fridge" ask
how he is to find suitable material for poetry in his well fed, comfortable life. A "nonharmonious, nonserene deliberately unproductive productiveness going against" nicely describes the result.
There are many great plays on clichés in an effort to stave off the
cliché of the poet, which any poet fears becoming, such as "Sym-
posium" and "They that Wash on Thursday". There is also a consciousness of memory and loss, that strange birthmark of middle
age, which only threatens to spread and overwhelm the poet.
There is "no immanent development of forms" considered in
Muldoon's oeuvre, no sense that the history of art is unfolding its
truths (a belief which, according to Meyer Shapiro characterised
Modernism), but there is instead a disorienting feeling that the
progression of form is associational and dreamlike, with no determinate end in sight beyond the record of sensation, the cataloguing of culture, the efforts of art to ride rather than order the
flux.[5]

The faith in art that characterises the Modernists is something
Muldoon finds particularly difficult to hold in place. He comes
close to having such a faith in "Incantata", but nevertheless it is
not the same belief as Yeats had in what he called the "sacred
book" of his poetry. A proclamation of belief common to thinkers
in the early twentieth century, made in this instance by Clive Bell
at the end of his book entitled *Art*, illustrates how difficult it is to
apply it to Muldoon's own style:

> Because the aesthetic emotions are outside and above life, it is
> possible to take refuge in them from life. He who has once lost
> himself in an "O Altitudo" will not be tempted to over-
> estimate the fussy excitements of action. He who can with-
> draw into the world of ecstasy will know what to think of cir-
> cumstance. He who goes daily into the world of aesthetic emo-
> tion returns to the world of human affairs equipped to face it
> courageously and even a little contemptuously. And if by

comparison with aesthetic rapture he finds most human passion trivial, he need not on that account become unsympathetic or inhuman. For practical purposes, even, it is possible that the religion of art will serve a man better than the religion of humanity. He may learn in another world to double the extreme importance of this, but if that doubt dims his enthusiasm for some things that are truly excellent it will dispel his illusions about many that are not. What he loses in philanthropy he may gain in magnanimity; and because his religion does not begin with an injunction to love all men, it will not end perhaps, in persuading him to hate most of them.⁶

This has all the hauteur we have come to expect from Modernist thinking and some of the wisdom we so often mistakenly miss. It is haughty, because we return to the world full of contempt for it, and wise, because through art, and not through politics and religion (Bell suggests) we avoid fanatical loves and hates. The passage appeals to an inhuman transcendental notion of the aesthetic, hovering above the accidents of human experience. It is so much more precarious for the postmodern poet to believe in anything approaching a religion of art or beauty. If "history is the root" and art "the small translucent fruit", as Muldoon maintains in "7, Middagh Street", then the aesthetic can offer no escape from history. There are times when Muldoon offers this opinion without the balance MacNeice's voice provides in "7, Middagh Street". In his poem "The Point", Muldoon takes the idea of Sato's "consecrated blade" from Yeats's poem "A Dialogue of Self and Soul" to discuss whether the point is indeed transcendental. Yeats's blade is "unsullied, keen", in Muldoon's paraphrase, but Muldoon's point is quite the opposite:

What everything in me wants to articulate
is this little bit of a scar that dates
from the time O'Clery, my schoolroom foe,

rammed his pencil into my exposed *thigh*
(not, as the chronicles have it, my calf)
with such force that the point was broken off.

For Muldoon, art does not remain above human suffering, unless, as in a recent poem, "Turkey Buzzards", it is there to feed off it. Poetry is often an expression of that scar. Human suffering is where the aesthetic begins and ends; yet human suffering is messy: unaesthetic, raw meat on the side of the road. This is one of the central paradoxes of Muldoon's art. He would fly high above on Pegasus's wings but knows we are all carrion eaters, like the Turkey Buzzards, and have to return to the earth to find our next meal. Yet Muldoon's scepticism is so profound that even a human-centred universe is questionable.

This detachment is closely connected to aesthetic distance, to the artist's objectivity, an idea which Muldoon explores beautifully if somewhat wistfully in "The Train". In this poem, Muldoon considers whether we as human beings are the centre of existence, or whether the world that spins round us, in this case embodied by the train rattling by two lovers at night in their home, is truly the centre, the "constant thing", in which our lives whirl. Listening to the freight train, the poet notices

> how it seems determined to give the lie
> to the notion, my darling,
> that we, not it, might be the constant thing.

The bearer of commodities, which is what the train signifies, "loaded with ballast so a track may rest / easier in its bed", seems to carry the weight of significance in the world. Human emotion seems insubstantial in comparison, or worse, a lesser commodity. If that is true, what worth is the stuff of poetry? The volume itself, taking one of the original commodities of agricultural culture as its symbol, hay, seems implicitly to ask this question. Throughout *Hay*, Muldoon is seeking a motif that will capture his predicament. From the very title we have a real sense of what is in the volume. There is the simple hay of grass cut or mown and dried for use as fodder, as we see in the title poem and in "The Plot". There are the sexual references, as in "to roll in the hay", as we see in many of the poems of the volume, but especially and perhaps most effectively in "Errata". There is also the sense of "to make hay", to seize the day – a theme underlying his humorous meditations on middle age and stoking his fervent sexual memories. And finally, perhaps underlying all, there is the idea of hay as a natural material, shaped and packaged for cultural consumption. Though some poems are indeed concerned with one or another meaning of 'hay', the many themes most often converge in any given poem. The theme of hay reaches its apogee in "Third Epistle to Timothy":

> The next haycock already summoning itself from windrow after
>   wind-weary windrow
> while yet another brings itself to mind in the acrid stink
> of turpentine. There the image of Lizzie
> Hardy's last servant girl, reaches out from her dais
> of salt hay, stretches out an unsunburned arm
> half in bestowal, half beseechingly, then turns away to appeal
> to all that spirit troop
> of hay treaders as far as the eye can see, the coil on coil
> of hay from which, in the taper's mild uproar,
> they float out across the dark face of the earth, an earth without
>   form, and void.

This image encapsulates the volume's main tensions between the visible and invisible world, the transformative process of poetry (making grass from the hay), as well as the struggles between material form and transcendent meaning. The close of the poem is one of the most haunting in Muldoon's verse, following Thomas Hardy into his deterministic universe. It seems to end in an image of dismal lifelessness, until one remembers that the hay treaders are there above the formless void, much as the dove sat brooding on the vast abyss. Muldoon's hopeful gestures are often so severely defined, so subtly implicit in the dark, as to be easily overlooked.

The themes, however, certainly come together from the first poem of the volume, "The Mudroom", which is based on the small room that serves as a cloakroom for muddy clothes in the deep and snowy northern winter, and which also serves as a type of a versatile storeroom. This versatility is at the heart of Muldoon's poetic. At the beginning of the poem, this space, much like the porch of the Stoic philosophers, contains a philosophical meaning. Its philosophical and religious significance seems to be tied into its role as a gathering place of odds and ends ("blanket from Valparaiso", etc.), as well as an altar upon which the food is laid. The religious function of food seems of special importance: from the Jewish Seder to the notion of sacrifice. The sacredness of its pastoral connections, rooted in the Jewish traditions of Muldoon's wife, comes to the fore quickly, as a memory of a trip in France seems bound to end in the confines of the mudroom:

> We followed the narrow track, my love, we followed the narrow
> track through a valley in the Jura
> to where the goats delight to tread upon the brink
> of meaning. I carried my skating rink,
> the folding one, plus
> a pair of skates laced with convolvulus,
> you a copy of the feminist Haggadah
> from last year's Seder.

"The Passover seder," notes Wills, "is the first of many meals to occur in this volume; the word 'Seder' means order."[7] During Passover, Jews commemorate the exodus from Egypt, but celebration of the Seder also includes separation: a line is drawn between the mess of ordinary life and Seder week. Purity is at stake and Jews draw a line between purity within and the unclean without, a line famously reinterpreted by Christ who contests that what is unclean comes from within. Wills notes insightfully that "another kind of separation may be hinted at here too: the 1967 border between Israel and Palestine, which is known as the green line (and the poem plays on the "blue-green, pine-ash" line in the goat cheese). Religion, politics, aesthetics all come into play in this meditation on the fertile miscellany of the mudroom.

After discussing the Seder, the miscellany is charted, and most of the meditations on their lives together, though they span the world, return to the mudroom and its objects. The poem lists them: foodstuffs, blankets, books, etc. Underneath them all is a sense of life as a journey and the sacrifice it takes to complete that journey, to compile the miscellany. Hence the closing image of the poem:

> It was time, I felt sure, to unpack the Suntory
> into the old fridge, to clear a space between *De Rerum Natura*
> and Virgil's *Eclogues,*
> a space in which, at long last, I might unlock
> the rink, so I drove another piton into an eighty-pound
> bag of Sakrete and flipped the half door on the dairy cabinet
> of the old Hotpoint
> and happened, my love, just happened
> upon the cross
> section of Morbier and saw, once and for all, the precarious
> blue-green, pine-ash path along which Isaac followed Abra-
>   ham
> to an altar lit be a seven-branched candelabrum,
> the ram's horn, the little goat whirligig
> that left him all agog.

Perhaps Muldoon is thinking of Kierkegaard here, especially of *Fear and Trembling*, to fill the space between the pastoral *Eclogues* and the meditation on the nature of things in Lucretius's *De Rerum Natura*. *Fear and Trembling* is concerned with Abraham's sacrifice of Isaac, implicit in the closing image of this poem. To Kierkegaard, absurdity underlies the resignation to fate and the faith that Abraham must place in the Lord's request to sacrifice his son. This belief is absurd in light of any rational ethical thinking. And so "faith" is "not an aesthetic emotion, but something far higher, exactly because it presupposes resignation; it is not the immediate inclination of the heart but the paradox of existence". This paradox leaves Muldoon all "agog".

Recognition of the absurdity of belief seems helpful. And Kierkegaard provides a frame for understanding some of the essential crises of aesthetics and faith in Muldoon, while he also points to something far higher, something that poet and philosopher are attempting to uncover outside of the tragic or poetic realms. Kierkegaard continues in more detailed argument:

Now the story of Abraham contains just such a teleological suspension of the ethical. [...] Abraham represents faith, and that faith finds its proper expression in him whose life is not only the most paradoxical conceivable, but so paradoxical that it simply cannot be thought [.] He acts on the strength of the absurd; for it is precisely the absurd that as the single individual he is higher than the universal. This paradox cannot be mediated; for as soon as he tries Abraham will have to admit that he is in a state of temptation, and in that case he will never sacrifice Isaac, or if he has done so he must return repentantly to the universal. On the strength of the absurd he got Isaac back. Abraham is therefore at no instant the tragic hero, but something quite different, either a murderer or a man of faith. The middle-term that saves the tragic hero is something Abraham lacks. That is why I can understand a tragic hero, but not Abraham, even though in a certain lunatic sense I admire him more than all others. [8]

This critique of universal ethical truths, the absurdity underlying the experience, the repudiation of the tragic hero as the highest form, the balancing of the murderer and the man of faith seem very Muldoonesque. It is not merely stylistic convention: the essential philosophical paradox that haunts the poet and drives the formal experimentation is exposed. This is what makes Muldoon more important than his whimsy sometimes allows. All around us is a dark intent and a demand of bloody sacrifice without proof of rational order to come of it.

In poems such as "Nightingales", "The Bangle", "The Plot", "White Shoulders", "Green Gown", "Now, Now", there is a nasty undertone to various plays – primarily on sex – that is marked by the same philosophical quandary as "The Mudroom", but which is less successful. This version of sexuality has become a familiar theme in Muldoon, but clearly he believes that there is some significance to it. Though the taste wearies a bit, there are poems like the translation of Rilke's "The Unicorn" that provide ballast. This translation is a beautiful evocation of sexuality and animal nature that hearkens back to Muldoon's own volume *Mules* and shows that the poem is not merely a transposition of another poet's theme, but is in fact an expression of Muldoon's own poetic. In the end, the translation is what it should be: an artistic mingling. The mythological embodiment of desire, and conflation of subject/object, human/animal, is striking. Similarly, the transcendental nature of the beast that never existed, that is "unsullied", was bound to make it an even more potent symbol of sexual power; its horn seems to be born of the human imagination, and reflects the human form:

> They brought it on, not with oats and corn,
> but with the chance, however slight,
> that it might come into its own. This gave it such strength
>
> that from its brow there sprang a horn. A single horn.
> Only when it met a maiden's white with white
> would it be bodied out in her, in her mirror's full length.

Notwithstanding the philosophical and poetic brilliance of this piece, balancing virginal beauty with the power of the beast, and of other poems like it, there is also another important element in this volume, and that is almost Japanese-like veneration for the depth of the simple image. In some ways, like any Western poet in the twentieth century, Muldoon is beholden to Imagism, but in others, he strikes out on his own. He understands the ability of haiku to allow images to work well off one another, to complement one another, that not all haiku must be fireworks, that some must be less fiery in order for the more brilliant ones to shine forth. In the poem "The Plover", which comes early in the volume, the design of this paradigm is apparent:

> The plovers come down hard, then clear again,
> for they are the embodiment of rain.

Muldoon somewhat uncharacteristically allows the beautiful to stand unchallenged, if only because it has such complex implications, combining bird and precipitation, and blurring the observer and reality. In "Hopewell Junction", the design is explored in a much lengthier way. The sequence of ninety haiku begins with a simple image (reminiscent in its farmyard simplicity of William Carlos Williams), placed in pastoral terms:

I

The door of the shed
open-shuts with the clangor
of red against red.

It shortly announces the seasons as underlying its main concerns:

VIII

Snow up to my shanks.
I glance back. The path I've hacked
is a white turf bank.

In both these haiku, reality seems difficult to distinguish. The shape of the poem mimics the shape of the image, with the aural rhyme echoing the visual one (red = red, snow = snow). Muldoon sensibly chooses rhyme to mimic the intricate use of form in the Japanese original, which, though unrhymed, has a series of hard and fast rules it must follow. This intricate echoing of sound and image continues to be the theme of this seasonal meditation on the unchanging, multi-layered nature of reality, that has both permanence and flux, terror and beauty, that is utilitarian and aesthetic: "The changeless penknife. / The board. The heavy trestles. / The changeless penknife" (XV). We see the same in another, "The finer the cloth / in your obi, or waist piece, / the finer the moth" (XVII). There are also comic touches that contain the same suburban ironies of other poems in the volume: "The first day of spring. / What to make of that bald patch / right under the swing?" (XVIII).

There are likewise erotic elements that have much less of the normal angst normally associated with the theme in Muldoon: "Jean stoops to the tap / set into a maple's groin / for the rising sap" (XXI). It is as if he has found a way merely to let the image speak and not interrupt, however much we like Muldoon's interruptions. The haiku number XXXIV moves similarly on this theme: "None more disheveled / than those who seemed most demure. / Our ragweed revels." There are also political themes, connected to paramilitary activity (XXIII), literary echoes of Melville (XXV, XXVI), even Christian symbols, set in natural imagery: "Good Friday. At three, / a swarm of bees sets its heart / on an apple tree" (XXVIII). Then there are poems that are perfect Muldoon poems within this form: "Raspberries. Red-blue. / A paper-cut on the tongue / from a billet-doux" (XXXV). Muldoon's identification with animals finds a homelier mirror, his cat, Pangur Ban, named after a famous cat of a medieval Irish monk: "The bold Pangur Ban / draws and quarters a wood thrush / by the garbage can." (XXXVII); the cat's death later takes on typical sceptically but poignant religious meaning: "From under the shed / a stench that's beyond belief. / Pangur Ban is dead" (XLVIII). Muldoon also makes a beautifully distinct connection between the erotic and the natural: "Jean paints one toenail. / In a fork of the white ash, / quick, a cardinal" (XLI). And, in the same vein, he comments on his changing sexuality in middle age: "Nowadays I flush / a long-drawn-out cry, at most, / from the underbrush" (XLII), which in XLVI, seems connected to his middle-class situation, the neatness, the clarity, the order, equalling sterility: "At my birthday bash, / a yellow bin for bottles / and a green for trash." Yet some hope remains in middle age: "While from the thistles / that attend our middle age / a goldfinch whistles" (LVII). There are haikus of philosophical interest and insight (LVIII, LXII), or of domestic provenance (LXI), many on the qualities of perception (LXXI, LXXII), some on Irish themes (LXXVII), and many on various natural themes (LIX, LX, LXV, LXVI, LXXVIII, LXXIX, LXXX, LXXXI, LXXXII, LXXXIV) increasing in frequency until near the end, when Muldoon ties his sequence together in a religious symbol:

LXXXVIII

That wavering flame
is the burn-off from a mill.
Star of Bethlehem.

Finally "Hopewell Haiku" closes with the humorous envoi one expects from Muldoon at this stage: "The maple's great cask / that once held so much in store / now yields a hip flask" (XC). In eastern fashion, the great becomes the small, but nevertheless the diminution provides the traveller lightness and portability; all this inside an Irish joke about drinking.

Some of the Japanese influences appear in other poems in similarly Muldoonesque guise:

> A sky. A field. A hedge flagrant with gorse.
> I'm trying to remember, as best I can,
> if I'm a man dreaming I'm a plowhorse
> or a great plowhorse dreaming I'm a man.

This poem, entitled "Horses", is a play on the famous, almost proverbial, poem by the Chinese philosopher Chuang Tse (*c*. 369 BC – *c*. 286 BC) that runs: "Now I do not know whether I was then a man dreaming I was a butterfly, or whether I am now a butterfly, dreaming I am a man." This play on reality has always been important to Muldoon, but instead of concentrating on the difference between material reality and the transcendent, as does Chuang Tse, Muldoon instead emphasises the tension between man and animal, using one of his favourite techniques of desublimation, bringing it back to the basics.

There are other poems in the volume that follow established patterns in Muldoon's poetry. The strangely beautiful "Aftermath" examines the relationship between sacrifice, bloodshed and beauty: "I imagine patriot cry to patriot / after they've shot / a neighbor in his own aftermath ... Christ ... wired up to the moon." It ends with a stunning indication of how beauty and love are shaped by suffering:

> Only a few nights ago, it seems, they set fire to a big house
>   and it got
> so preternaturally hot
> we knew there would be no reprieve
> till the swallows' nests under the eaves

had been baked into these exquisitely glazed little pots
from which, my love, let us now drink.

In "Wire" Muldoon contemplates a pastoral setting in Connecticut (while playing on Wallace Stevens's famous abstract
poem "The River of Rivers in Connecticut") which is then interrupted by memories of Northern Ireland, illustrating how close
the pastoral and anti-pastoral conventions are:

> Then a distant raking through the gearbox
> of a truck suddenly gone haywire
> on this hillside of hillsides in Connecticut
> brought back some truck on a bomb run,
> brought back so much with which I'd hoped to break –
> the hard line […]

For Muldoon, it is difficult to move beyond such knowledge
into the type of aesthetic argument on which Steven so beautifully
arranges his poem: "… a river, an unnamed flowing, // Space-
filled, reflecting the seasons, the folk-lore / Of each of the senses;
call it, again and again, / The river that flows nowhere, like a
sea."[9] History, as so often noted, intrudes inescapably no matter
how much Muldoon wants to "break the hard line." That he does
want to is what makes his artistry notable. For he may be too self-
conscious an artist, but he has a purpose: to fight against reality.
This is what makes his poetry "boxing clever". His poetry often
displays the ability, as in this stanza from "Burma", to capture the
shape of the experience in the shape of the poem in such a way as
to show how important felt-life is:

> Thunder and lightning. The veil of the temple rent
> in twain
> as I glimpse through the flickering flap of the tent
> the rain […]

The elephants in Burma, like Muldoon, want to "escape the
Pavilion" which we watched them "hoist"; that is, both the poet

and the circus animals want to return to the wildness that their art
and circus acts domesticate.

Perhaps this desire to escape, or to return to basics, is one of
the reasons why Muldoon so often ends his volumes with long
poems, as if one of the contemporary masters of the sonnet, which
Muldoon can rightly claim to be, wanted to unleash the epic form.
And yet, it is often the case that the long poem is a collection of
short ones. In the case of *Hay*, the last poem "The Bangle (Slight
Return)" is actually a sequence of sonnets. It begins with an invocation of a previous epic, *The Aeneid*, as it begins in the ashes of
Troy. The next sonnet sequence alludes to the figures of the Children of Lir, making clear the connection in themes of exile, family
and longing between the Irish and Greek mythic traditions. As in
many other myths, there are references to food, to love, to sexuality and war. A recurring phrase is Virgil's "The Beauty of it",
functioning as much as an interrogative as a declaration of intent.
A main figure in Muldoon's retelling is Creusa, a daughter of
Priam and Hecuba. She is almost a forgotten figure of history,
brought back to life by Muldoon in order to highlight the loss inherent in the epic cycle. She married Aeneas, leader of the Darda-
nian allies of the Trojans, and bore Ascanius. She was captured by
the Greeks, but saved by Cybele and Aphrodite. Later she disap-
peared as her family was escaping from the burning city of Troy,
and was presumed dead. At the beginning of "The Bangle", Aeneas steals "back a look for Creusa" and is left only with a flame
in his "flame burnished arms", as Virgil tells us. By the end of the
poem, Creusa is addressed by our poet:

> A scattering to the four winds of the street arabs.
> Creusa cutting me an intolerable deal
> of slack as she gave me a wave of her razor-sharp
> middle claw, half appalled, half in appeal,
>
> and slipped forever from my arms.

She is a figure of all his mistakes, personal, public, and poetic.
All that he deserves for years of making hay: a poetic rebuke and

a profound sense of loss that threatens to overwhelm him. And like all such figures, Creusa reflects some of the threats – in this case, the flames that would engulf Dido and Carthage – which Aeneas and Muldoon consciously or unconsciously present to all who love them.

Endnotes

---

[1] W. B. Yeats *The Collected Works of W. B. Yeats Vol. III: Autobiographies* (London: Macmillan, 1963), 551.

[2] Renato Barilli, *A Course on Aesthetics*, trans. Karen E. Pinkus (Minnesota; University of Minnesota Press, 1993), 133.

[3] Clair Wills, *Reading Paul Muldoon*, 186.

[4] Edward Said, *On Late Style* (London: Bloomsbury, 2006), 7.

[5] See Meyer Shapiro, "Style: Form-and-Content", *Aesthetics Today*, ed. Morris Philipson (New York: Meridian, 1961), 87.

[6] Clive Bell, *Art* (New York: Capricorn, 1958; originally published in 1914), 190.

[7] Wills, *Reading Paul Muldoon*, 190.

[8] Søren Kierkegaard, *Fear and Trembling* (New York; Penguin, 2005), 53.

[9] Wallace Steven, *Collected Poems* (New York: Vintage, 1990), 533.

9

Moy Sand and Gravel (2002)

"MOST INTELLECTUALLY AMBITIOUS contemporary poetry inclines to the abstract," writes the unnamed reviewer of *Moy Sand and Gravel* (2002) for *The Economist*; the reviewer then explains the method behind Muldoon's mode of writing in this, his ninth book: "The words please themselves. They are non-representational, or less representational – there as paint rather than likeness; squeak or drone or rattle rather than melody. Such venerable stand-bys as lyrical states of feeling, description or narrative are, if not absent, then complicated or mangled. For the reader, it can appear a bumpy and unenticing prospect. But then, we are not talking about a popular art."

Besides being a bit too general (for surely there is some lyricism in abstract poetry, especially in Muldoon's), and besides taking a rather depressing view of poetry's place in mainstream culture, this comment does characterise the work of Muldoon to some extent, and indeed the marginalised place of poetry. The reviewer goes on to say: "His latest book is about deracination and reorientation, the move, as he puts it with the emblematic adspeak so characteristic of this volume, from 'the Orchard County' to 'the Garden State'",[1] that is from Northern Ireland to New Jersey. We know that this theme has been outlined much earlier in Muldoon's work, and that it is not so much adspeak as a gift for using and defusing our cliché-ridden language. Even though Muldoon had used this technique in earlier volumes, it is increasingly apparent in both *Hay* and *Moy Sand and Gravel*. And with that acknowledgement we must admit that, in many ways, these volumes cover some of the same ground as earlier ones. There is parody and pastiche aimed as much at Muldoon's own poetic as at poetry at large. While *The Annals of Chile* may have seemed to mark a turning point in Muldoon's work, in fact, it just allowed some new elements into the mix, mainly the elegiac note of "Incantata" and "Yarrow". Even with this new element, some critics remain unconvinced. Tom Payne writes of *Moy Sand and Gravel* in the *Daily Telegraph*: "Trying to use these tricks and still make sense is a daunting task, and I'm not convinced Muldoon always manages it."[2] Ian Samson, on the other hand, appreciates the trickiness of the volume: "The book is full of the usual small juicy magnificences, and the vast farings of a literary mind, the clearly excellent but obscure intentions, the abundance, the precision, the witty superiority that readers of Muldoon have come to expect. It's all utterly bonzer, and ever so slightly bonkers."[3] Others have more mixed reactions.

In *The New York Review of Books*, Mark Ford notes: "*Moy Sand and Gravel* is unlikely to strike Muldoon aficionados as a great leap forward, but it still offers a number of poems that demonstrate why he is regarded by many as the most sophisticated and original poet of his generation."[4] And Peter Davison, in *The New York Times Book Review*, is aware of Muldoon's technique: "*Moy Sand and Gravel* [...] shimmers with play, the play of mind, the play of recondite information over ordinary experience, the play of observation and sensuous detail, of motion upon custom, of Irish and English languages and landscapes, of meter and rhyme. Sure enough, everything Muldoon thinks of makes him think of something else, and poem after poem takes the form of linked association." Nevertheless, Davison has real reservations: "There's something piquant, not to say perverse, about Muldoon's imagination. Some of his long poems strike me as artificially enriched, over-informed doggerel. 'At the Sign of the Black Horse,' by contrast, seems to me to contain true feeling at its center. Muldoon is so varied and lavish a poet that no reader will find him wholly accessible, for while on one page he may speak simply of his dog or cat, on the next he'll spread his learning thickly ..." Davison concludes his admiring review with real ambivalence: "If the task of the poet, as Auden suggested, is 'the clear expression of mixed feelings', Muldoon has fulfilled only the second half."[5]

Where does this leave us as we try to make our way through the penultimate and ultimate volumes of Muldoon's career? Is it enough to say with Ford that they are not leaps forward? Do they have to be? Or, are we better off saying with Samsom that whether Muldoon is a great poet or not is irrelevant if we like his work. Better then to ask ourselves whether we enjoy him and why. For the present writer, it is not always the jokiness that pleases most; rather it is Muldoon's bitter snarl behind his laugh, a certain tragic insistence that makes him to want to escape into poetry and makes him first disgruntled with poetry for not really offering an escape and, secondly, with himself for wanting to escape into the aesthetic at all. For the aesthetic offers only brief shelter and never escape. This is an old theme in Muldoon's poetry that takes us back to the earliest volumes, to poems such as "Lunch with Pancho Villa" and it has been treated throughout his career. In "Hard Drive", the first poem of *Moy Sand and Gravel*, Muldoon reminds us once more of his purpose. It is his favoured form, a sonnet, though in a chastened tetrameter rather than the more emotionally open pentameter, and it plays with clichés as a way of testing words for what meaning they may hold. If clichés are phrases that have been overused so much they have no meaning left, then Muldoon's purpose is to refresh them by being fresh, so to speak. The poem concludes:

> With a toe in the water
> and a nose for trouble
> and an eye to the future
> I would drive through Derryfubble
>
> and Dunnamanagh and Ballynascreen,
> keeping that wound green.[6]

The notion of the landscape bearing the wounded consciousness of the poet is an old one, and, like Muldoon's anti-aesthetic, is found in poets before him, but it is central to his poems. One needs only to remember "Wind and Tree" from *New Weather* (1973).

The wound must be kept green, but where is his wound and what inflicted it? Is it psychological or historical, or both? In the title poem "Moy Sand and Gravel", the dirty laundry of history and humankind is there to be washed, "as if washing might make it clean". There are connections made in the poem to two great towers, which even if not a conscious allusion to September 11 act as allusions, much as do the towers in Seamus Heaney's most recent collection, *District and Circle*. In many ways, in a poem like "The Otter" Muldoon takes that famous phrase from Shirley, "the glories of our blood and state",[7] and makes it read "the darkness of our blood and state". The subtle links between human nature, the nature of the self, the act of writing and the body politic are so beautifully made in this poem, so lyrical in inflection, so under-stated in tone, that they might be missed:

> That was the year S------- told him how on the Queen's desk
> there lay a great six-by-four-foot blotter
> of such a blackness, she would aver,
> a blackness so dense
> and a grain so close, so compact,
> no one could hope to hold
> a mirror up to it
> and thereby ... and thereby hit
> on any evidence of clandestine contracts of covenants, of old
> enemies having entered a secret pact
> to which she might be a party or affix her hand, any evidence
> of the treachery he now saw written all over her,
> rising as she did to meet him like the otter
> that had risen once to meet him from Lough Eske.

In his recent book of essays Muldoon discusses "the tension between surface and core"[8] in Marianne Moore's poetry, which he says suits both her poetry and H.D.'s. Obviously, it also fits Muldoon's own. In that tension between the blackness of the desk and that of the lake lies the source of his poetic. Marianne Moore's comment on the otter in the poem "New York" has a similar bearing:

it is not the atmosphere of ingenuity,
the otter, the beaver, the puma skins
without shooting-irons or dogs;
it is not the plunder,
but 'accessibility to experience'. [9]

The tension between surface and core, as ravaging as it can be, is explored in Muldoon as a way into the depths of experience. Muldoon quotes Moore's comment on H.D. as applicable to the former poet's work. It is also appropriate for Muldoon: "We have in these poems an external world of commanding beauty – the erect, the fluent, the unaccountably brilliant. Also, we have that inner world of interacting reason and unreason in which are comprehended the rigor, the succinctness of hazardous emotion." [10] That latter phrase, the "succinctness of hazardous emotion" aptly describes Muldoon's lyric gift.

One of the chief strengths of *Moy Sand and Gravel* is the lyric mode, contrary to the assumptions of the reviewer from *The Economist*; some of them are translations, some woven from particular experiences or from memory. The translations, like those from *Hay*, are also satisfying, and many of the topics seem tailor-made for Muldoon. This may be an individual quality of Muldoon's ability as a translator, for whether translating from the Irish, from French, Italian or Latin, there is something in the translations that make the poems feel like Muldoon poems. Not that they efface the image of the original author, but the overlay of Muldoon's hand reveals what is Muldoonesque in the original. This is not always true, but is so remarkably often. In "Paul Valéry: Pomegranates", the image of the fruit resonates both ways toward author and translator alike:

should the wizened gold of your skin
give way to pressure from within
and explode in red juice-gems,

that light-shedding fracture
might bring a soul such as I had to dream
of its own hidden architecture.

The inherent violence and sexuality in this image of the fruit of paradise and "the Fall" is echoed in the next poem dedicated to Yehuda Amichai, entitled "Pineapples and Pomegranates" (not a translation but germane), in which the gestures of art and war are too closely aligned (like the words Pineapples and Pomegranates) even though they have opposite meanings:

> ... As if the open hand
> might, for once, put paid
> to the hand grenade
> in one corner of the planet.
> I'm talking about pineapples – right ? – not pomegranates.

Muldoon's translation of Eugenio Montale's famous poem "The Eel" ("*L'anguilla*") invites the reader to see human life mirrored in the journey of the eel, while his beautiful translations of Horace's Odes contain the epic themes of love and war.

Muldoon's translation of Horace has the type of thunder he is often criticised for lacking. He hits the major chords without the usual self-conscious undercutting, and does so in a very satisfying way, as in the music of the translation of Book I, Ode XV:

> For though Achilles and his fleet, consumed as they are with
>   ire,
> may delay the course of events, by the time ten years have
>   rolled round
> the Greeks will have set the fire
> that will burn Troy to the ground.

It is not that Muldoon should write like this, for he has reasons for not doing so, but rather it is remarkable how well he can. He is able to sound the same impersonal note with a very different tone, in the next translation from Horace, Book III, Ode XVIII:

> Faunus, you who love the nymphs, from whom the nymphs
>   love to run,
> may you look kindly, as you cross in and out of my farm,
> on its boundary posts and pastures already blessed by the sun,

and deliver the littlest of my flock from harm [...]

One admires Muldoon's poetic powers for a variety of reasons, not least for his virtuosity, and in these translations we feel that quality keenly, but it is his translation of "Caedmon's Hymn" that may be most surprising:

> Now we must praise to the skies   the Keeper of the heavenly
>   kingdom
> The might of the Measurer,   all he has in mind,
> The work of the Father of Glory,   of all manner of marvel,
>
> Our eternal Master,   the main mover.

One doesn't often hear religious strains in Muldoon without a healthy dose of scepticisim.

In certain lyrics of his own, there is a real sense that he is testing the utilitarian as well as the moral nature of the aesthetic. In "The Killdeer" this seems very evident:

> Why was he trying to clear
> a space in the forest of beech
> by turning beech posts and, by beech pegs,
> fitting each to each?
>
> For the reason at which the killdeer
> seems to be clutching
> when she lays her four pear-shaped eggs
> with the pointed ends touching.

This interest in the utility of the aesthetic, and how the latter graces the former, is taken from Frost's poem "Two Tramps in Mud Time" (where "vocation and avocation" unite "as two eyes make one in sight"). Muldoon's own version of Frost's "Mending Wall", entitled "Whitethorns", combines themes from Frost's poems above and provides an eloquent example of how the aesthetic and practical are linked:

The paling posts we would tap into the ground with the flat of
   a spade
more than thirty years ago,
hammering them home then with a sledge
and stringing them with wire to keep our oats from Miller's
   barley,

are maxed-out, multilayered whitethorns, affording us a
   broader, deeper shade
than we ever decently hoped to know,
so far-fetched does it seem, so far-flung from the hedge
under which we now sit down to parley.

This union of form and utility can also have metaphysical implications ("The Breather"):

Think of this gravestone
as a long, low chair
strategically placed
at a turn in the stair.

The lyric mode is one of the most satisfying ones Muldoon
employs, precisely because of its range.

When the lyric mode combines with public issue, the result
can be very forceful, as Muldoon approaches political and social
issues with so much scepticism. In "A Brief Discourse on Decommissioning", that is, the decommissioning of weapons by the IRA,
he concludes: "you can't make bricks without the straw / that
breaks the camel's back", exposing the difficulties inherent in the
task of decommissioning – how the very stuff that would bring
peace could destroy it. This tortured sense underlies the brilliance
of Muldoon's bitterest verse. In poems such as "Homesickness" or
"The Goose", the feeling that all suffering is the result of some divine indifference, often mirrored in familial pain, gives the poems
real power as Muldoon endeavours to show this with humour
and spite. In the second stanza of the former, it is made apparent:

The black-winged angel leaning over the sandstone parapet
of the bridge wears a business suit, dark gray.
His hair is slick with pomade.
He turns away as my mother, Brigid,
turned away not only from her sandstone pet
but any concession being made.
The black-winged angel sets her face to the unbending last ray
of evening and meets rigid with rigid.

The meaning of homesickness changes. One is sick because of home not because one is far away. In "The Goose" Hermes' gift of the goose that lays the golden egg is paralleled to the gift of disease, especially of cancer, that species of transmigration we know too well, which comes like a thief in the night. Here we must remember that Hermes is a Christ-like god of transmigration as well as of thieves. Muldoon's arch and angry poetry on the suffering he witnesses is one of the chief strengths of his oeuvre; however, there are not that many poems a poet can actually write on the subject, one imagines. Unwelcome events, such as disease and death, have to intervene and no one would wish that on any poet, for the consolations of poetry are not those of philosophy; as Boethius tells us, they open rather than heal the wound.[11] Yet, Muldoon, as we know, wants to keep the wound green, never shying away from painful inconsolable subjects, and so poetry is the appropriate métier, "seductive", as it is, "unto destruction".[12]

In certain poems from this volume, we sense that Muldoon has been an outcast since his early days. In "The Whinny", "A Collegelands Catechism" and "Beagles", the artist appears to be isolated from his society. This is not a new theme in Muldoon, but perhaps is something the poet must consistently work through in light of his developing subject matter. Another theme explored in early volumes, and present here too, is the link between art, perversity and religion. "The Misfits" echoes the Joycean use of this theme from the first story of *Dubliners*, "The Sisters". The poem begins with a nod to the pastoral:

If and when I did look up, the sky over the Moy was the very
   same gray-blue
as the slow lift
of steam-smoke over the seam
of manure on a mid-winter morning. I noticed the splash of
   red lead
on my left boot as again and again I would bend
my knee and bury my head in the rich

black earth the way an ostrich
was rumored to bury its head.

The connections between creativity and excrement in this first stanza (the black earth is black because of manure) will lead to the connections between the perversity of the character called "Monk" and his ability with the guitar – an ability Muldoon wants to share. The Monk "Had spent twenty-odd years as a priest in South Bend" and "Fred Crew said something strange about how he liked to 'lift' / his shirt-tail". Muldoon's father is adamantly against Muldoon riding in the car with the Monk, which only makes the boy plaintive:

'... If you think, after that, I'd let the Monk give you a lift

into the Moy to see Montgomery bloody Clift
you've another think coming. I'll give him two barrels full of
   twelve-gauge lead
if he comes anywhere near you. Bloody popinjay. Peacock.
   Ostrich.'
All I could think of was how the Monk was now no more
   likely to show me how to bend
that note on the guitar – 'like opening a seam
straight into your ear' – when he played Bessie Smith's 'Cold
   in Hand Blues'
than an ostrich to bend
its lead-plumed wings and, with its two-toed foot, rip out the
   horizon-seam
and lift off, somehow, into the blue.

Again we see how the transcendent effect of the poetic is hope-lessly rooted in the devil's work. Transcendence is always com-promised in Muldoon's poetry. Still, like similar themes of deliv-erance, it is one of his most interesting ideas, even as he undoes it:

> It seemed that Bap, who buried two milk-churns
> like two zig-zaggy funerary urns
>   between the posts of a gate
> would now be most likely to castigate
>   me for daring to explode
>   the myth of the mother–lode.

And the fault, as we see in the end of this poem, entitled "Guns and Butter", is not always attributable to the myth makers, but to the hard practical men of action, who have "contempt" for the speaker "for daring to spread the butter / meant to save his guns from rust / on my small bit of a crust".

One of the personal themes of the book, which is explored in various single poems and carried into the long closing poem, "At the Sign of the Black Horse", is the relationship between Muldoon and his wife. The conversation of the poem "The Grand Conversa-tion" is between Jean Korelitz's Jewish background and Mul-doon's Irish one:

> *She.* My people came from Korelitz
> where they grew yellow cucumbers
> and studied the Talmud.
> *He.* Mine pored over the mud
> of mangold- and potato-pits
> or flicked through kale plants from Comber
> as bibliomancers of old
> went a-flicking through deckle-mold.

If her family was "trained to make a suture / after the bomb and bombast", his people were the makers of bombs ("Peep O'Day Boys") and bombast. Yet, as Muldoon says, "we may yet construct our future / as we have reconstructed our past". Can it be so easy? The conclusion of the poems points out the complications:

> *She.* Each from his stand of mountain ash
> will cry out over valley farms
> spot-lit with pear blossom.
> *He.* There some young Absalom
> picks his way through cache after cache
> of ammunition and small arms
> hidden in grain-wells, while his nag
> tugs at a rein caught on a snag.

Absalom is a hit-man carrying out a vendetta (this of course not only points to Ireland but to modern-day Israel as well). Absalom's sister Tamar had been raped by David's eldest son, Amnon, who was in love with her. Absalom, after waiting two years, revenged by sending his servants to murder Amnon at a feast to which he had invited all the king's sons (2 Samuel 13). The familial nature of this plot appeals to all politically-charged societies, whether Irish or Jewish. The same concerns surface in the colonial meditations "The Turn" and "The Ancestor", in which family problems are translated into the political context. By now we have become familiar with this theme.

Another type of poem, the haiku, that emerged in *Hay*, emerges once again in *Moy Sand and Gravel*. "News Headlines from the Homer Noble Farm" is a collection of nineteen haikus on a number of themes, though, like the sequence "Hopewell Haiku", many are centred round domestic suburban life and many are fine examples of Muldoon's eye for detail – humorous, quirky or otherwise. One plays on the famous grassy knoll of John F. Kennedy's assassination, from where a shot was supposed to be fired in one of the conspiracy theories that surround that event:

> From his grassy Knoll
> he has you in his cross-hairs,
> the accomplice mole.

Another captures the filmic quality of a chipmunk's movements, remembering, of course, that most Europeans' first image of the chipmunk came from television (unless Muldoon did not watch cartoons as a child):

> He has, you will find,
> two modes only, the chipmunk:
> fast forward; rewind.

Muldoon's favourite theme of mixed breeds comes into the sequence as well:

> Steady, like a log
> riding a sawmill's spill-way,
> the steady coydog.

The coydog being the offspring of mating between dog and coyote. Coyotes, traditionally a Western American animal, have in recent years migrated East and in the process grown somewhat larger from the wealth of food they found there. The mongrel and migrant elements suit Muldoon very well. The closing haiku brings us to the confrontation of the natural world and artificial intelligence:

> How all seems to vie
> not just my sleeping laptop
> with the first firefly.

The strange electric beauty of the firefly or lightening bug is matched by that of the computer and the electrified world that produced the laptop.

In other poems in the volume, there are themes and styles reminiscent of earlier volumes. A poem like "The Loaf" has become a signature item in his repertoire, being as "whimful" a poem as anything he has written, especially its refrain, but containing historical tension and tragic consequence at least in the margins of its attempt. In the third stanza, the suffering of the Irish navies from Raritan to Delaware is given the Muldoon treatment:

When I put my nose to the hole I smell the flood-plain
of the canal after a hurricane
and the spots of green grass where thousands of Irish have lain

with a stink and a stink and a stinky-stick.[13]

In the poem "Two Stabs at Oscar", Muldoon meditates on
Wilde's time in Reading Gaol for the "crime" of "indecent behaviour" with men.[14] Muldoon was commissioned to write this poem
by the Reading Borough Council to be incorporated in the Oscar
Wilde Memorial Walk. It shows the deep sympathy for the life of
the prisoner that Wilde had exhibited in his famous long poem,
"The Ballad of Reading Gaol", as we see in Muldoon's lines: "that
I serve some sentence / is so ingrained in me / that I still wait for a
warder / to come and turn the key." The two stabs at Wilde are
psychological, as we have just seen, and symbolic, as the second
part attests:

A stone breaker on his stone bed
lay not less tightly curled
than opposite-leaved saxifrage
that even now, unfurled,
has broken through its wall of walls
into this other world.

The beautiful closing brings together a number of strengths in
Muldoon's work: his eye for natural detail, his sense of the
strangeness of the world itself, his bitter feeling that nature rather
than art tells our tale most truly. Art takes a stab at reality and so
duplicates the violence. "Each man kills the thing he loves", as
Wilde insisted in *The Ballad of Reading Gaol*, "by each let this be
heard".[15]

"Tell" is a fabulistic reflection on the role of hero or artist in
the colonies. We may say hero because William Tell is so like
Abraham, and artist because of his expertise with the arrow. The
son may also be the artist in question as he hears the apple split
above his head. "Tell" is based on the story of William Tell and
his son. As the *Encyclopedia Britannica* notes:

The historical existence of Tell is disputed. According to popular legend, he was a peasant from Bürglen in the canton of Uri in the 13th and early 14th centuries who defied Austrian authority, was forced to shoot an apple from his son's head, was arrested for threatening the governor's life, saved the same governor's life en route to prison, escaped, and ultimately killed the governor in an ambush. These events supposedly helped spur the people to rise up against Austrian rule.[16]

Muldoon takes this story and gives it a North American setting, having tepees stand in for the Alps:

The red-cheeked men put down their knives
at one and the same
moment. All but his father, who somehow connives
to close one eye as if taking aim

or holding back a tear,
and shoots him a glance
he might take, as it whizzes past his ear,
for another Crow, or Comanche, lance

hurled through the Tilley-lit
gloom of the peeling-shed
were he not to hear what must be an apple split
above his head.

For Muldoon, there seems to be the sense that art cannot transcend the violence of the historical incident. In some renderings of the Tell legend, the father had two arrows in his quiver, and when asked why he had two, he said that if he missed the apple and killed his son, he would aim the second at the man who made him do it in the first place. The conditional ending of Muldoon's version of the poem ("were he not to hear what must be an apple split") highlights the symbolic aspect of the story. Something else might have happened, something else might be construed from what happened. "Tell" represents the oppressed in Switzerland, or the oppressed in North America in order to fight back. His feat requires putting his children in danger, as Muldoon feels he has done on a personal level, just by being a father and experiencing a miscarriage, and as the Native Americans have done. All colonial people in some ways must risk the welfare of their children in order to be free, that is "the gloom of the peeling-shed".

The people who are lost in this carnage have always been important to Muldoon. In this volume, there are Sitting Bull, Oscar Wilde, Marilyn Monroe, Bessie Smith, and most importantly, the miscarried child. These losses have mythic inheritances, as Muldoon demonstrates in his elegy for the miscarriage, "The Stoic":

> ... This was more like the afternoon last March
> when I got your call in St Louis and, rather than rave
> as one might rant and rave at the thought of the yew
> from Deirdre's not quite connecting with the yew from Nao-
>   ise's grave,
>
> rather than shudder like a bow of yew or the matchless Osage
>   orange
> at the thought of our child already lost from view
> before it had quite come into range,
> I steadied myself under the Gateway Arch.

The "Gateway Arch" is the famous arch in St Louis built to celebrate the city's position as a gateway to the west, a gateway which lead to the slaughter of the Indians on the western range ("where the Missouri // had not as yet been swollen by the Osage"). The loss of the child mirrors the loss of the Osage tribe. The closing image of the poem brings Irish navies, construction workers in the creation of canals and railways, to the fore of the poem. They stand like statues of the anonymity of these losses. Men whose lives and deaths took place in the shadows of history. Simply put, all are miscarriages.

These themes surface in the closing poem of the volume, which many reviewers hailed as one of the best of the volume, "At the Sign of the Black Horse, September 1999". The first stanza, read in the light of what has just been discussed, illustrates how subtly Muldoon can weave together his concerns:

> Awesome, the morning after Hurricane Floyd, to sit out
>   in our driveway and gawk
> at yet another canoe or kayak
> coming down Canal Road, now under ten feet of water.
>   We've wheeled to the brim
> the old Biltrite pram
> in which, wrapped in a shawl of Carrickmacross
> lace and a bonnet
> of his great-grandmother Sophie's finest needlepoint,
> Asher sleeps on, as likely as any of us to find a way across ...

Asher is the second of Muldoon's two children; his oldest is a girl named Dorothy. In the poem preceding this last one, "Cradle Song for Asher", emphasises the universal nature of the child, for, as Muldoon says, "beyond your wicker / gondola ... whole continents flicker". The hurricane represents the coming of Europeans to America, and the loss of his child; it is the sublime force which Muldoon both parodies and acknowledges. The choice of the word "Awesome" is intentional. It is now an overused word in contemporary American English, but has it roots in the aesthetics of the sublime. The forces of the sublime are still to be felt, but their presence has becomes hackneyed. The poem as a whole covers various subjects, many of them alluding to his wife's or his family backgrounds, and is punctuated by various emergency or warning phrases, such as "No Turn on Red", "Please Secure Your Own Oxygen Mask / Before Attending to Children", etc. Much of the family and/or national history contains a certain controversy or crime, as if familial or national wrongs are always waiting to resurface in the lives of the newest generation, much as present day history, in this case represented by Hurricane Floyd, threatens the existence of all who live on its grounds.

Behind the poem is Yeats's "A Prayer for My Daughter", and its meditation on how best to stay afloat among hostile historical tides. Throughout the poem, Muldoon seems obsessed by the losses he has incurred, the miscarriages of justice, and in the following lines quotes Yeats directly ("... no obstacle / But Gregory's wood and one bare hill ..."):[17]

          ... The hacking through a babby bone.
No obstacle but Gregory's wood
and one bare hill, Slippery When Wet,
bringing back the morning Dr Patel had systematically drawn
the child from Jean's womb, For Hire,
Uncle Arnie all the while hanging a whitewall tire
about the draft mule's neck ...

The loss of the child is paralleled by the domestic chores of the Uncle, as something so momentous as the miscarriage becomes the routine. The flood that resulted from the hurricane made boats floating along town streets seem the order of the day. The close of the poem, using all the devices at Muldoon's disposal, and once again echoing Yeats ("Once more the storm"), gives us a litany of family problems, celebrity and heroics, only to leave us again with the sad image of the starving Irish navy (while the Jewish-Irish phrases "Irish schlemiel" and "Irish schmucks" mirror the parentage of the poem) who built the canal, standing on the berm ("a narrow space or ledge, sometimes left between the ditch and the base of the parapet", often "opposite the tow path")[18] where the rising waters will first flood:

          ... Once more the storm is howling as it howled
when Isaac shouted down the board of Yale, the Black
Horse Tavern still served ale,
when Sophie was found dead in the bath, a ringed plover
with all her rings stolen, Please Cover,
when Sam discontinued his line of Berbecker and
Rowland upholstery nails, For Sale,

when we might yet have climbed the hill and escaped by
   Coppermine
when Uncle Arnie was gut-shot [by George McManus?]
for non-payment of tight-lipped, poker-faced debts, when
   Helene Hanff, the celeb,
was found asleep
in the De Witt nursing home in the arms of Bulwer-Lytton,
   Follow Detour,

when Fanny tried to stop the leak
of a so-called confession by one Joseph Gluck
which fingered her ex-husband, Nicky Arnstein, when
    the trebucket of my lonely *túr*

was tripped for the very last time by Joe Hanff, No Egress,
when a cantankerous
young Reinhart or Abrams, No Children Beyond This Point,
was borne along at shoulder height by the peaked cap,
    Out of Bounds,
when the cry went up from a starving Irish schlemiel who
    washed an endosperm
of wheat, deh-dah, from a pile of horse-keek
held to the rain, one of those thousands of Irish schmucks
    who still loll, still loll and lollygag,
between the preposterous tow-path and the preposterous
    berm.

What is preposterous is the preposterousness of a random history that leaves us vulnerable, that leads to such loss as this volume laments, the child, the endosperm the navy washes, whom Muldoon will not carry on his shoulders because he/she is "Out of Bounds". This is the flotsam and jetsam that Hurricane Floyd washes out of the canal, and Muldoon is there to collect the remains.

Endnotes

---

[1] "Reasons for Rhyme", *The Economist*, 6 February 2003. See http://www.complete-review.com/reviews/muldoonp/moysand.htm.

[2] Tom Payne, "Four Ostriches and an Orange", *Daily Telegraph*, 9 September 2003.

[3] Ian Samsom, "Awesome in Armagh", *The Guardian*, 2 November 2002.

[4] Mark Ford, "A Review of *Hay* by Paul Muldoon", *The New York Review of Books*, 25 September 2003

[5] Peter Davison, "Darkness at Muldoon", *The New York Times Book Review*, 13 October 2002.

[6] Muldoon, *Moy Sand and Gravel* (London: Faber, 2002).

[7] James Shirley (1596–1666), "The Glories of our Blood and State", *Harvard Clas-*

sics, ed. Charles W. Eliot (New York: P. F. Collier & Son, 1909–14.) The first stanza of the original is:

> The glories of our blood and state
> Are shadows, not substantial things;
> There is no armour against fate;
> Death lays his icy hand on kings:
> Sceptre and Crown
> Must tumble down,
> And in the dust be equal made
> With the poor crooked scythe and spade.

[8] Paul Muldoon, *The End of The Poem: Oxford Lectures* (New York: Faber, 2006), 267.

[9] Quoted in Muldoon, *The End of The Poem: Oxford Lectures,* 268.

[10] Muldoon, *The End of the Poem,* 267.

[11] Boethius writes: "When she saw that the Muses of poetry were present by my couch giving words to my lamenting, she was stirred a while; her eyes flashed fiercely, and said she, 'Who has suffered these seducing mummers to approach this sick man? Never do they support those in sorrow by any healing remedies, but rather do ever foster the sorrow by poisonous sweets. These are they who stifle the fruit-bearing harvest of reason with the barren briars of the passions: they free not the minds of men from disease, but accustom them thereto. I would think it less grievous if your allurements drew away from me some uninitiated man, as happens in the vulgar herd. In such an one my labours would be naught harmed, but this man has been nourished in the lore of Eleatics and Academics; and to him have ye reached? Away with you, Sirens, seductive unto destruction! leave him to my Muses to be cared for and to be healed.' Book I, *The Consolation of Philosophy* translated by W. V. Cooper (London: J. M. Dent and Company, 1902), 3.

[12] See above, "Away with you, Sirens, seductive unto destruction! leave him to my Muses to be cared for and to be healed." Boethius, Book I, *The Consolation of Philosophy* translated by W. V. Cooper (London: J. M. Dent and Company, 1902), 3

[13] For a video clip of Muldoon reading this poem see http://opticnerve.co.uk/PoSMuldoonVideo.htm

[14] Richard Ellmann, *Oscar Wilde* (New York: Vintage), 474.

[15] Oscar Wilde, *Complete Works* (London: Blitz, 1990), 823.

[16] "Tell, William." *Encyclopædia Britannica.* 2007. *Encyclopædia Britannica* Online, 7 January 2007: http://search.eb.com/eb/article-9071605

[17] Yeats, *Poems,* 236.

[18] *Oxford English Dictionary,* Fifth Edition.

10

Horse Latitudes (2006)

MULDOON'S POETRY INCREASINGLY burns with the question of art's complicity in suffering. Is an artist a purveyor of atrocities? Answering this question creates some of Muldoon's best poems, which are great because they are so deeply self indicting; this is true throughout his career, but especially evident in this volume. If sometimes, in *Hay* and *Moy Sand and Gravel*, he seemed to engage in too much self-parody and seemed to lack a subject, this is not true of this, his tenth volume. *Horse Latitudes* has a number of truly lacerating poems: "Turkey Buzzards", "Tithonus", "The Outlier", and "Sillyhow Stride: *In Memory of Warren Zevon*". Such poems prove that this period in Muldoon's career is as formative as any earlier one, or perhaps more so, displaying, as they do, his always formidable talents. That art bears the brunt of Muldoon's sharp sardonic edge is what in the end makes this volume so important. While insisting that art has a positive role to play, Muldoon has simultaneously felt that art was complicit in suffering, and this has provided an edge to his satire. The satiric bite is now very deep, and the sadness that comes after the pain is often tragic in proportions. Rather than trying "to dehumanize art ... to avoid living forms ... to consider art as play and nothing else ... to be essentially ironical ... to regard art as a thing of no transcending consequence," as Ortega y Gassett proposed, Muldoon is trying to point out how inhuman, even cruel the artistic gaze has always been. He indicts it and wishes it were otherwise.[1] For Muldoon, if art only repeats the devastation of the world and reflects the atrocities of war and disease, it is of little use. One is not certain that he is proposing a different use, but certainly in his savage indignation he highlights the right attitude of moral despair, which makes *Horse Latitudes* among his most notable volumes to date.

Critical reception of *Horse Latitudes* so far supports this estimation. If we remember that the prominent poetry critic Helen Vendler had once said of Muldoon's poetry, as quoted at the beginning of this book, that there's "a hole in the middle where the feeling should be", her attitude towards this volume is revealing: "Paul Muldoon seems to me a more convincing poet now than he was ten or fifteen years ago." What accounts for this change in perception? It is mainly recognition of Muldoon's subversive, but nevertheless brilliant uses of tradition. Muldoon is a revolutionary traditionalist in the best sense of Irish art. Vendler writes: "Critics have found Muldoon useful as an example of post-this and post-that (post-colonialism and postmodernism, mostly); but he is both too mercurial and too traditional to be so easily confined and defined. He looks more often backward than forward, and delights in tracking today back not only into yesterday, but into yesteryear and yester-era, as he does here in a charming shaggy-dog poem called 'Tithonus'. [...] Although it could be said that the comic succession of ancestral sounds is an example of eclectic postmodernism, it could equally well be argued that Muldoon, in joining his poem to Greek myth, to Milton's cricket on the hearth, to Keats's grasshopper, and to Tennyson's 'Tithonus', is sustaining an uninterrupted tradition."[2] We might add Swift, Yeats, Beckett and Joyce to that tradition (as might Vendler), but in the phrase "mercurial and traditional", she has captured what is best in Muldoon's work. Emphasising the apparent importance of Muldoon's work is not to minimise the difficulties of reading it, however.

Some of the old difficulties persist in confronting Muldoon's work, and one supposes that they always will, considering how much this poet relies on both formal and thematic complexity for his power. Muldoon explains some of this complexity in a discussion with Charles McGrath, who writes of their conversation: "Just about everyone except Muldoon thinks his poetry is often difficult. When I suggested to him once that his work is some-times hard to follow, he shook his head and seemed almost of-fended. "I'm not all that keen on the idea that every poem should be full of allusions," he said, and he added that what he strove for always was clarity. "It's mostly a matter of clearing away," he said, "the way Frost did." But then after a pause, he added: "It's hard to make a poem these days that is absolutely clear and direct – if the poem is really to be equal to its era. This is not an era in which clarity and directness, however much we hope for them, are entirely justifiable, because so much is unclear and indirect. I'm not just talking about willed obfuscation and crookedness, though, God knows, there's plenty of that. I'm just talking about a realization that very little is as it seems, that everything has within it massive complexities – maybe even the inappropriateness of being certain about things. A proper awareness that things are just not at all as they seem – one would wish for more of that, par-ticularly on the political front. Wouldn't you love to hear the president or someone say, 'Well, you know, I'm not absolutely clear on that'?"[3] Regarding the difficulty of reading Muldoon, James Fenton writes in *The Guardian*: "Muldoon, who lives and teaches at Princeton, has a strong following among students and academics and anyone who can put up with a certain element of the brain-teaser, in poetry as in his prose. When he lectured at Ox-ford, the audience used to listen slack-jawed as he pursued an ar-gument by means of etymology, mythology, analogy and some personal theory of correspondences. He is a brilliant poet, even at those moments when he makes you shake your head in disbelief."

Fenton goes on to describe a reading Muldoon gave and how much it helped to hear Muldoon's introduction of his work, which is true of so many poets, and should stand as a reminder to read-ers of poetry of how important it is to hear poets read, even if, as we all know, poetry readings can be demanding.

> Muldoon tells us that he started work on the 19 sonnets that form the title sequence of his new collection, *Horse Latitudes*, "as the US embarked on its foray into Iraq. The poems have to do with a series of battles (all beginning with the letter 'B' as if

to suggest a 'missing' Baghdad) in which horses or mules played a major role. Intercut with those battle-scenes are accounts of a 'battle' with cancer by a former lover, here named Carlotta, and a commentary on the agenda of what may only be described as the Bush 'regime'." [...] This information, the sort of thing Muldoon is happy to tell an audience at a reading, is useful to the reader on the page, because these battles-beginning-with-B, in which horses or mules played a major role, are not all going to be very familiar (at least, they weren't to me). Here is the list: Beijing, Baginbun, Bannockburn, Berwick-upon-Tweed, Blaye, Bosworth Field, Blackwater Fort, Benburb, Boyne, Blenheim, Bunker Hill, Brandywine, Badli-Ke-Serai, Bull Run, Bronkhorstspruit, Basra, Bazentin, Beersheba, Burma [...] Muldoon's method might be taken as playful, but there is nothing funny in what he is talking about when he is talking about Bush and Baghdad. Nor is there anything funny about a former lover's cancer. [4]

As both Fenton and Vendler note, the theme of cancer, and with it mortality, recurs again and again in a collection that is dedicated to the memory of the poet's sister, Maureen Muldoon, who died of the same cancer that killed his mother thirty years ago. The context in which we gather this detail is a poem in memory of the singer Warren Zevon, another cancer victim, with whom Muldoon had worked and whom he revered. That takes us to the end of the volume, the final poem, the long eulogy to Zevon, where so many of the volume's political, cultural, and personal concerns come together; however, such themes are apparent from the outset, in the tales of death, political stagnation and colonial mayhem that are implicit in the very title of the book.

Introducing the volume's title, the book jacket tells us:

Horse Latitudes ... refers to those areas thirty degrees north and south of the equator where sailing ships tend to stand becalmed in mid-ocean, where stasis (if not stagnation) is the order of the day, and where sailors, in the days when Spanish vessels transported horses to the West Indies, would throw their live cargo overboard to lighten the load and conserve food and water.

One feels certain that such an image first occurred to Muldoon when he visited North Carolina's Outer Banks many years ago. Feral horses have been found on the barrier islands of Georgia, North Carolina and Virginia since the early explorers first visited the continent. Some of the horses swam to shore as a result of shipwrecks. Others were cast overboard when Spanish ships had to lighten their load because they were stuck on the sandbanks which made that part of the eastern seaboard such hazardous sailing. Others perhaps got free from, or were abandoned by early settlers. Many went to the mainland, while others remained on the numerous sandbars where there are still herds. In any case they are symbolic of an early dating before the full-scale European invasion of the new world; and they represent freedom. This fact, coupled with the sense of entropy these latitudes sustain, must make us pause. Is the invasion of Baghdad meant to mirror the invasion of America, and the subsequent bringing of democracy? One might have reason to think so.

The main figures in "Horse Latitudes" are a speaker and his woman companion, named Carlotta (who, in another poem, points out that her name is an anagram for "oral tact"). They seem to be staying at the Vanderbilt Hotel in Nashville, falling into the horse latitudes, much like the dreaded Bermuda Triangle, where ships and planes are mysteriously lost. The speaker and Carlotta inhabit the doldrums or "horse latitudes" (the 30th to 35th parallels) of middle age, "trying simply to bear the light of day [they] had tried to seize" ("Beijing"). Vendler makes a brilliant formal analysis of one of the sonnets of *Horse Latitudes* ("Beersheba") to tell us "what the Muldoon style sounds like when it is resisting intelligibility". It is the type of critical performance that sets Vendler apart as a critic, and is worth quoting here in order to give the reader a sense of what can be done with the formal qualities of Muldoon's work. Here is the sonnet:

> Now summoned also the young Turk
> who had suddenly arisen
> from that great pile of toot, heehaw,

as from one of Beersheba's wells.
Like the sail that all of a sudden swells
or the yawl that all of a sudden yaws,
a wind finding meaning in a mizzen
and toppling a bouncy castle.
Her grandfather fain to wrastle
each pack mule to a rubber mat
whereat ... whereat ... whereat ... whereat ... whereat ...
he would eftsoons get down to work,
reaching into its wide-open wizen
while a helper clamped back its jaws. [5]

And here is Vendler's discussion of it:

We find here familiar Muldoon turns: the arbitrary title (the individual poems in Muldoon's 1990 sequence "Madoc" bore the names of philosophers, scientists, and so on); the historical allusions; the jokey language (from Spenserian "eftsoons" to Wild West "wrastle"); the slang ("toot" for "dung"); the interpolated low-style commentary phrase ("heehaw," and the poet as mule – Muldoon's second volume was called *Mules*); the puns and the sonic play ("the yawl that yaws"); the glance at contemporary absurdity, here the inflatable structures put up for children's parties ("a bouncy castle"); the break in syntax (the repetitive "whereats," which I suppose call up the successively mutilated mules); and the indistinct connection of all these to the historical battle of Beersheba or to the relations between the speaker and Carlotta. This sonnet (like its eighteen companions) rhymes in the "concealed" manner characteristic of Muldoon: the rhymes of the first three lines (*Turk, arisen, heehaw*) match the rhymes of the last three lines (*work, wizen, jaws*), while inside these brackets, three couplets ("wells/swells"; "castle/wrastle"; and "mat/whereat") sit next to two lines (ending in "yaws" and "mizzen") that rhyme with members of the first and last tercets. [6]

The only slip in this fine interpretation is the possible misreading of toot, which can also mean cocaine.

Not all the sonnets resist intelligibility quite as much as that above, but many of similarly impressive formal qualities. Some of them are openly political and fiercely topical, punning the various intrigues of the day (Texaco for Bush's Texas, "gross imports", etc.):

> As I held Carlotta close
> that night we watched some Xenophon
> embedded with the 5th Marines
> in the old Sunni Triangle
> make a half-assed attempt to untangle
> the ghastly from the price of gasoline.
> There was a distant fanfaron
> in the Nashville sky, where the wind
> had now drawn itself up and pinned
> on her breast a Texaco star.
> "Why," Carlotta wondered, "the House of *Tar*?
> might it have to do with the gross
> imports of crude oil Bush will come clean on
> only when the Tigris comes clean?"

Clearly in this sonnet "Blackwater Fort", the Sunni Triangle mirrors the Bermuda Triangle in that military operations seemed stalled there, and equally clearly it is time to dump the horses overboard, so to speak. In Xenophon's *Anabasis*, the Greek general Clearchus is quoted as saying that "a soldier ought to be more frightened of his own commander than of the enemy" – something that for Muldoon might well apply to Bush. In a later sonnet in the sequence on the Battle of the Boyne, the famous battle that spelled the end of Jacobite dreams in Ireland, "the blood" is "slick from the horse slaughter". Horse and mule imagery prevails in the sequence, being that image for Muldoon of animal nobility on the one hand, and sterile hybridity (stand in for the Irish poet), on the other. Either way, slaughter is the end result of this stalemate. The final sonnet, "Burma", recounts Carlotta's grandfather having to slit the vocal-chords of the army pack-mules in order to keep them silent in battle. This type of sacrifice haunts Muldoon, reflecting, as it does, the arbitrary disruptions of fate that elsewhere in the volume appear as death and disease. The poem "Alba" repeats this message. In this, we are all mules who, despite our ancestry and sterility, deserve better treatment.

One of the most striking aspects of the sequence, however, is the constant linking of personal grief and loss, in this case Carlotta's disease, with the larger public issues of war. For Muldoon, the terms of engagement are the same. This interconnection of the personal and public is one of Muldoon's most tried and tested themes. In the sonnet entitled "Brandywine", which is part of the opening sequence, the links are implicit. The title is taken from the Battle of Brandywine, one of the largest engagements of the Revolutionary War, fought significantly on September 11, 1777, between the Continental Army led by General George Washington and the British forces headed by General William Howe. The only references to the battle or era in which it was fought – and they are oblique at best – is in the tools and implements that surface in the poem: "the great cast-ironpot", the "man-size barrel or butt". The poem is about the discovery of a cancerous tumor in Carlotta, but takes place pool-side at a hotel. The images that surround it are not only of the revolutionary war period, but contain those terms of venery (hunting and war) and Venus, which since Elizabethan times has been the play of poets seeking to link desire and violence. The inherent violence of disease makes its discovery and survival a theatre of war unto itself. Muldoon's touch on such a subject is one of his surest in all poetry; in fact, for Muldoon it is self-reflecting, a metanarrative imagining of the creation of poetry itself.

Such a consideration brings this reader back to the opening sonnet of the sequence, "Beijing", where art, war, desire and disease merge into sculpture of our inevitable destiny, death and decay:

> I could still hear the musicians
> cajoling those thousands of clay
> horses and horsemen through the squeeze

> when I woke beside Carlotta.
> Life-size, also. Also terra-cotta.
> The sky was still a terra-cotta frieze
> over which her grandfather still held sway
> with the set square, fretsaw, stencil,
> plumb line, and carpenter's pencil
> *his* grandfather brought from Roma.
> Proud-fleshed Carlotta. Hypersarcoma.
> For now our highest ambition
> was simply to bear the light of the day
> we had once been planning to seize.

The famous Chinese clay soldiers so recently discovered bear with them the history of art's epic claims in war. Linking war and love, Carlotta is also made from the earth (terra-cotta meaning baked earth); this is an unhappy connection because how can the inner world or inner life survive the larger conflagration of war. There is also a play on her "proud-flesh" and hypersarcoma (etymologically meaning "beyond or above the flesh"), as if ironically pride and cancer had become interchangeable. Like Dido in Carthage, whose flames of love eventually become the flames that destroy the city, the devastation is complete. Such claims are trying to this poet and seem to want to burst the sonnet form. The *carpe diem* is now only a meager attempt to survive the day.

Following on this criticism of Bush and the war in such personal terms of longing and loss, "Tithonus", as well as being securely in the tradition, as Vendler notes, seems also to contain an embedded critique of the decadence of Southern culture, the "Rebel yell", that informs so much of the backward-looking but harshly radical ethos of elements of the current Republican party. At the close of the poem, it is the sense of political and cultural senescence that marks the poem most strongly:

> heard by your great-great-grandfather, the Rebel yeller
> who happened to lose a stirrup
> and come a cropper
>
> at the very start of the Confederate offensive in the west,

> nor even the phatic
> whittering of your great-great-grandmother ("such a good *seat*")
> whose name was, of all things, Blanche,
>
> nor again the day-old cheep of a smoke detector on the blink
> in what used to be the root cellar
> but what turns out to be the two-thousand-year-old chirrup
> of a grasshopper.

That "chirrup" makes us think of the cricket's burden in *Ecclesiastes*, and with it, the thought that politically there is nothing new under the sun. Things have indeed become phatic; that is, redolent "of designating, or relating to speech, utterances, etc., that serve to establish or maintain social relationships rather than to impart information, communicate ideas".[7] If politically that is true, culturally there is more hope, if only because Muldoon's belief in poetry, as filled with distrust as it is, continues to keep him afloat.

Muldoon's poem to Bob Dylan, "Bob Dylan at Princeton, November 2000", contains a belief in Dylan's apocalyptic message:

> It's that self-same impulse that has him rearrange
> both 'The Times They Are A-Changin' and 'Things Have
>   Changed'
>
> so that everything seems to fall within his range
> as the locusts lock in on grain silo and grange.

Muldoon's love of popular music isn't always so serious, however. Sometimes it is downright sentimental ("mother of pearl"), though always with a twist ("a deepening sense of regret"), as is in this paean to the "Duke of Earl" entitled "Soccer Moms", placing these mothers in Muldoon's own age-group:

> Their hearts, Mavis and Merle,
>
> hanker for the time when it was not yet revealed
> failure's not less literal than figurative,
> the time of day when light fails on the field
>
> and gives back a sky more muddy than mother-of-pearl,

so it's with a deepening sense of regret
they remember Gene Chandler topping the charts with 'Duke
    of Earl'
and winning their hearts, Mavis and Merle.

This interest in music takes a sinister turn in "Flags and Emblems", a poem which uses and abuses the refrain of many a traditional Irish song as well as one of the major types of Jacobite poetry, the *aisling* or vision poem . It is an inverted or perverted *aisling* in which a woman is gang-raped by a group of paramilitaries (to the refrain of "Riddle-me-O"). "At Least They Weren't Speaking French" uses a similar musical motif. Many critics have recognised (and some have criticised) Muldoon's investment in language – foreign, archaic, local, dialectical, learned, and recherché.[8] In "At Least They Weren't Speaking French", Muldoon takes his son to see his parents' house in Ireland. The title, and the comic refrain it provides, is an allusion to the anti-French feelings in the US during the beginning of the war in Iraq. As Fenton notes, it is the "the sheer number of words in modern English (by comparison with modern French) [that] makes Muldoon's exuberant linguistic variety possible".[9] Fenton continues:

> Showing off as usual, Muldoon builds the whole of this thirty-six line poem (except for its refrain '*fol-de-rol fol-de-rol fol-de-rol-di-do*') on three rhyme-sounds (-ench, -one, and -oth). *French, bench, trench, clench, stench, wrench,* and *blench* are, for example, the '-ench' words; and Muldoon, seeking them out one by one and writing lines around them, enjoys cramming his ancestors into this tragicomic Procrustean bed. Yet the linguistic highjinks have not been allowed, here, to occlude feeling; Muldoon keeps both fanciness and fatality in focus.[10]

Both "At Least They Weren't Speaking French" and "Flags and Emblems" are driven by family secrets, a recurrent theme in Muldoon's work, as by now the reader must be aware.

In the middle of the volume is a poem called "Eggs", concerning a family secret, in this case, the time Muldoon's grandmother got drunk while taking some newly laid eggs to market. "It ends," as McGrath notes, "with the image of the poet himself as a chick pecking his way out not just from an eggshell but, if we apply just a little stunt-reading, the whole carapace of his family and his history."[11] The sonnet sequence "The Old Country", in which the last line of one sonnet is the first of the next, makes a commentary through this form on the inevitability of Irish history, the nightmare from which all artists have tried to awaken. Taken in this light, the surreal or exaggerated end of each line seems historically predetermined. "Each runnel was a Rubicon"? Of course. "Every resort was a last resort?" Who could have thought otherwise? All this is the undoing of the pastoral ideal with which the poem begins and ends ("every town was a tidy town"), for the second line, "every garden was a hanging garden", is what tells the tale.

This same theme underlies the mythos of the poem "The Outlier", a sequence of two trimester sonnets, in which Muldoon is reduced to a character from myth. "The Outlier" insists on the importance of the detached poetic gaze, while simultaneously questioning its morality. This double-take is typical of Muldoon, but reaches its height in this volume. Muldoon had earlier remarked that, as a child, his father sat on a bench "at the end of a lane marked by two white stones". In this succinct autobiography, "The Outlier", the stones have become the speaker's parents. As Vendler notes, "'The Outlier' rhymes in immobile fashion on 'one-eyed' words (all formed on the single template 'vowel + n'). In each of its two parts, the stanzas gradually 'grow' from two lines to three to four to five, enacting the process by which nurture distorts an already distorted nature."[12] The "Fomorians" mentioned in the poem, original nature gods of Ireland, were sometimes said to have only one eye. Balor in particular is famous for his eye that would turn the enemy to stone, but he couldn't open it without the help of his fellow soldiers. For Muldoon, this ancient trait, rooted in nature, resurfaces in the poetic gaze, which turns his subjects to stone. This unflinching stony gaze serves Muldoon in a number of ways. In "Turtles" it allows him to record the moral cloudiness that underlies the peace process in Northern Ireland. Those "sentries and scouts" who had banged bin lids in order to warn their side of the approach of the police have now been "enlisted by some police forces / to help them recover corpses".

It is in "Turkey Buzzards", however, that the stony satirical gaze of Muldoon's poetic finds its most fitting subject. As Muldoon tells it in poetry readings,[13] the range of these birds had been confined to the Southeastern states, until (with the advent of the highway system under Eisenhower) the subsequent roadkill enlarged their range dramatically. The alternating four beat, two beat line perhaps mirrors the flight of the buzzards above the road; certainly echoes are heard from Swinburne's famous poem "Faustine". The line length and rhyme scheme are the same, as is the rank mood. Here are three stanzas from Muldoon:

> They've been so long above it all,
>> those two petals
> so steeped in style they seem to stall
>> in the kettle
>
> [...]
>
> the kettle where it all boils down
>> to the thick scent
> of death, a scent of such renown
>> it's given vent
>
> to the idea buzzards can spot
>> a deer carcass
> a mile away, smelling the rot
>> as, once Marcus ...

Marcus is Marcus Aurelius, which is another connection to the Roman decadence that so moved Swinburne in the images of bloodlust and gladiatorial struggle that define "Faustine". Here are three stanzas from the latter:

> She loved the games men played with death,
>> Where death must win;
> As though the slain man's blood and breath
>> Revived Faustine.

Nets caught the pike, pikes tore the net;
   Lithe limbs and lean
From drained-out pores dripped thick red sweat
   To soothe Faustine.

She drank the steaming drift and dust
   Blown off the scene;
Blood could not ease the bitter lust
   That galled Faustine.

Muldoon has said that poets must reflect the difficult reality they confront. In this he is much like Eliot. Yet for Muldoon, savage satire is the heartfelt response to the obscenities and difficulties he faces. Socially, Muldoon satirises the decadence of a culture that has given rise to the prevalence of turkey buzzards. As they now complain of Muldoon's poetry, though in somewhat different terms, reviewers once complained of the decadence of Swinburne, to which the Victorian poet replied: "I have heard that even the little poem of 'Faustine' has been to some readers a thing to make the scalp creep and the blood freeze. It was issued with no such intent. Nor do I remember that any man's voice or heel was lifted against it when it first appeared, a new-born and virgin poem, in the *Spectator* newspaper for 1862. Virtue, it would seem, has shot up surprisingly in the space of four years or less – a rank and rapid growth, barren of blossom and rotten of root."[14] Such an indictment of society seems important if not central to Muldoon's poem: the turkey buzzards' new-found importance links a "theologian's and the thug's / twin triumphings // in a buzzard's shaved head and snood". The decadence of society is more perhaps evocatively painted in other poems; here it reflects the despair that circles around the main theme of the poem, his sister's illness and, with it, the meditation on the artistic process, characterised by the birds themselves.

The birds contain resemblances of religion and art, living off death as they do. The buzzards, digging their head in the corpses, become not only an image of cancer eating at his sister's vitals, but an image of belief, of a "soul in bliss". In the first of a series of complicated allusions, the buzzards digging at the entrails ("like a rose in over its head / among brambles") are symbolic of Mount Ararat, "on which the Ark would come to grief", that is, where it would finally land. Having reached the shore, Noah must return to the world and all its exigencies. The flight through the deluge is over. The buzzards descending to feed are therefore recurrent images of this coming to grief. Clearly, it is a landing that to Muldoon is richly ambivalent and echoes his own descent from formal beauty to the cancer that eats away at the content of art. Like art, the birds live off death and destruction, circling high above to catch sight of their next meal. Like art, the birds seem to be immune from the suffering they depict ("their poop containing an enzyme / that's know to boost // their immune systems, should they prong / themselves on small / bones"). In the end, the grotesque image of the birds descending into a deer's carcass implies the last end of his sister, as well as Muldoon's own carrion reckonings, "sinking fast":

> in a deer crypt
> buzzards getting the hang at last
> of being stripped

> of their command of the vortex
> while having lost
> their common touch, they've been so long
> above it all.

Is the force of this poem not derived from being stripped of its command of the vortex, and being clumsy on the ground because it's been so long above it? Vendler puts it succinctly: "The viciousness of the poet's dissection finally turns on the buzzards themselves, as they take infection from a corpse and learn at last, like all artists, their own mortality, realising in the end that their aesthetic disengagement has removed them from warm proximity to life."[15]

This tilt against art itself, this sardonic grief, is one of Muldoon's most moving poems. For all of the redemptive beauties of an elegy like "Incantata" from *The Annals of Chile* (1994), there is something in a poem like "Turkey Buzzards" that has unleashed more of Muldoon's carnivorous poetic powers. In a poem like "Hedge School" Muldoon is seen at last tracing the root of *metastasis*, to see that this spreading of cancer comes from a Latin rhetorical figure (meaning: "rapid transition from one point or type of figure to another"),[16] which only secures his conviction that art, like disease, depends upon cruel and rapid change. Poems such as "Now Pitching Himself like a Forlorn Hope", "Perdu" and "The Last Time I saw Chris", as one can tell from their titles, reflect on similarly despairing themes. In "Glaucus", referring to the King of Corinth (and not the sea-god), we see how hubris towards the gods is repaid. Having angered Venus, Glaucus, as the myth recounts, is eaten by horses he had readied for battle by having fed them on human flesh. Again, the figure of art and/or politics, for surely Glaucus unites these images, leads to a perversion of nature. It is significant that this poem was first published in an anthology celebrating the environmentalist Rachel Carson's most famous book, *Silent Spring*, aimed, as it was, at the use of DDT.[17]

The final poem of the volume contemplates many of these themes; it is the elegy to Warren Zevon entitled "Sillyhow Stride". Zevon is a difficult man to eulogise, as, during his bout against cancer, he came up with some of his own best epitaphs: "It's a damned hard way to make a living, having to die to get 'em to know you're alive"; or "I'll sleep when I'm dead".[18] Yet, Muldoon is well suited to the task of remembering this sardonic man of song who was also known for his literary muscle. Janet Maslin sums up the personality she gleans from the book by his estranged wife Crystal Zevon: "The Mr Zevon on these pages is surprisingly image-conscious, abusive, petty, jealous, sordid, vain, shopaholic and even banal; among his obsessive-compulsive tics was buying the same kind of gray T-shirt over and over again."[19] She does admit, however, that the book "captures a lovable but wildly aberrant personality".[20] Muldoon's long poem (some ten pages) also captures much of the wild and literary nature of his friend's talent, beginning from the opening stanzas:

I want you tell me if, on Grammy night, you didn't get one
  hell of a kick
out of all those bling-it-ons in their bulletproof broughams,
all those line managers who couldn't manage a line of coke,

all those Barmecides offering beakers of barm –
if you didn't get a kick out of being as incongruous
there as John Donne at a junior prom.

Zevon thereafter becomes part of Muldoon's meditation on the postcolonial and the subaltern, specifically the child soldiers of Africa, echoing the theme of "Excitable Boy", Zevon's early hit. Soon Muldoon considers all the people in his life who have been claimed by the cancer, his mother and most recently his sister, whose suffering he recounts to Zevon.

I knelt and adjusted the sillyhow

of her oxygen mask, its vinyl caul
unlikely now to save Maureen from drowning in her own spit.
I thought of how the wrangling schools

need look no further than her bed
to find what fire shall burn this world – or that heaven
which 'is one with' this world – to find how gold to airy
  thinness beat

may crinkle like cellophane
in a flame, like a cellophane or the flimmerings of gauze
by which a needle is held fast in a vein.

Again, we have Muldoon's insistence that respite from suffering is the only real transcendence. Donne's metaphysical "gold to airy thinness beat" is brought down to the needle that brings the drug's relief. And so he advises Warren to remember drugs and rock 'n' roll in the middle of his Christian passion:

So break off, Warren, break off the last lamenting kiss
as Christ broke with Iscariot
and gave himself to those loosey-goosey
Whiskey A Go Going mint julep – and margarita –

and gimlet-grinders, those gin fizz-
ignomists.

Yet Muldoon never makes any directive as to a course of action without some important equivocation. Alluding to Zevon's
song "Werewolves of London", Muldoon notes of Zevon's famous addictions: "the werewolf ... realised it ain't that pretty at
all to be completely wasted when you're testing your chops, hint
hint, / on a Gibson Les Paul." What the world of Zevon does offer
is a catalogue of the hodgepodge of late twentieth-century experience, the "G-men", "fishionistas", the "boy-soldiers", "Scottish
Mormons" and last, by not least, a New Critical image of the postmodern imagination: "our last few grains of heroin ash stashed in
a well-wrought urn." The question of what will purge the poem of
its inherent suffering is the same as the turkey buzzards, a quality
which inures it to the carrion it must feed on: the cleansing quality
of poetic detachment. The closing image of the poem reminds us
of this connection (*Cathartes aura* being the Latin name for turkey
buzzard):

> turkey buzzards waiting for you to eclipse and cloud them
>   with a wink
>
> as they hold out their wings and of the sun his working vigor
>   borrow
> before they parascend through the Viper Room of the Whisky
>   A Go Go,
> each within its own 'cleansing breeze,' its own *Cathartes aura*.

Of course, in order to have that capacity, your evolution must
depend on such a ghoulish meal. In *Horse Latitudes*, we see that
this rendering of the survival-of-the-fittest form of art has evolved
into one of Muldoon's most trenchant moral themes.

Endnotes

---

[1] See Mark Helprin, "Against the dehumanization of art", *The New Criterion* Vol. 13, No. 1, September 1994.

[2] Helen Vendler, "Fanciness and Fatality", *The New Republic*, 9 November 2006.

[3] Interview with Paul Muldoon, Charles McGrath, "Word Freak", *The New York Times*, 19 November 2006.

[4] James Fenton, "A Poke in the Eye with a Poem", *The Guardian*, 21 October 2006.

[5] *Horse Latitudes* (London: Faber and Faber; New York: Farrar, Straus and Giroux, 2006).

[6] Vendler, "Fanciness and Fatality", *The New Republic*, 9 November 2006.

[7] *Oxford English Dictionary*, fifth edition.

[8] James Fenton, "A Poke in the Eye with a Poem", *The Guardian*, 21 October 2006.

[9] Fenton, "A Poke in the Eye with a Poem".

[10] Fenton, "A Poke in the Eye with a Poem".

[11] McGrath, "Word Freak", *The New York Times*, 19 November 2006.

[12] Vendler, "Fanciness and Fatality", *The New Republic*, 9 November 2006.

[13] Poetry reading April 18, during conference "Befitting Emblems of Adversity": Lyric and Crisis in Northern Irish Poetry 1966–2006" Georgetown University, April 17–18, 2007; Poetry Reading for the opening of library exhibit, "Nobel Times Four: Yeats, Shaw, Beckett, Heaney", University of North Carolina, Chapel Hill, 9 October 2006.

[14] Algernon Charles Swinburne, *Notes on Poems and Reviews* (London: John Camden Hotten, 1866); edited in *Complete Works* by Sir Edmond Gosse and Thomas James Wise, *Prose Works*, Vol. VI (London: William Heinemann, Ltd., 1926), 364.

[15] Vendler, "Fanciness and Fatality", *The New Republic*, 9 November 2006.

[16] *Oxford English Dictionary*, fifth edition

[17] See *Wild Reckoning: An Anthlogy Provoked by Rachel Carson's Silent Spring* (Calouste Gulbenkian Foundation, 2004).

[18] Janet Maslin, "It Ain't that Pretty, That Life of Zevon's", review of *I'll Sleep When I'm Dead* by Crystal Zevon, *The New York Times*, 30 April 2007.

[19] Maslin, "It Ain't That Pretty".

[20] Maslin, "It Ain't That Pretty".

Conclusion

IN THE TRADITION OF IRISH NATURE writing, emphasising alle-gorical and mythological renderings of nature, and reflecting the pressures of a colonial history, Muldoon's first volume, *New Weather* (1973), is organised around the themes of landscape, na-ture and family/community/nation. The connection between na-ture and original sin has a long lineage in Irish literature — in all literature, of course – but in Ireland it takes on specific historical forms. Though Muldoon's poems are universal in significance, they are also local in character. By his second volume, *Mules* (1977), Muldoon sardonic wit is guided by the following Swiftian aims: he wishes to argue against the abstract, theoretical tenden-cies of rationalism; he doubts the capacity of human reason to at-tain metaphysical and theological truth; he contests the attitudes of experimental and theoretical science; he opposes the Romantic conception of man, which was the result of both rationalism and science, and which taught the essential goodness of human na-ture; he questions the increasing power of centralised government and the corruption of English colonialism, whether in Ireland, Britain or America.

Both Swift and Muldoon create fables of social and political experience that uncover dark truths of human nature. Behind their complex political position is a sovereign intellectual satire of humanity which seeks to uncover the most primitive transgres-sions of power, cruelty, and lust. Both Swift and Muldoon stage a confrontation between our animal and rational characteristics. Muldoon's *Mules* is a type of bestiary of human aspirations. There also is a strong element of the anti-pastoral in this volume, meant to counter the first volume's emphasis on the landscape, which is very much a part of Muldoon's keen considerations of how human endeavours become entangled in the net of nature's designs; however, by the next volume these deliberations are given topical values because of the rising intensity of the violence in Northern Ireland.

Since the Irish Literary Renaissance, Irish literature has been a testament to twentieth-century experience: the political, religious and ethnic strife, the struggles and grief of colonisation and decolonisation, in which questions of identity and place have been paramount. In Paul Muldoon's poetry, home and family are a place and situation one can never leave behind. Personal and familial reflections inevitably have public resonance, and aesthetic choices political implications. In *Why Brownlee Left* (1980), the family is investigated in very intimate terms and are seen to have inevitable and perhaps regrettable public demonstrations. In the aesthetics and politics of Irishness there is a constant endeavour to find a way of recreating the familiar, of healing the wounds of history with images of shared reality, one which Paul Muldoon's engages throughout his career. *Why Brownlee Left* explores Ireland's history of colonisation and decolonisation, and presents a post-colonial critique of family and civility that is torn by the uneasy relationship between aesthetics and politics.

Muldoon's penchant for violence in his poetry reaches its height in *Quoof* (1983), his fourth collection of poetry, which was published in the period right after the hunger strikes in Ireland. It is a volume for a difficult time, juxtaposing and confusing poems of violence with nostalgic celebrations of childhood and home, and is one in which his father figures largely. The father's presence in Muldoon's imagination and his absence, following his death, form a central motif of the volume; perhaps the misogynistic tone of many of the poems result from his mother's role in this relationship, as Muldoon's mother appears to have always disrupted the affections between father and son. The Muldoon family romance is settled in different ways and raises various questions. Is the depiction of home liberating or confining? Is the father corrupting or benign? Muldoon is seeking a solution, but dubious as ever regarding the curative abilities of poetry.

From the eighteenth to the twentieth century, the idea of family remained a ruling aesthetic and political concept in Irish writing. Though this is obviously true of many Irish writers, it is particularly true of Muldoon, especially as we approach the poetry of *Meeting the British* (1987), where there is a sublimation of the family romance onto the landscape in his lyric poems, a poetic gesture which is taken from Louis MacNeice. Importantly for Muldoon, Louis MacNeice's aestheticisation is not mere escapism or retreat, but another starting point for discussions of history and nature within Ireland, Britain, and Europe. Muldoon himself establishes a similar starting point for such reflections. One difference between these two poets may be that Muldoon's family is written into the landscape and nature rather than sublimated as they are in MacNeice. Muldoon is more like John Montague or Seamus Heaney in this respect. He places himself and his ancestors on the land and considers how history, nature, politics and personal/familial life have shaped them in very specific ways. Another aspect of Muldoon's poetic in *Meeting the British*, which is worth mentioning, is the American influence. Muldoon has increasingly become American in certain aspects of his writing as well as citizenship, having become a citizen and having won the Pulitzer Prize. It is safe to say that he experiments with form, resists moralising and emphasises surfaces, play, process, improvisation and chance as few Irish poets have done before him (in prose, of course, there are James Joyce, Flann O'Brien and Samuel Beckett). He also has a very postmodern sense of the place and uses of popular culture; yet there is always something in Muldoon's love of traditional forms that seems to remind his American admirers of his roots in Irish poetry, that make it difficult not to be drawn to understanding the Irish dimension of his poetry.

After his move to the US in 1987, Paul Muldoon published the complex amalgam of puzzles that is *Madoc: A Mystery* (1990). The title poem is a strange recapitulation of individual and public his-

tory: that is, the birth of the individual recapitulating or summa-
rising the development of the species, just as the history of philosophical thought condenses the history of colonisation. It makes
sense, however, to combine these two recapitulations. In reading
the poem we chart the development of various characters who
have come to America from Britain, and see how their trials and
tribulations mirror the developing colony. Also, the birth of a nation almost presupposes the return to a primitive state of mind.
That we go through so many centuries of philosophy so quickly
says something about the accelerated pace of development in the
New World. The sequence endeavours to prove that sensual experience is the only kernel of truth that we might have. The measure of man is made through perception. "Madoc" thereby measures the philosophical quandary and diseased body politic of
Western civilisation, as it appears in the New World.

It would not be news to say that Paul Muldoon is one of the
most exemplary postmodern poets of Ireland and the US, but it
was "Madoc" that confirmed this assessment. While accepting
some notable differences between a poet such as Yeats and Muldoon, any understanding of the post-"Madoc" Muldoon must
discuss how conceptions of aesthetics apply to the question of the
stability of the subject, to politics, history and landscape, as well
as to postmodernity and postcoloniality within an Irish frame –
thereby sharpening the comparisons between Yeats and Muldoon.
The philosophical and aesthetic dilemmas of postmodernism and
Modernism are remarkably similar; no matter how "incorrigibly
plural" we've become, poets want to achieve some sort of stability
in the subject, to clear a space in which poetry can be created, to
illuminate form. Even if Muldoon seemed to have delineated the
ways in which such an illumination is interrupted in "Madoc: A
Mystery", in *The Annals of Chile* (1994) he had personal reasons
(the elegy for his friend Mary Powers, the birth of his daughters,
the elegy for his mother) for this aesthetic illumination, as well as
for the consideration of its redemptive capacity.

Having acknowledged the importance of that capacity, having
admitted the ways in which the deaths of those near to you, of

those whose spirits have ruled your particular star, may in turn reshape your aesthetic, may force you to rethink some of your essential premises, Muldoon was confronted with what he would next use as the basis of his subject and his style. For Muldoon, changes in style and content have been quite evident. In *Hay* (1998), Muldoon entered what might be said to be the later stages of his mature style, and is now open to parody. In this vein, Muldoon knowingly mocks himself. There are many great plays on clichés in an effort to stave off the cliché of the poet. There is also a consciousness of memory and loss, that strange birthmark of middle age, which only threatens to spread and overwhelm the poet. In Muldoon's *oeuvre*, there is no sense that the history of art is unfolding its truths, but there is instead a disorienting feeling that the progression of form is associational and dreamlike, with no determinate end in sight beyond the record of sensation, the cataloguing of culture, the efforts of art to ride rather than order the flux. *Moy Sand and Gravel* (2002), Muldoon's ninth book, extends the example of *Hay* and is concerned with deracination and reorientation. Even though Muldoon had used this technique in earlier volumes, it is particularly visible in both *Hay* and *Moy Sand and Gravel*. With that recognition, we must admit that in many ways the volumes cover some of the same ground as earlier ones. There is parody and pastiche aimed as much at Muldoon's own poetic as at poetry and society at large.

While *The Annals of Chile* may have seemed to mark a turning point in Muldoon's work, it may have just admitted some new elements into the mix, mainly the complex elegiac notes of "Incantata" and "Yarrow". And we have seen that, even with this new element, some critics remain unconvinced. Yet a question increasingly burning from Muldoon's poetry is that of art's complicity in suffering. Answering this question creates some of Muldoon's best poems, which are great because they are so deeply self indicting; this is true throughout his career, but especially true in his most recent collection of poems, *Horse Latitudes* (2006). *Horse Latitudes* has a number of poems proving that this period in Muldoon's career may be the culmination of his always impressive talents. Sometimes Muldoon insists that art has a positive role to play, at other times, that it is of no use whatsoever and merely feeds off the carnage. For Muldoon, art should not merely repeat the devastation of the world, although he is afraid that it does, and engages in bitter moral despair that makes some poems of *Horse Latitudes* among the very best he has written.

Bibliography

By Paul Muldoon:

Poetry Volumes

New Weather. London: Faber and Faber, 1973.

Mules. London: Faber and Faber; Winston-Salem: Wake Forest UP, 1977.

Why Brownlee Left. London: Faber and Faber; Winston-Salem: Wake Forest UP, 1980.

Quoof. London: Faber and Faber; Winston-Salem: Wake Forest UP, 1983.

Mules and Earlier Poems. Winston-Salem: Wake Forest UP, 1985.

Selected Poems 1968–1983. London: Faber and Faber, 1986.

Meeting the British. London: Faber and Faber; Winston-Salem: Wake Forest UP, 1987.

Selected Poems 1968–1986. New York: Ecco Press, 1987.

Madoc: A Mystery. London: Faber and Faber; New York: Farrar, Strauss, and Giroux, 1990.

The Annals of Chile. London: Faber and Faber; New York: Farrar, Strauss and Giroux, 1994.

New Selected Poems 1968–1993. London: Faber and Faber, 1996.

Hay. London: Faber and Faber; New York: Farrar, Straus, and Giroux, 1998.

Poems 1968–1998. London: Faber and Faber; New York: Farrar, Straus and Giroux, 2001.

Moy Sand and Gravel. London: Faber and Faber; New York: Farrar, Straus and Giroux 2002.

Horse Latitudes. London: Faber and Faber; New York: Farrar, Straus and Giroux, 2006.

Pamphlets and Selections

Knowing My Place. Belfast: Ulsterman Publications, 1971.

Poetry Introductions 2. London: Faber and Faber, 1972.

Out of the Blue: A Selection of Poems, by Muldoon and James Simmons. Belfast: Arts Council of Northern Ireland, 1974.

Spirit of Dawn. Belfast: Ulsterman Publications, 1975.

Names and Addresses. Belfast: Ulsterman Publications, 1978.

Immram. Oldcastle, Co. Meath: Gallery Press, 1980.

Out of Siberia. Oldcastle, Co. Meath: Gallery Press, 1982.

The Wishbone. Oldcastle, Co. Meath: Gallery Press, 1984.

The Prince of the Quotidian. Oldcastle, Co. Meath: Gallery Press; Winston-Salem: Wake Forest UP, 1994.

Incantata. Dublin: Graphic Studio, 1994.

Kerry Slides, with photographs by Bill Doyle. Oldcastle, Co. Meath: Gallery Press, 1996.

From the Mud Room. Deerfield, MA: Deerfield Press, 1997.

Hopewell Haiku. Easthampton: Warwick Press, 1997.

The Bangle (Slight Return). Princeton: The Typography Studio, 1998.

Unapproved Road. Hopewell, NJ: Pied Oxen, 2002.

Medley for Morin Khur. London: Enitharmon Press, 2005.

Sixty Instant Messages to Tom Moore. Evanston, IL: Modern Haiku Press, 2005.

Libretti

Shining Brow. London: Faber and Faber, 1993.

Bandanna: An Opera in Two Acts and a Prologue. London: Faber and Faber, 1999.

Vera of Las Vegas. Oldcastle, Co. Meath: Gallery Press, 2001

Screenplay

Monkeys. BBC, 1989.

Play

Six Honest Serving Men. Oldcastle, Co. Meath: Gallery Press, 1995.

Books for Children

The O-O's Party, New Year's Eve. Oldcastle, Co. Meath: Gallery Press 1980.

The Last Thesaurus. London: Faber and Faber, 1995.

The Noctuary of Narcissus Batt. London: Faber and Faber, 1997.

Reverse Flannery: Magical Tales of Ireland. New York: Random House, 2003.

Translations

The Biggest Egg in the World, by Martin Sorescu, translated by Muldoon and others. Newcastle upon Tyne: Bloodaxe, 1987.

Pharaoh's Daughter, by Nuala Ní Dhomhnaill, translated by Muldoon and others. Oldcastle, Co. Meath: Gallery Press; Winston-Salem: Wake Forest UP, 1990.

The Astrakhan Cloak: Poems in Irish by Nuala Ní Dhomhnaill with translations into English by Paul Muldoon. Oldcastle, Co. Meath: Gallery Press; Winston-Salem: Wake Forest UP, 1992.

When the Tunnels Meet: Contemporary Romanian Poetry, translated by Muldoon and others. Newcastle upon Tyne: Bloodaxe, 1996.

The Birds, translated from Aristophanes by Muldoon, with Richard Martin. Oldcastle, Co. Meath: Gallery Books, 1999.

The Fifty Minute Mermaid, by Nuala Ní Dhomhnaill, translated by Muldoon. Oldcastle, Co. Meath: Gallery Press, 2006

The Hebrew Book of Psalms, with Michael Thomas Davis. London: Faber and Faber; New York: Farrar, Straus and Giroux, 2007.

The Drowned Blackbird. Princeton: Princeton UP, 2007.

Edited or Introduced

The Scrake of Dawn: Poems by Young People from Northern Ireland. Belfast: Blackstaff Press, 1979.

The Faber Book of Contemporary Irish Poetry. London: Faber and Faber, 1986.

The Essential Byron. New York: Ecco Press, 1989.

The Faber Book of Beasts. London: Faber and Faber, 1997.

Ploughshares Spring 2000: Stories and Poems. 26.1 Boston: Ploughshares Books, 2000.

Irish Fairy and Folk Tales. Ed. W. B Yeats. New York: The Modern Library, 2003.

The Best American Poetry 2005. New York: Scribner, 2005.

Critical Works

"Getting Round: Notes towards an *Ars Poetica*", *Essays in Criticism* 48.2 (1998), 107–28.

"The Point of Poetry." *Princeton University Library Chronicle* LIX.3 (1998), 503–16.

To Ireland, I: The 1998 Clarendon Lectures. Oxford: Oxford UP, 2000.

The End of the Poem: All Soul's Night by W. B. Yeats: An Inaugural Lecture Delivered before the University of Oxford on 2 November 1999. Oxford and New York: Oxford UP, 2000.

"The End of the Poem: 'The Mountain' by Robert Frost", *American Poetry Review* 30.1 (2001), 41–46.

"Polar Expeditions: 'I tried to think a lonelier Thing' by Emily Dickinson." *New England Review* 24.2 (2003), 6–24.

"Zigzag." *Parnassus: Poetry in Review* 27.1–2 (2003), 213–32.

The End of the Poem: Oxford Lectures on Poetry. New York: Farrar, Straus and Giroux, 2006.

Articles and Critical Discussions on Muldoon:

Adams, Michael. *Censorship: The Irish Experience*. Tuscaloosa: University of Alabama Press, 1968.

Adamson, Ian. *The Identity of Ulster: The Land, the Language, and the People*. Belfast: Adamson, 1982.

Allison, Jonathan. "Questioning Yeats: Paul Muldoon's '7, Middagh Street.'" *Learning the Trade: Essays on W. B. Yeats and Contemporary Poetry*. Ed. Deborah Fleming. West Cornwall, CT: Locust Hill, 1993, 3–20.

Allnutt, Gillian, Fred D'Aguiar, Ken Edwards and Eric Mottram, eds. *The New British Poetry*. London: Collins, 1988.

Anderson, Benedict. *Imagined Communities: Reflections on the Origin and Spread of Nationalism*. London: Verso, 1983.

Andrews, Elmer. *Contemporary Irish Poetry: A Collection of Critical Essays*. Basingstoke: Macmillan, 1992.

—. *Paul Muldoon: Poems, Prose, Drama*. Gerrards Cross: Colin Smythe, 2006.

—. "'Some Sweet Disorder' – The Poetry of Subversion: Paul Muldoon, Tom Paulin and Medbh McGuckian". *British Poetry from the 1950s to the 1990s: Politics and Art*. Ed. Gary Day and Brian Docherty. London: Macmillan, 1997, 118–42.

Arthur, Paul and Keith Jeffery. *Northern Ireland Since 1968*. Oxford: Blackwell, 1988.

Ashcroft, Bill, Garreth Griffiths, and Helen Tiffin. *The Empire Writes Back: Theory and Practice in Post-Colonial Literature*. London: Routledge, 1989.

Auge, Andrew J. "To Send a Shiver through Unitel: Imperial Philosophy and the Resistant Word in Paul Muldoon's *Madoc: A Mystery*", *Contemporary Literature* 46.4 (2005): 636–66.

Banville, John. "Slouching Toward Bethlehem", *New York Review of Books*, 30 May 1991.

Barry, Sebastian, ed. *The Inherited Boundaries: Younger Poets of the Republic of Ireland*. Dublin: Dolmen, 1986.

Batten, Guinn. "'He Could Barely Tell One from the Other': The Borderline Disorders of Paul Muldoon's Poetry", *South Atlantic Quarterly* 95.1 (1996), 171–204.

—. "'Where All the Ladders Start:' Identity, Ideology, and the Ghosts of the Romantic Subject in the Poetry of Yeats and Muldoon". *Romantic Generations: Essays in Honor of Robert F. Gleckner*. Ed. Guinn Batten and Barry Milligan. Lewisburg, PA: Bucknell UP, 2001, 245–80.

Baucom, Ian. "Found Drowned: The Irish Atlantic", *Nineteenth-Century Contexts* 22.1 (2000), 103–38.

Berensmeyer, Ingo. "Identity or Hybridization? Mapping Irish Culture in Seamus Heaney and Paul Muldoon", *Etudes Irlandaises* 28.1 (2003), 65–83.

Bolton, Jonathan. "Irish Stew at the Café du Monde: Heterogeneity and the Emigré Experience in Paul Muldoon's 'Yarrow'", *South Atlantic Review* 64.1 (1999), 48–71.

Boyce, D. George. *Nationalism in Ireland*. Baltimore: Johns Hopkins UP, 1982.

Boyleston, J. Matthew. "To Sing the Magic Words that Raise the Dead: Form and Allusion in Paul Muldoon's 'Incantata'", *South Carolina Review* 38.1 (2005), 128–35.

Bradley, Anthony and Maryann Gialanella Valiulis. *Gender and Sexuality in Modern Ireland*. Amherst: University of Massachusetts Press, 1997.

Brearton, Fran. *The Great War in Irish Poetry: W. B. Yeats to Michael Longley*. Oxford: Oxford UP, 2000.

—. "'Ploughing by the Tail:' Longley, Muldoon, and Anxiety of Influence", *Nordic Irish Studies* 2.1 (2003), 1–16.

Brewster, Scott. "'Something Else, Then Something Else Again:' Transformation and Translation in Paul Muldoon", *Nordic Irish Studies* 2.1 (2003), 17–28.

Brewster, Scott. et al. eds. *Ireland in Proximity: History, Gender, Space*. London: Routledge, 1999.

Brown, John. *In the Chair: Interviews with Poets from the North of Ireland*. Clare: Salmon Press, 2002.

Brown, Richard. "Bog Poems and Books Poems: Doubleness, Self-Translation and Pun in Seamus Heaney and Paul Muldoon", *The Chosen Ground: Essays on the Contemporary Poetry of Northern Ireland*. Ed. Neil Corcoran. Bridgend: Seren, 1992, 153–157.

Brown, Terence. *Northern Voices: Poets from Ulster*. Dublin: Gill and Macmillan, 1975.

—. *Ireland: A Social and Cultural History, 1922–1985*. 1981. London: Fontana, 1985.

Brown, Terence and Nicholas Grene, eds. *Tradition and Influence in Anglo-Irish Literature*. London: Macmillan, 1989.

Buchanan, Barbara. "Paul Muldoon: 'Who's to know what's knowable?'", *Contemporary Irish Poetry*. Ed. Elmer Andrews. London: Macmillan, 1992, 310–327.

Buckland, Patrick. *A History of Northern Ireland*. Dublin: Gill and Macmillan, 1981.

Burris, S. "Some Versions of Ireland: The Poetry of Tom Paulin and Paul Muldoon." *Kenyon Review* VII.4 (1985), 129–135.

Burt, Stephen. "Paul Muldoon's Binocular Vision", *Harvard Review* 7 (1994): 95–107.

Buxton, Rachael. *Robert Frost and Northern Irish Poetry*. Oxford: Clarendon Press; New York: Oxford UP, 2004.

—. "'Structure and Serendipity:' The Influence of Robert Frost on Paul Muldoon." *Critical Ireland: New Essays in Literature and Culture*. Ed. Alan A. Gillis and Aaron Kelly. Dublin: Four Courts, 2001, 14–21.

Campbell, Matthew, ed. *The Cambridge Companion to Contemporary Irish Poetry*. Cambridge: Cambridge UP, 2003.

Cahill, Eileen. "A Silent Voice: Seamus Heaney and Ulster Politics", *Critical Quarterly* 29.3, 1987, 55–9.

Cairns, David and Toni O'Brien Johnston, ed. *Gender in Irish Writing*. Milton Keynes: Open UP, 1991.

Cairns, David and Shaun Richards. *Writing Ireland: Colonialism, Nationalism and Culture*. Manchester: Manchester UP, 1988.

Cleary, Joe, and Claire Connolly, eds. *The Cambridge Companion to Modern Irish Culture*. Cambridge: Cambridge UP, 2005.

Cliff, Brian. "Paul Muldoon's Community on the Cusp: Auden and MacNeice in the Manuscripts for '7, Middagh Street'", *Contemporary Literature* 44.4 (2003), 613–36.

Clifton, H. "Available Air: Irish Contemporary Poetry", *Krino* 7 (1989), 20–30.

Clyde, T. "An Ulster Twilight: Poetry in Northern Ireland." *Krino* 5 (1988), 95–102.

Conner, Lester I. "Paul Muldoon", *Poets of Great Britain and Ireland since 1960*. Ed. Vincent B. Sherry, Jr. Ann Arbor: Gale, 1985, 400–405.

Connolly, Claire, ed. *Theorizing Ireland*. Basingstoke: Macmillan, 2003.

Corcoran, Neil. *After Yeats and Joyce*. Oxford: Oxford UP, 1997.

—. ed. *The Chosen Ground: Essays on the Contemporary Poetry of Northern Ireland*. Bridgend: Seren Books, 1992.

—."In Ireland or Someplace: A Second Generation from Northern Ireland." *English Poetry Since 1940*. London: Longman, 1993, 205–220.

—."'A Languorous Cutting Edge:' Muldoon versus Heaney?" *Princeton University Library Chronicle* 59.3 (1998), 559–80.

—. *Poets of Modern Ireland: Text, Context, Intertext*. Carbondale: Southern Illinois UP, 1999.

Cosgrove, Kevin P. "Paul Muldoon's Explorer Myth: From Madoc to Raleigh", *New Hibernia Review/Iris Éireannach Nua: A Quarterly Record of Irish Studies* 4.2 (2000), 67–83.

Coulter, Carol. *Ireland: Between the First and the Third Worlds*. Dublin: Attic Press, 1990.

Crozier, Maurna, ed. *Cultural Traditions in Northern Ireland*. Belfast: Institute of Irish Studies, 1991.

Davison, Peter. "Darkness at Muldoon", *The New York Times Book Review*, 13 October 2002.

Dawe, Gerald. *Against Piety: Essays in Irish Poetry*. Belfast: Lagan Press 1995.

—. *False Faces: Poetry, Politics and Place*. Belfast: Lagan Press, 1994.

—. *How's the Poetry Going: Literary Politics and Ireland Today*. Second edition. Belfast: Lagan Press, 1993.

—. *A Real Life Elsewhere*. Belfast: Lagan Press 1995.

—. ed. *The Younger Irish Poets*. Belfast: Blackstaff, 1982.

Dawe, Gerald and Edna Longley, eds. *Across a Roaring Hill: The Protestant Imagination in Modern Ireland*. Belfast: Blackstaff, 1985.

Denvir, Gearoid. "Continuing the Link: An Aspect of Contemporary Irish Poetry", *Irish Review* 3 (1998), 40–54.

DeShazer, Mary. "Michael Longley and Paul Muldoon", *Concerning Poetry* 14.2 (1981), 125–131.

Donahue, Joseph. "Paul Muldoon (1951–)." *British Writers: Supplement IV*. Ed. Carol Howard and George Stade. New York: Scribner, 1997, 409–32.

Dorgan, Theo, ed. *Irish Poetry since Kavanagh*. Dublin: Four Courts Press, 1996.

Dunne, Tom. "New Histories: Beyond 'Revisionism.'" *Irish Review* 12 (1992), 1–12.

Drexel, John. "Threaders of Double-Stranded Words: News from the North of Ireland", *New England Review and Bread Loaf Quarterly* 12.2 (1989), 179–192.

Easthope, Anthony and John O. Thompson, eds. *Contemporary Poetry Meets Modern Theory*. Hemel Hempstead: Harvester Wheatsheaf, 1991.

Farrell, Michael. *Northern Ireland: The Orange State*. London: Pluto, 1980.

Ford, Mark. "A Review of *Hay*, by Paul Muldoon", *The New York Review of Books*, 25 September 2003.

Foster, Roy. "We Are All Revisionists Now", *Irish Review* 1 (1986), 1–5.

—. *Modern Ireland, 1600–1972*. Hammondsworth: Penguin, 1988.

Foster, Thomas C. "'Enough to Be Going on With': Uncertainty in Paul Muldoon's Recent Sequences", *Nua: Studies in Contemporary Irish Writing* 4.1–2 (2003), 37–52.

Frazier, Adrian. "Juniper, Otherwise Known: Poems by Paulin and Muldoon", *Eire-Ireland* 19.1 (1984), 123–133.

Garratt, Robert F. *Modern Irish Poetry: Tradition and Continuity from Yeats to Heaney*. Berkeley: University of California Press, 1986.

Gering, August. "To Sing of '98: The United Irishmen Rising and the Ballad Tradition in Heaney and Muldoon", *Lit: Literature Interpretation Theory* 10.2 (1999), 149–79.

—. "Following the Conundrum: The Irish Diaspora and Imperialism in Paul Muldoon's *Madoc: A Mystery*", *Notes on Modern Irish Literature* 12 (2000), 32–42.

Gitzen, Julian. "Northern Ireland: The Post-Heaney Generation", *Poesis* 6.2 (1985), 47–64.

Goodby, John. "'Armageddon, Armagh-geddon:' Language and Crisis in the Poetry of Paul Muldoon." *Anglo-Irish and Irish Literature: Aspects of Language and Culture.* Ed. Birgit Bramsbäck and Martin Croghan. Vol. 2. Uppsala: Uppsala UP, 1988, 229–236.

—. "Hermeneutic Hermeticism: Paul Muldoon and the Northern Irish Poetic." *In Black and Gold: Contiguous Traditions in Post-War British and Irish Poetry.* Ed. C.C. Barfoot. Amsterdam: Rodopi, 1994, 137–68

—. *Irish Poetry Since 1950: From Stillness into History.* New York: St Martin's Press, 2000.

—. "'The Narrow Road to the Deep North:' Paul Muldoon, the Sonnet, and the Politics of Poetic Form", *Swansea Review* 14, 26–35.

Graham, Colin and Richard Kirkland, ed. *Ireland and Cultural Theory: The Mechanics of Authenticity.* London: Macmillan, 1998.

Grant, Patrick. *Breaking Enmities: Religion, Literature and Culture in Northern Ireland, 1967–97.* New York: Macmillan, 1999.

—. *Literature, Rhetoric, and Violence in Northern Ireland, 1968–98: Hardened to Death.* New York: Palgrave, 2001.

Grgas, Stipe. "Paul Muldoon and the Context of Postmodernity", BELLS: *Barcelona English Language and Literature Studies* 11 (2000), 89–100.

Gregson, Ian. *Contemporary Poetry and Postmodernism: Dialogue and Estrangement.* New York: St Martin's Press, 1996.

Grennan, Eamon. *Facing the Music: Irish Poetry in the Twentieth Century.* Omaha: Creighton UP, 1998.

Hancock, Tim. "Identity Problems in Paul Muldoon's 'The More a Man Has, the More a Man Wants'", *The Honest Ulsterman* 97 (1994), 57–64.

—. "'Mad Images and a Very Fixed Landscape': Paul Muldoon and the New Narrative", *Critical Review* 37 (1997), 133–40.

Harmon, Maurice, ed. *Irish Poetry after Yeats.* Dublin: Wolfhound Press; Boston: Little, Brown, 1979.

Heaney, Seamus. *Place and Displacement: Recent Poetry of Northern Ireland*. Grashmere: Trustees of Dove Cottage, 1984.

—. "The Pre-Natal Mountain: Vision and Irony in Recent Irish Poetry", *The Place of Writing*. Atlanta: Scholar's Press, 1989, 36–34.

Hena, Omaar. "Playing Indian/Disintegrating Irishness: Globalization and Cross-Cultural Identity in Paul Muldoon's "Madoc: A Mystery", *Contemporary Literature*, 49:2 (forthcoming).

Hollo, Kaarina. "From the Irish: On *The Astrakhan Cloak*", *New Hibernia Review/Iris Éireannach Nua: A Quarterly Record of Irish Studies* 3.2 (1999), 129–41.

Hoffman, Michael. "Muldoon – A Mystery", *London Review of Books*, December 20, 1990.

Howe, Stephen. *Ireland and Empire: Colonial Legacies in Irish History and Culture*. Oxford: Oxford UP, 2000.

Hughes, Eamonn, ed. *Culture and Politics in Northern Ireland, 1690–1990*. Milton Keyes: Open UP, 1991.

Hufstader, Jonathan. *Tongue of Water, Teeth of Stone: Northern Irish Poetry and Social Violence*. Lexington: UP of Kentucky, 1999.

Johnston, Dillon. *The Poetic Economies of England and Ireland, 1912–2000*. London: Macmillan, 2001.

—. "Poetic Discoveries and Inventions of America", *Colby Quarterly* 27.4 (1992), 202–214.

—. "Toward a Broader and More Comprehensive Identity", *Irish Poetry After Joyce*. Notre Dame: U of Notre Dame P, 1985, 247–272.

Kearney, Richard, ed. *Across the Frontiers: Ireland in the 1990s*. Dublin: Wolfhound Press, 1990.

—. ed. *The Irish Mind: Exploring Intellectual Tradition*. Dublin: Wolfhound Press, 1985.

—. *Postnationalist Ireland: Politics, Culture, Philosophy*. London: Routledge, 1997.

—. *Transitions: Narratives in Modern Irish Culture*. Dublin: Wolfhound Press, 1990.

Keller, Lynn. "An Interview with Paul Muldoon", *Contemporary Literature*, 35: 1 (1994)

Kelleher, Margaret and Philip O'Leary. eds. *The Cambridge History of Irish Literature. Vol. 2. 1890–2000*. Cambridge: Cambridge UP, 2006.

Kendall, Tim. "'Parallel to the Parallel Realm:' Paul Muldoon's *Madoc: A Mystery*", *Irish University Review: A Journal of Irish Studies* 25.2 (1995), 232–41.

—. "Paul Muldoon and the Art of Illusion." *Verse* 11.1 (1994), 78–83.

—. *Paul Muldoon*. Chester Springs, PA: Dufour, 1996.

Kendall, Tim and Peter McDonald. *Paul Muldoon: Critical Essays*. Liverpool: Liverpool UP, 2004.

Kenneally, Michael, ed. *Poetry in Contemporary Irish Literature*. Gerrards Cross: Colin Smythe, 1995.

Kerrigan, John. "Ulster Ovids", *The Chosen Ground: Essays on the Contemporary Poetry of Northern Ireland*. Ed. Neil Corcoran. Bridgend: Seren, 1992, 235–269.

Kiberd, Declan. *Anglo-Irish Attitudes*. Derry: Field Day Publications, 1984.

—. *Identity Parades: Northern Irish Culture and Dissident Subjects*. Liverpool: Liverpool UP, 2002.

—. *Inventing Ireland: The Literature of the Modern Nation*. Cambridge: Harvard UP, 1995.

Kirkland, Richard. *Literature and Culture in Northern Ireland Since 1965: Moments of Danger*. New York: Longman, 1996.

—. "Paul Muldoon's 'Immram' and 'Immrama:' Writing for a Sense of Displacement", *Essays in Poetics: The Journal of the British Neo-Formalist Circle* 17.1 (1992), 35–43.

Liddy, J. "Ulster Poets and the Catholic Muse", *Eire-Ireland: A Journal of Irish* 13.4 (1978), 126–37.

Lloyd, David. *Anomalous States: Irish Writing and the Post-Colonial Moment*. Dublin: Lilliput Press, 1993.

Longley, Edna. *Culture in Ireland: Division or Diversity?* Belfast: Institute of Irish Studies, 1991.

—. *The Living Stream: Literature and Revisionism in Ireland*. Newcastle upon Tyne: Bloodaxe Books, 1994.

—. "Poetic Forms and Social Malformations", *Tradition and Influence in Anglo-Irish Poetry*. Ed. Terence Brown and Nicholas Grene. Totowa, NJ: Barnes & Noble, 1989, 153–180.

—. "Poetry and Politics in Northern Ireland", *Crane Bag* 9.1 (1985), 26–37.

—. *Poetry and Posterity*. Newcastle: Bloodaxe Books, 2000.

—. *Poetry in the Wars*. Newcastle upon Tyne: Bloodaxe Books, 1990.

Mahony, Christina Hunt. *Contemporary Irish Literature: Transforming Tradition*. Basingstoke: Macmillan, 1998.

Malone, Christopher T. "Writing Home: Spatial Allegories in the Poetry of Seamus Heaney and Paul Muldoon", *ELH* 67.4 (2000), 1083–1109.

Marken, Ronald. "Paul Muldoon's 'Juggling a Red-Hot Half-Brick in an Old Sock:' Poets in Ireland Renovate the English Language Sonnet", *Eire-Ireland: A Journal of Irish Studies* 24.1 (1989), 79–91.

Marshall, Alan and Neil Sammels, ed. *Irish Encounters: Poetry, Politics and Prose*. Bath: Sulis Press, 1998.

Mason, David: "In praise of artifice", *Hudson Review* 54:4, Winter (2002).

Matthews, Steven. *Irish Poetry: Politics, History, Negotiation: The Evolving Debate, 1969 to the Present*. London: Macmillan, 1997.

Matthias, John. "From Mauberley to Middagh Street: Ways of Meeting the British", *PN Review* 20.5 (1994), 44–47.

McCracken, Kathleen. "A Northern Perspective: Dual Vision in the Poetry of Paul Muldoon", *Canadian Journal of Irish Studies* 16.2 (1990), 92–103.

McCurry, Jacqueline. "Crafty Inklings: Sonnets by Paul Muldoon", *Notes on Modern Irish Literature* 9 (1997), 35–43.

—."A Land 'Not 'Borrowed' but 'Purloined:' Paul Muldoon's Indians." *New Hibernia Review/Iris Éireannach Nua: A Quarterly Record of Irish Studies* 1.3 (1997), 40–51.

—. "'Scrap:' Colonialism Indicted in the Poetry of Paul Muldoon", *Eire-Ireland: A Journal of Irish Studies* 27.3 (1992), 92–109.

McDonald, Peter. *Mistaken Identities: Poetry and Northern Ireland*. Oxford: Clarendon, 1997.

McGrath, Charles. "Word Freak", *New York Times Magazine*, 19 Novemner 2006, 60–65.

McIvor, P.K. "Regionalism in Ulster: An Historical Perspective", *Irish University Review* 13.2 (1983), 180–8.

MacLaughlin, James. *Ireland: The Emigrant Nursery and the World Economy*. Cork: Cork UP, 1994.

Mari, Allison. "A Pilgrim's Progress: Paul Muldoon's 'Immram' as a Journey of Discovery", *Canadian Journal of Irish Studies* 21.2 (1995), 44–51.

Maxwell, D.E.S. "Imagining the North: Violence and the Writers", *Eire-Ireland: A Journal of Irish Studies* 8.2 (1973), 91–107.

Miller, Kerby A. *Emigrants and Exiles: Ireland and the Irish Exodus to North America*. Oxford: Oxford UP, 1985.

Murphy, Shane. "'The Eye that Scanned It:' The Picture Poems of Heaney, Muldoon, and McGuckian." *New Hibernia Review/Iris Éireannach Nua: A Quarterly Record of Irish Studies* 4.4 (2000), 85–114.

—. "Obliquity in the Poetry of Paul Muldoon and Medbh McGuckian", *Eire-Ireland: A Journal of Irish Studies* 31.3–4 (1996), 76–101.

—. "Remapping America: Paul Muldoon's *Madoc: A Mystery*", *Nua: Studies in Contemporary Irish Writing* 2.1–2 (1998–1999), 103–12.

—. "Sonnets, Centos and Long Lines: Muldoon, Paulin, McGuckian and Carson." *The Cambridge Companion to Contemporary Irish Poetry*. Ed. Matthew Campbell. Cambridge: Cambridge UP, 2003, 189–208.

O'Brien, Sean. *The Deregulated Muse: Essays on Contemporary British and Irish Poetry*. Newcastle upon Tyne: Bloodaxe Books, 1998.

O'Donoghue, Bernard. "'The Half-Said Thing to them is Dearest:' Paul Muldoon." *Poetry in Contemporary Irish Literature*. Ed. Michael Kenneally. Gerrards Cross: Colin Smythe, 1995, 400–18.

O'Dowd, Liam. "Neglecting the Material Dimension: Irish Intellectuals and the Problem of Identity", *Irish Review* 3 (1988), 8–17.

O'Neill, Charles L. "Paul Muldoon's *Madoc: A Mystery* and the Romantic Poets", *The Wordsworth Circle* 24.1 (1993), 54–56.

Ormsby, Frank, ed. *Poets from the North of Ireland*. Belfast: Blackstaff, 1979.

Osborn, Andrew. "Skirmishes on the Border: The Evolution and Function of Paul Muldoon's Fuzzy Rhyme", *Contemporary Literature* 41.2 (2000), 323–58.

Payne, Tom. "Four Ostriches and an Orange", *Daily Telegraph*, 9 September 2003

Putzel, Steven D. "Fluid Disjunction in Paul Muldoon's 'Immram' and 'The More a Man Has the More a Man Wants'", *Papers on Language and Literature: A Journal for Scholars and Critics of Language and Literature* 32.1 (1996), 85–108.

Riordan, Maurice. "Eros and History: On Contemporary Irish Poetry", *Crane Bag* 9 (1985), 49–55.

Roberts, Neil. *Narrative and Voice in Postwar Poetry*. London: Longman, 1999.

Robinson, Peter. "Muldoon's Humour." *Shiron* 35 (1996), 53–72.

Rumens, Carol. "Taig-Tickling and Prod Picking: Some Northern Irish Poets and their Critics", *Thumbscrew* 7 (1997), 20–8.

Ryan, Ray, ed. *Writing in the Irish Republic: Literature, Culture, Politics 1949–1999*. London: Macmillan; New York: St Martin's, 2000.

Russell, Richard Rankin. "The Yeatsian Refrain in Paul Muldoon's *Moy Sand and Gravel*." *ANQ: A Quarterly Journal of Short Articles, Notes, and Reviews* 19.3 (2006), 50–56.

Sailer, Susan Shaw. "On the Redness of Salmon Bones, the Communicative Potential of Conger Eels, and Standing Tails of Air: Reading Postmodern Images", *Word & Image: A Journal of Verbal/Visual Enquiry* 12.3 (1996), 308–25.

Sales, Rosemary. *Women Divided: Gender, Religion and Politics in Northern Ireland*. London: Routledge, 1991.

Sansom, Ian. "Awesome in Armagh", *The Guardian*, 2 November 2002.

Schirmer, Gregory A. *Out of What Began: A History of Irish Poetry in English*. Ithaca and London: Cornell UP, 1998.

Smith, Stan. "The Language of Displacement in Contemporary Irish Poetry." *Poetry in Contemporary Irish Literature*. Ed. Michael Keneally. Gerrards Cross: Colin Smythe, 1995.

—. *Inviolable Voice: History and Twentieth Century Poetry*. Dublin: Gill and Macmillan, 1982.

Smyth, Gerry. *Decolonisation and Criticism: The Construction of Irish Literature*. London: Pluto, 1998.

Stanfield, Paul Scott. "Another Side of Paul Muldoon", *North Dakota Quarterly* 57.1 (1989), 129–43.

Swann, Joseph. "Theology as Cultural Parameter: Sign and Meaning in Four Contemporary Irish Poets", *Hungarian Journal of English and American Studies* 5.1 (1999), 61–79.

Tell, Carol. "In the American Grain? Paul Muldoon's *Madoc*." *Canadian Journal of Irish Studies* 21.2 (1995), 52–62.

—. *Part-Time Exiles: Contemporary Irish Poets and Their American Migrations*. Bethesda, MD: Academic Press Llc, 2001.

—. "Paul Muldoon: A Postmodern Ulysses?" *The Classical World and the Mediterranean*. Ed. Donatella Badin and Giuseppe Serpillo. Cagliari, Italy: Tema, 1996, 208–14.

Vance, Norman. *Irish Literature: A Social History*. Dublin: Four Courts Press, 1999.

Watson, George. "The Narrow Ground: Northern Poets and the Northern Irish Crisis", *Irish Writers and Society at Large*. ed. Masaru Sekine. Gerrards Cross: Colin Smythe, 1985.

Wheatley, David. "The Aistriúchán Cloak: Paul Muldoon and the Irish Language", *New Hibernia Review/Iris Éireannach Nua: A Quarterly Record of Irish Studies* 5.4 (2001), 123–34.

—. "An Irish Poet in America." *Raritan: A Quarterly Review* 18.4 (1999), 145–57.

—. "'That Blank Mouth:' Secrecy, Shibboleths, and Silence in Northern Irish Poetry", *Journal of Modern Literature* 25.1 (2001), 1–16.

Wheeler, Susan. "Paul Muldoon: Irish Weather over New Jersey", *Publishers Weekly* 2001 May 7; 248 (19), 216–17.

Whyte, John and Garrett Fitzgerald. *Interpreting Northern Ireland*. Oxford: Oxford UP, 1996.

Wichert, Sabine. *Northern Ireland Since 1945*. London: Longman, 1999.

Wills, Clair. *Improprieties: Politics and Sexuality in Northern Irish Poetry*. Oxford: Oxford UP, 1993.

—. "The Lie of the Land: Language, Imperialism, and Trade in Paul Muldoon's *Meeting the British*", *The Chosen Ground: Essays on the Contemporary Poetry of Northern Ireland*. Ed. Neil Corcoran. Bridgend: Seren; 1992, 121–49.

—."Paul Muldoon: *The Annals of Chile*", *Essays and Studies* 49 (1996), 111–39.

—. *Reading Paul Muldoon*. Newcastle upon Tyne: Bloodaxe, 1998.

Wilson, William A. "The Grotesqueries of Paul Muldoon, 'Immram' to *Madoc*", *Eire-Ireland: A Journal of Irish Studies* 28.4 (1993), 115–32.

—. "Paul Muldoon and the Poetics of Sexual Difference." *Contemporary Literature* 28.3 (1987), 317–31.

—. "Yeats, Muldoon, and Heroic History", *Learning the Trade: Essays on W. B. Yeats and Contemporary Poetry*. Ed. Deborah Fleming. West Cornwall, CT: Locust Hill, 1993, 21–38.

Zinnes, Harriet. "Paul Muldoon: 'Time-Switch Taped To The Trough'", *The Hollins Critic* 33.1 (1996), 1–12.

Selected Reviews of Muldoon's Most Recent Volumes:

Horse Latitudes (2006):

Burt, Stephen. "Connection charge", *Times Literary Supplement*, 24 Novmber 2006.

Cole, Judith. "Muldoon: putting the world to WRITES", *Belfast Telegraph*, 26 October 2006.

Fenton, James. "A poke in the eye with a poem", *The Guardian*, 21 October 2006.

Ford, Mark. "The Call of the Stallion", *New York Review of Books* 53.20, 21 December 2006, 78–80.

Huston, Karla. "Horse Latitudes", *Library Journal*. 131.14, 1 September 2006, 151.

James, Jamie. "Amazing Grace." *Los Angeles Times*, 5 November 2005.

Longenbach, James. "Paul Muldoon: The poet of giddiness", *Slate* 28 November 2006.

Lucas, David. "Make what you can of poet Paul Muldoon", *Plain Dealer* (Cleveland), 15 October 2006.

McCue, Jim. "*Horse Latitudes* by Paul Muldoon." *The Independent*, 5 November 2006.

—. "MacNeice knew when to stop", *ABC Magazine*, 5 November 2006, 28.

McLane, Maureen N. "Paul Muldoon's poems and essays pulse with emotional and intellectual vigor", *Chicago Tribune*, 8 October 2006.

McGrath, Charles. "Word Freak", *The New York Times*, 19 November 2006.

Munson, Sam. "The Magpie Artist", *The New York Sun*, 5 December 2006.

O'Brien, Sean. "Daring to be difficult", *The Sunday Times*, 12 November 2006.

Porte, Rebecca. "Paul Muldoon at full sail with two new works." *Star Tribune* (Minneapolis, MN), 15 October 2006.

Potts, Robert. "Far more going on than first meets the eye", *The Daily Telegraph*, 21 October 2006.

Schmidt, Michael. "Poetic thoroughbred has winning lines", *Scotland on Sunday*, 29 October 2006.

Vendler, Helen. "Fanciness and Fatality", *The New Republic*, 6 November 2006.

Moy Sand and Gravel (2002):

Davison, Peter. "Darkness at Muldoon", *New York Times Book Review*, 13 October 2002.

Fallon, Peter. "Grains of lasting truth and beauty", *The Irish Times*, 19 October 2002.

Ford, Mark. "At Arm's Length", *New York Review of Books* 50.14, 25 September 2003.

Kilroy, Ian. "Transatlantic poet Paul Muldoon's *Moy Sand and Gravel* has won him a Pulitzer Prize in poetry. The master of wordplay talks to Ian Kilroy", *The Irish Times*, 19 April 2003.

Knight, Stephen. "More than just clever-dickery", *Independent on Sunday*, 20 October 2002.

Macfarlane, Robert. "High and dry in the flood", *Times Literary Supplement*, 11 October 2002, 24.

Padel, Ruth. "It's not painting by numbers", *The Independent*, 5 October 2002.

Payne, Tom. "Four ostriches and an orange", *The Daily Telegraph*, 11 September 2002.

Sansom, Ian. "Awesome in Armagh", *The Guardian*, 2 November 2002.

Quinney, Laura. "In the Studebaker", *London Review of Books*, 23 October 2003.

Scharf, Michael and Jeff Zaleski."*Moy Sand and Gravel*", *Publishers Weekly* 249.24, 17 June 2002, 57.

Skloot, Floyd. "Bearing Sorrow." *Southern Review*, 39.1 (2003), 219– 236.

Smith, Dinitia. "Times Are Difficult, So Why Should The Poetry Be Easy?" *New York Times*, 19 November 2002.

Utley, Alison. "Paul Muldoon", *Time High Education Supplement*, 11 March 2003.

Poems 1968–1998:

Sanger, Richard. "How the Northern Irish saved poetry", *The Globe and Mail* (Canada), 9 June 2001.

Hobsbaum, Philip. "Gliding the Lily Pond", *The Scotsman*, 19 May 2001.

Clifton, Harry. "Remembering the redemptive power of art", *The Irish Times*, 26 May 2001.

Brownjohn, Alan. *The Sunday Times*, 22 July 2001.

Downing, Ben. "Poetry and Parlor Tricks", *Wall Street Journal*, 13 March 2001.

Eder, Richard. "To Understand Is to Be Perplexed", *The New York Times Book Review*, 10 June 2001.

MacKinnon, Lachlan. "A sceptic's passion", *The Daily Telegraph*, 6 February 2001.

Newey, Adam. "Walking on air", *New Statesman*, 11 June 2001.

Nye, Robert. *The Times*, 22 July 2001.

Romer, Stephen. "A poet of perfect poise", *The Guardian*, 16 June 2001.

Hay (1998):

Burt, Stephen. "*Hay*: Paul Muldoon", *Boston Review*, April/May 1999.

Cardwell, Colin. "Piano poetry", *Scotland on Sunday*, 18 October 1998.

Frisardi, Andrew. "Of life and culture, from the playful to the satirical", *Boston Globe*, 27 December 1998.

Hass, Robert. "Poet's Choice", *Washington Post Book World*, 21 February 1999.

Imlah, Mick. "*Hay*, by Paul Muldoon", *The Observer*, 15 November 1998.

Jenkins, Nicholas. "For 'mother' read 'other'", *Times Literary Supplement*, 29 January 1999.

Kendall, Tim. "Maps of life's detour", *The Guardian*, 17 October 1998.

Kirsch, Adam. "The Virtuoso", *The New Republic*, 30 November 1998.

Lewis, Leon. "*Hay*" *Magill Book Reviews*, 8 January 1999.

O'Rourke, Meghan. *Los Angeles Times*, 7 February 1999.

Polito, Robert. "*Hay*, by Paul Muldoon", *Book Forum*, Winter 1998.

Pratt, William."Verse", *World Literature Today* 73.2 (1999), 338.

McDonald, Peter. "The poet at play", *The Irish Times*, 24 October 1998.

Index